CHANTAL MOUFFE

Chantal Mouffe's writings have been innovatory with respect to democratic theory, Marxism and feminism. Her work derives from, and has always been engaged with, contemporary political events and intellectual debates. This sense of conflict informs both the methodological and substantive propositions she offers. Determinisms, scientific or otherwise, and ideologies, Marxist or feminist, have failed to survive her excoriating critiques. In a sense she is the original post-Marxist, rejecting economisms and class-centric analyses, and also the original post-feminist, more concerned with the varieties of 'identity politics' than with any singularities of 'women's issues'.

While Mouffe's concerns with power and discourse derive from her studies of Gramsci's theorisations of hegemony and the post-structuralisms of Derrida and Foucault, her reversal of the very terms through which political theory proceeds is very much her own. She centres conflict, not consensus, and disagreement, not finality. Whether philosophically perfectionist, or liberally reasonable, political theorists have been challenged by Mouffe to think again, and to engage with a new concept of 'the political' and a revived and refreshed notion of 'radical democracy'.

The editor has focused on her work in three key areas:

- *Hegemony: From Gramsci to 'Post-Marxism'*
- *Radical Democracy: Pluralism, Citizenship and Identity*
- *The Political: A Politics Beyond Consensus*

The volume concludes with a new interview with Chantal Mouffe.

James Martin is Professor of Politics at Goldsmiths, University of London, UK. He has published widely on Italian political thought, contemporary political theory and rhetoric.

Routledge innovators in political theory
Edited by Terrell Carver, University of Bristol and Samuel A. Chambers, Johns Hopkins University

Routledge Innovators in Political Theory focuses on leading contemporary thinkers in political theory, highlighting the major innovations in their thought that have reshaped the field. Each volume collects both published and unpublished texts, and combines them with an interview with the thinker. The editorial introduction articulates the innovator's key contributions in relation to political theory, and contextualises the writer's work. Volumes in the series will be required reading for both students and scholars of twenty-first-century politics.

1 William E. Connolly
Democracy, pluralism and political theory
Edited by Samuel A. Chambers and Terrell Carver

2 Carole Pateman
Democracy, feminism, welfare
Edited by Terrell Carver and Samuel A. Chambers

3 Michael J. Shapiro
Discourse, culture and violence
Edited by Terrell Carver and Samuel A. Chambers

4 Chantal Mouffe
Hegemony, radical democracy, and the political
Edited by James Martin

CHANTAL MOUFFE

Hegemony, radical democracy, and the political

Edited by
James Martin

Routledge
Taylor & Francis Group

LONDON AND NEW YORK

First published 2013
by Routledge
2 Park Square, Milton Park, Abingdon, Oxon OX14 4RN

Simultaneously published in the USA and Canada
by Routledge
711 Third Avenue, New York, NY 10017

Routledge is an imprint of the Taylor & Francis Group, an informa business

British Library Cataloguing in Publication Data
A catalogue record for this book is available from the British Library

Library of Congress Cataloging in Publication Data
Mouffe, Chantal.
Chantal Mouffe : hegemony, radical democracy, and the political / edited by James Martin.
pages cm. -- (Routledge innovators in political theory ; 4)
Includes bibliographical references and index.
1. Political sociology. 2. Hegemony. 3. Democracy. I. Martin, James, 1968- editor of compilation. II. Title. III. Title: Hegemony, radical democracy, and the political.
JA76.M68 2013
306.2--dc23
2012048805

ISBN: 978-0-415-82521-4 (hbk)
ISBN: 978-0-415-82522-1 (pbk)
ISBN: 978-0-203-78890-5 (ebk)

Typeset in Bembo
by Integra Software Services Pvt. Ltd.

CONTENTS

ACKNOWLEDGEMENTS

I would like to express my gratitude to the series editors, Terrell Carver and Sam Chambers, for their support during the preparation of this volume. Thanks also go to Chantal Mouffe, who patiently tolerated the delays and passed on helpful suggestions concerning the collection's content. Paulina Tambakiki kindly offered wise advice at various stages and, like my colleague, Saul Newman, cast a glance at the Introduction. I am grateful to them both. Naturally, responsibility for all editorial choices is mine alone.

INTRODUCTION

Democracy and conflict in the work of Chantal Mouffe

James Martin

Chantal Mouffe's work challenges democrats to acknowledge the antagonistic dimension of political life and to embrace democracy as a stage for managing disagreement, not building consensus. This important and controversial innovation sets Mouffe apart from so much of mainstream Anglo-American political theory, whose philosophical assumptions and socially integrative orientations she vigorously contests. It also distinguishes her from traditional 'radical' approaches to politics that draw upon the romantic imagery of a stable community whose full integrity will arrive only *après la lutte*. Mouffe's innovation as a political theorist has been to insist upon the conflictual aspect of democracy as the fundamental source of its virtues.

The essays gathered in this collection of Mouffe's own work survey some of the principal interventions in the evolution of her theoretical *corpus*, and they demonstrate the consistency and breadth of her critique of mainstream theory and politics. Her writing has always been engaged, in the sense of contesting the purported foundations of social and political theory, as well as challenging the wider policies and practices it often sustains. Indeed, Mouffe's theoretical orientation emerged from the continental Marxist and feminist traditions, with their focus firmly on the struggles of social movements against the material and intellectual power of dominant groups and forces. Conflict, then, is not simply a condition of democratic politics for her; it is an integral dimension of her understanding of society and a characteristic of her own style as a critic. Unashamedly theoretical, her writings nevertheless refuse extended abstraction or system building. Instead, they regularly take issue with prevalent intellectual currents, focusing theoretical labour on exposing the unexamined assumptions and prejudices of the mainstream in order, ultimately, to stimulate a radically different politics.

Mouffe's readiness to embrace conflict reflects, in part, the fortunes of her generation, which came to maturity in the mid-1960s and 1970s when the post-war consensus on the welfare state started to fray, as so-called new social movements (feminism, ecologism, anti-racism, and so on) began to eclipse traditional class politics, and as anti-colonial struggles contested the dominance of the imperial superpowers across the globe. Her career as a theorist is inextricably linked, then, with the advancing and retreating waves of emancipatory struggles that have marked late capitalist societies following the euphoria of the events of May '68 in Paris. Let us first of all survey her major publications and the theoretical disputes and social conflicts that have animated them.

Gramscian interventions

Born in Charleroi, Belgium, Mouffe studied philosophy at the Catholic University of Louvain before moving to Paris. In the 1960s, she attended the seminars of the Marxist philosopher Louis Althusser, whose anti-humanist reconstruction of Marxism dominated the intellectual scene and strongly influenced her intellectual formation. In the early 1970s, she worked at the National University of Colombia in Bogotá. Returning in the middle of the decade to postgraduate study at the University of Essex, Mouffe arrived in a Britain marked by the ascendance of the New Right and the deepening crisis of Labour's social democracy (see Mouffe 2001–2, p. 10).

As the Reagan and Thatcher governments consolidated the new dominance of conservative, market-oriented ideology with an assault on the legacies of social democracy and the left-libertarian values of the previous decade, Mouffe went on to take up research positions in the USA, including posts at Harvard and Princeton universities. Between 1989 and 1995 – as Soviet and East European communism and South African apartheid collapsed, and while ethnic conflict raged in the Balkans – she was Programme Director at the Collège Internationale de Philosophie in Paris. Mouffe eventually took up a position at the Centre for the Study of Democracy at the University of Westminster in the UK, where she became Professor of Political Theory in 2001.

Mouffe's major contributions to political theory are quite inseparable from these momentous events and their impact in shaping contemporary democratic politics. Her critical engagements with Marxism in the late 1970s and early 1980s, for example, reflected wider discussions about how to reconcile movements such as feminism and ecologism with prevailing assumptions about the explanatory and political primacy of social classes. Her first book, the edited collection *Gramsci and Marxist Theory* (Mouffe 1979), gathered contributions to prevailing theoretical debates on the European continent concerning the meaning and application of the work of the Italian Marxist, Antonio Gramsci (1891–1937), whose elaboration of the concept of hegemony remains of seminal importance in Mouffe's political theory. More than that of any other Marxist, particularly in the 1960s and 1970s, it was the legacy of Gramsci which opened the way to an appreciation of the *complexity* of politics in advanced capitalist states. By foregrounding struggles over ideology and popular consent in civil society, Gramsci attended to the contingent, fluctuating dimensions of class power rather than to the abstract necessity of economic relations of production. As the debates in that volume demonstrated, Gramsci supplied a rich seam of ideas with which to conceptualise the connections between class struggles and the demands and values of non-class groups and ideologies.

The culmination of Mouffe's early interventions into such debates, however, came in the slim yet ground-breaking volume, *Hegemony and Socialist Strategy: Towards a Radical Democratic Politics*, co-written with Ernesto Laclau and published in 1985 (Laclau and Mouffe 2001). A major innovation in the theorisation of radical politics, the book combined a sophisticated interrogation of Marxism by way of Gramsci's concept of hegemony, newly recast in light of insights from contemporary poststructuralist philosophy, particularly deconstruction from the work of Jacques Derrida, Foucault's reading of power and discourse, and Jacques Lacan's rendering of psychoanalysis. Gramsci's insistence on the primacy of political and ideological relations over economic structures was uniquely combined with analyses of the relational and unstable character of all social identities. The conclusions the authors drew fundamentally challenged the defining precepts of Marxist thinking: namely, the economistic logic that configured society as a coherent object with a stable essence; the displacement of politics to a contingent status supplemental to an underlying necessity; and the primacy granted in socialist political discourse to the interests of the working class in the formation of alliances, democratic or otherwise.

The break made by Mouffe and Laclau from the conceptual framework of Marxism was, without a doubt, profound. In time, it would spawn a whole new lexicon (anti-essentialism, discourse, articulation, chains of equivalence, and so on) as well as the inevitable hostile reactions from the Marxist Left. But what remained of Marxism was also significant. The authors retained a focus on relations of power and domination as the driving undercurrent of radical politics and social change. But hegemony now designated the ongoing assemblage of all social identities without privilege, and no longer merely indicated the connecting of economic classes to non-class groups and ideas.

Central to this recalibration of hegemony was the concept of antagonism – the clash between different groups and classes revealed in numerous hostilities, conflicts and forms of violence. Where Marxism had been inclined to treat class conflict as the moving force of a teleological view of history – whereby social differences would ultimately harmonise with the onset of socialism – Mouffe and Laclau gave antagonism a permanent and ontological function. Antagonism, they claimed, was the 'limit of all objectivity': social groups and relations exist only by means of their symbolic differentiation from other possible relations and identities, through exclusion from or opposition to certain conditions. This antagonistic differentiation supplies a fictive coherence and objectivity to social identity through the demarcation of a threatening 'other' often regarded as irrational, hostile or beyond reasonable comprehension (selfish capitalists, envious foreigners, cold-hearted bureaucracies, and so on), thus promising an illusory fullness of identity once the antagonist has been overcome.

Mouffe and Laclau both pluralised antagonism and refused the utopia of a fully-reconciled society. In dispensing with the primacy of class, antagonisms were never reducible to one (economic) difference alone. As the decline of social democracy demonstrated, conflicts over race, ethnicity, gender or class could coexist and mutually distort each other in public discourse. Hegemonic politics, in their view, therefore entailed the ongoing management and displacement of numerous antagonisms, but never their final resolution. The Left had therefore something to learn from the successes of the New Right and neo-conservatism, which were based precisely on the ability to rearticulate their messages in ways that refashioned various conflicts and identities around opposition to institutions of welfare and discourses of equality.

If recent transformations in capitalism remained the dominant (but not the necessary, that is, ontologically privileged) ground of social antagonisms, a radical socialist politics built exclusively around class was never going to resolve social conflicts once and for all. *Hegemony and Socialist Strategy* instead offered the prospect of modern socialism as a radical and pluralist democracy, a deepening of the modern democratic revolution in which numerous groups and identities would be recognised in their autonomy and joined together in ongoing coalitions of citizens unified by their antagonism to various aspects of late capitalist society. Far from being eliminated, then, such antagonisms were the underlying condition of any plural, democratic community.

Rethinking democracy

After *Hegemony and Socialist Strategy* was published, Mouffe expanded on the principles and arguments originally set out in that volume. Significantly, these efforts coincided with the collapse of Soviet communism, which opened the way to a notorious triumphalism on the part of the now hegemonic neo-liberal discourses of the market (Gray 2009). With Marxian socialism in steady retreat across the world, political philosophers were drawn to debates that had once been marginal but in which the Left now had an increasing stake, for example, the meaning and significance of postmodernity, the relationship between individual identity and community, and the prospects for democracy in an age of rights. In her edited collection, *Dimensions of Radical Democracy* (Mouffe 1992), Mouffe gathered together essays by various American and European authors in order to discuss a democratic and pluralist politics in the post-communist age without adopting the individualist and rationalist assumptions of liberal political philosophy. The volume included contributions by feminist, neo-republican and communitarian political theorists seeking to rethink democratic citizenship.

Mouffe's next volume, and the first in her own name alone, *The Return of the Political* (Mouffe 1993), adopted a distinctive, polemical stance in relation to developments in Anglo-American political theory in the 1980s and 1990s. Returning to the question of pluralism and antagonism, she took issue with the legalistic style of reasoning and unacknowledged assumptions of consensus that permeated the political philosophies of John Rawls, Ronald Dworkin and their followers. The political dimension – that is, the contingent and antagonistic ground of any community and consensus – in her view had been suppressed in the post-communist urge to imagine liberal capitalism as the final and inclusive setting for all differences. A similar view, this time elaborated around an exchange between two other critics of rationalism and universalism, Richard Rorty and Jacques Derrida, was the theme of Mouffe's next edited volume, *Deconstruction and Pragmatism* (Mouffe 1996a). Neither rationalism nor anti-foundationalism, she argued, was sufficient to generate a democratic politics unless 'we accept that every consensus exists as a temporary result of a provisional hegemony, as a stabilisation of power, and that it always entails some form of exclusion' (Mouffe 1996b: 10). Mouffe also explored this deconstructive train of thought in dialogue with the work of Wittgenstein, co-editing a collection of papers from a conference on his legacy in 1999 (see Nagl and Mouffe 2001).

One figure who regularly reappears in Mouffe's work from the 1990s onwards is the German jurist and philosopher, Carl Schmitt (1888–1985). A conservative and unapologetic supporter of Nazism, Schmitt claimed that the political dimension consists, fundamentally, in the existential distinction between friend and enemy. This stark, potentially authoritarian claim has made Schmitt a controversial thinker, not least because of his explicit political alignment. To Mouffe, however, Schmitt's critique of liberalism (where, in principle, all rational people can supposedly become friends, without exclusion) provides insights that inform democratic theory, even as she emphatically rejects his anti-democratic conclusions.

Such was the perspective she encouraged in her edited collection, *The Challenge of Carl Schmitt* (Mouffe 1999), and it continued in her subsequent writings. For Schmitt understood, uniquely in Mouffe's view, the ever-present prospect of violence that circumscribes all political relations, and he therefore refused to reduce politics to an ethics without antagonism. Such a benign ethical outlook, common in the early post-communist years, could not even begin to grasp the nature of intense hostilities such as religious fundamentalism or the break-up of Yugoslavia, where liberation from Soviet control led not to the peaceful flowering of liberal toleration but to an unrelenting bloodbath of ethnic hatred and violence.

Mouffe's next book, *The Democratic Paradox* (Mouffe 2000), explored the theme of enmity further in light of the resurgence of the centre-left across Europe and the USA. For both the Clinton presidencies and for the governments of Tony Blair (UK) and Gerhard Schröder (Germany), social democratic goals of social inclusion and partial wealth redistribution were now possible only by accommodating the demands of globalising markets and reducing the burdens of public welfare on the state, and lightening the burden of taxation. In this capitulation by the centre-left to the neo-liberal hegemony of the previous decade – with their claims to have transcended the conflicts of state *versus* markets, equality *versus* liberty, left *versus* right, and so on, by harnessing the strengths of globalisation for progressive ends – Mouffe offered a timely and succinct riposte. The opposition between equality and liberty, she argued, is a constitutive antagonism of modern politics. Any pretensions to have overcome the conflict between them threaten the tension that sustains democratic identities.

Mouffe detected, in various forms – from centre-left appeals to a Third Way in social democracy to Anthony Giddens's treatises on globalisation or the ever-proliferating ruminations on deliberative models of democracy – a pervasive tendency to evade the irresolvable conflict between equality and liberty, and the clashes of principle that underscored them. In their place, she defended a reformulation of radical democracy as an agonistic politics. An agonistic democratic theory, she argued, begins from the impossibility of reconciling all social demands without exclusion or violence. But if differences cannot be harmonised, as liberals and neo-liberal social democrats envisaged, nevertheless they can engage each other in democratic encounters. A successful democratic order, again, is not one that erases division and conflict, but rather one that reduces outright antagonism in favour of a managed conflict. That entails, as Mouffe coins it, a conflictual consensus, where contrasting differences of principle acknowledge each other's legitimacy but still remain opposed. Only by providing a stage (or stages) for the airing of radical differences can dangerous forms of hostility and violence be reduced.

A succinct reiteration of Mouffe's political theory can be found in her short volume, *On the Political* (Mouffe 2005), where the framework of hegemony, the poststructuralist theorisation of social identity, and the critique of efforts to suppress the political dimension are once again brought to bear on contemporary issues and problems. Published after the terrorist attacks of 11 September 2001 and the subsequent invasions of Iraq and Afghanistan, Mouffe remains clear that the danger for democratic theory and practice lies, fundamentally, in what she terms the post-political orientation that informs domestic and international politics in the twenty-first century, even its most radical currents. In this book, Mouffe extends her analysis to debates over, for example, cosmopolitan democracy and right-wing populism.

I have argued that Mouffe's innovations stem from a consistent challenge – to political theorists, to all of us – to think democratic politics from the perspective of conflict, and not against it. In this endeavour, her published work has always been theoretically sophisticated and engaged with the cutting edge; but also practically informed by the struggles and conflicts that define the scenes of contemporary politics.

Structure of the book

This volume is divided into three Parts that take as their headings key terms in the subtitle of the book: Hegemony, Radical Democracy, and 'the Political'. These terms signify themes that, despite their linear order of succession here, have all been intimately connected in Mouffe's work from the beginning. Yet they also mark out notable phases and preoccupations in her career when certain key ideas were formulated. The works collected here appear in a largely chronological order (according to the original date of delivery or publication), but readers will note the interweaving and reiteration of similar ideas and claims.

Hegemony: from Gramsci to post-Marxism

Part I, 'Hegemony: from Gramsci to post-Marxism', comprises writings that represent the early formulation of Mouffe's political theory, namely, her work on hegemony and its elaboration in a so-called post-Marxist framework informed by philosophical critiques of foundational claims. As is evident in the more recent, final chapters of the book, the framework of hegemony remains the guiding thread of Mouffe's philosophical outlook. It informs her understanding of the contingent formation of power relations, their fundamental relationality, and consequently their openness to contestation. The concept of hegemony supplies Mouffe's work with a standpoint from which to hold to account dogmatic claims to objective reason or the pretence of a smooth universality untroubled by difference and exclusion.

Chapter 1, 'Hegemony and ideology in Gramsci' (pp. 15–44), is Mouffe's first major publication, her contribution to the volume on Gramsci she edited. Here, still informed by an Althusserian-Marxian analysis, Mouffe sets out the enduring novelty of Gramsci's work through a concept of hegemony that is resolutely anti-reductionist and anti-economistic. Dispensing with class as the essential agent of radical change, she argues, Gramsci conceived hegemony as the generation of a new subjective identity – a 'collective will' – and not simply the imposition of a class ideology.

In Chapter 2, 'Hegemony and new political subjects: towards a new concept of democracy' (pp. 45–57), Mouffe further develops her approach to hegemony around an explicitly poststructuralist agenda concerning the instability and malleability of subjective identity. Furthermore, she explores the prospect for conceiving radical democratic politics in light of the emancipatory demands of new social movements, which she renames 'democratic movements' in order to distinguish them from other, sometimes reactionary groups. The scandal of these theoretical positions, among Marxists at least, was demonstrated in the extensive critique of *Hegemony and Socialist Strategy* by Norman Geras in the pages of *New Left Review* (Geras 1987).

Chapter 3, 'Post-Marxism without apologies (1987)' (pp. 58–87), comprises the detailed, robust response given by Mouffe and Laclau in the same journal. The authors helpfully clarify the conceptual apparatus that informs their joint work – particularly the theory of discourse – and vigorously fend off the charge of idealism directed at them by Geras.

Radical democracy: pluralism, citizenship and identity

Part II, 'Radical democracy: pluralism, citizenship and identity', consists of essays written through the late 1980s and early 1990s that clarified and expanded the theory of a radical and plural democracy announced in *Hegemony and Socialist Strategy*. Whereas the earlier phase of Mouffe's writings had engaged the preoccupations of Marxist theorists and socialist politics (both, at that time, the dominant platforms for the radical Left), her subsequent writings brought the challenge of radical democracy to the broader concerns of contemporary political theory, and consequently to a wider constituency of readers. Mouffe demonstrated how the framework of hegemony and the critique of identity had serious, critical consequences for mainstream approaches to pluralism and citizenship.

Chapter 4, 'Radical democracy: modern or postmodern?' (pp. 91–102), finds Mouffe clarifying the relationship between the – then proliferating – reflections on the postmodern condition and the project of radical democracy. For thinkers such as Habermas, postmodernism entails conservatism, in so far as it refuses a foundation for social and political critique. But in Mouffe's view, radical democracy does not simply involve the postmodern renunciation of rational and universal foundations; rather, it remains inextricably linked to the modern project of emancipation. Thus, radical democracy 'could be defined as being both modern and postmodern' (p. 92).

In Chapter 5, 'Democratic citizenship and the political community' (pp. 103–114), Mouffe examines the question of citizen identity and its connection with the idea of community, drawing on Michael Oakeshott's discussion of *societas* or civil association. Against the consensus-oriented conceptions proffered by Kantian liberals, civic republicans and communitarians, she argues for an idea of community in which conflict and antagonism are central to the experience of citizenship.

Mouffe reflects in a more focused way in Chapter 6 on the claims to neutrality and rationality that underscore the obsession with consensus in liberal political philosophy. In 'Politics and the limits of liberalism' (pp. 115–131), she engages in particular with its dominant figures, Rawls and Charles Larmore, arguing that pluralism can neither be wholly inclusive nor impartial. Rather, it is the outcome of a hegemonic politics whose limits are always open to contestation.

The vitally important contribution of modern feminism to the debates about democratic citizenship and identity is explored in Chapter 7, 'Feminism, citizenship and radical democratic politics' (pp. 132–145). Here Mouffe critically surveys the contribution of notable feminists to the critique of patriarchy and of the fixed, binary conceptions of identity that support it. However, she takes issue with the ideas of differentiated citizenship promoted by, for example, Carole Pateman and Iris Marion Young. Anti-essentialist feminism, she argues, goes beyond merely defending women *as* women; it offers the prospect of exploring the articulation of women's subordination to wider relations of power and domination.

Finally, Chapter 8, 'For a politics of nomadic identity' (pp. 146–153), consists of a short, theoretical reflection on the idea of social identity as intrinsically multiple and unstable, and always the object of political contest. Democratic theory, she affirms, must refuse to censure this instability, as nationalist politics, then prevalent across Europe, sought to do. Rather, she argues, we must give it scope to play out within the terms of a democratic politics.

The political: a politics beyond consensus

Part III comprises Mouffe's work on the conception of 'the political' and its application to various domains of contemporary politics and theory. Her critique of consensus established, Mouffe now regularly employs the concept of 'the political' as a figure for the antagonistic dimension that is persistently disavowed in other theories. In this phase of her work, she underlines the importance not only of acknowledging antagonism but, moreover, of transforming antagonists from enemies to adversaries – that is, endorsing the legitimacy of one's foes, despite deep disagreement, so as not to exclude them altogether.

In Chapter 9, 'The radical centre: a politics without adversary' (pp. 157–166), Mouffe focuses her gaze on the ideas that informed the British Labour Party and other centre-left political parties across Europe in the late 1990s. Despite Labour's electoral successes, Mouffe locates the illusions of so-called Third Way politics in its renunciation of the political dimension, namely, by denying alternative approaches to globalisation and refusing the possibility of dissent towards neo-liberal thinking.

Chapter 10, 'Carl Schmitt and the paradox of liberal democracy' (pp. 167–180), sets out Mouffe's views on the contribution of Schmitt to conceptualising 'the political' as the experience of antagonism at the heart of any communal identity. Making clear her rejection of his repugnant politics, nevertheless she endorses the theoretical value of his distinction between friend and enemy. Democracy, she argues, *contra* both liberal and deliberative philosophies, 'always entails relations of inclusion-exclusion' (p. 171), an unstable frontier that makes possible a negotiation over what and who constitutes 'the people'.

Mouffe's Inaugural Lecture as Professor of Political Theory at the University of Westminster forms Chapter 11, 'Politics and passions: the stakes of democracy' (pp. 181–190). Here, with great clarity, she affirms her view of the ineradicability of the political dimension with reference to the role of passions in sustaining commitments to democratic politics. Without these, she argues, democracy threatens to become an arid realm unable to recruit the identifications necessary to nourish it.

The agonistic model of democracy that Mouffe advocates is explored in detail in Chapter 12, 'For an agonistic model of democracy' (pp. 191–206). Agonistic democracy is here contrasted with the consensus orientation of the deliberative model promoted in different ways by theorists such as Jürgen Habermas, Seyla Benhabib and Joshua Cohen. Mouffe disputes the role attributed by the latter to rules of argumentation and insists, instead, on the importance of the wider practices that sustain democratic allegiances. That way, adversarial disputes between a plurality of contrasting ideological positions can be allowed to clash within a common political space without recourse to violence.

With a scope that is wider than the circumscribed domains of public reasoning common to mainstream liberalism and democratic theory, Mouffe's work has been of long-standing interest to artists and cultural theorists. In Chapter 13, 'Cultural workers as organic intellectuals' (pp. 207–215), she extends her theory of agonism to encompass the work they do. Returning to ideas from her earliest writings, she employs Gramsci's conception of the organic intellectual to illustrate the critical role of cultural workers in the production of new subjectivities and the formation of a new hegemony. In this chapter she also takes issue with the work of Michael Hardt and Antonio Negri – whose two books, *Empire* and *Multitude*, became popular theoretical manifestos for a new generation of political activists at the turn of the twenty-first century – which she believes fail adequately to grasp changes in capitalism as part of a hegemonic process that remains fractured and contestable.

Chapter 14, 'Democracy in a multipolar world' (pp. 216–227), extends Mouffe's reflections on adversarial politics to new domains; this time, to the question of democracy at the level of the international order. Although critical of the unipolarity of international politics in the post-Cold War era, Mouffe disagrees with the logic of cosmopolitan democrats who, she argues, seek 'a world beyond hegemony and beyond sovereignty, therefore negating the dimension of the political' (p. 219). Instead she advocates an alternative view characterised by the pluralisation of hegemonies: 'a multi-polar, agonistic world organised around several big, regional units with their different cultures and values' (p. 219). Such a view, she continues, holds open the prospect that different kinds of democracy might emerge, not only the Western one based on the idea of human rights.

The volume closes with a short interview (Chapter 15) in which Mouffe discusses her views on a number of topics, including Gramsci, Schmitt, art and the uprisings of 2011 in the Middle East and North Africa (the so-called Arab Spring), which she regards, to some extent, as an affirmation of the ideas she has formulated across the years. A neat summary of many of the views set out in the chapters of this volume, the interview offers an insightful glimpse of the way that Mouffe sees her own contribution and the prospects for democratic theory in a world forever shaped by conflict.

It is a mark of Mouffe's sense of vocation as a democratic theorist that she takes her cue not simply from abstract principles but, moreover, from a constant theoretical interrogation of the arguments, disputes and conflicts in the real world. Almost by definition, there is much with which to take issue in her work and many adversarial exchanges to be had over her theoretical framework and the conclusions she draws. Controversy and disagreement have been integral elements in her innovative style of theorising from the beginning. But, more than this, her writing invites us to undertake, perhaps paradoxically, a positive and hopeful task: to respond to the challenge that conflict, rather than consensus, can help make better democrats of us all.

References

Geras, N. 1987. 'Post-Marxism?' *New Left Review* (Series 1), no. 163 (May–June), pp. 40–82.
Gray, J. 2009. *False Dawn: The Delusions of Global Capitalism*, 2nd edn. London: Granta.
Laclau, E. and Mouffe, C. 2001. *Hegemony and Socialist Strategy: Towards a Radical Democratic Politics*, 2nd edn. London: Verso.
Mouffe, C. 1979. *Gramsci and Marxist Theory*. London: Routledge.

——(ed.). 1992. *Dimensions of Radical Democracy*. London: Verso.

——1993. *The Return of the Political*. London: Verso.

——(ed.). 1996a. *Deconstruction and Pragmatism*. London: Routledge.

——1996b. 'Deconstruction, Pragmatism and the Politics of Democracy', in C. Mouffe (ed.). *Deconstruction and Pragmatism*. London: Routledge, pp. 1–12.

——(ed.). 1999. *The Challenge of Carl Schmitt*. London: Verso.

——2000. *The Democratic Paradox*. London: Verso.

——2001–2. 'Interview with Chantal Mouffe', *CSD Bulletin* 9:1 (Winter), pp. 10–13.

——2005. *On the Political*. London: Routledge.

Nagl, L. and Mouffe, C. (eds.). 2001. *The Legacy of Wittgenstein; Pragmatism or Deconstruction*. Frankfurt am M: Peter Lang.

PART I
Hegemony
From Gramsci to 'post-Marxism'

1

HEGEMONY AND IDEOLOGY IN GRAMSCI (1979)[1]

The theory of ideology was for a long time one of the most neglected areas of the Marxist analysis of society. Yet this is a key area involving some extremely important issues which are not only theoretical but also political. It is vital, therefore, to attempt to understand the nature of those obstacles which have hindered the formulation of a theory which offers an adequate explanation of the significance and role of ideology, since it is no exaggeration to say that these have constituted the main impediment to the development of Marxism, both as a theory and as a political movement.

At first sight, the answer seems fairly simple. The various obstacles all seem in effect to proceed from the unique phenomenon which a vast body of contemporary literature has termed *economism*. However, the apparent obvious simplicity of the term hides a whole series of problems which begin to emerge as soon as one attempts a rigorous definition of its specificity and extent. Although it is clear that all forms of economism imply a misrecognition of the distinct autonomy of politics and ideology, this generic definition is inadequate, as it gives rise to two possible spheres of ambiguity. The first stems from the fact that the notion of the economic is indeed ambiguous and far from being clear itself (it is not clear, for example, what is the relative importance attributed to the forces of production and the relations of production in this area). The second is the result of the vagueness and imprecision characterising the mechanism of the subordination of politics and ideology to economics, since this is always defined resorting to purely allusive metaphors ('subordination', 'reduction', 'reflection'). In this way one is left with the possibility of the existence of complex forms of economism which are not easy to detect since they do not appear as such at first sight.

Economism and ideology

It is here that we can locate the reason for the complexity of the problem of economism in relation to the theory of ideology, since the former occurs in numerous forms, some of which have only rarely been identified. The economistic problematic of ideology has two intimately linked but quite distinct facets. The first one consists in seeing a causal link between the structure and the superstructure and in viewing the latter purely as a mechanical reflection of the economic base. This leads to a vision of ideological superstructures as epiphenomena which play no part in the historical process. The second facet is not concerned with the role of the superstructures but with their actual nature, and here they are conceived as being determined by the position of the subjects in the relations of production. This second aspect is not identifiable with the first since here it is in fact possible to attribute 'differential time sequences' and even a certain efficacy to the ideological superstructures.

It is important to understand the various forms in which these two aspects have been combined in the Marxist tradition. They can in fact be divided into three main phases: the first, which is the one in which the two aspects have combined, constitutes the pure and classic form of economism; in the second there is a move away from the classic view as the two aspects begin to be dissociated; finally, in the third phase there is a break with the two aspects of economism, and the theoretical bases for a rethinking of historical materialism in a radically anti–economistic perspective are established.

There are various reasons why the distinction of these three moments is necessary for an accurate understanding of economism. First of all, although it is generally agreed that the Second and Third Internationals were economistic, the particular forms of economism involved have not been adequately specified, with the result that reductionism and epiphenomenonism have tended to be identified with each other, or at least to be seen in a relation of mutual implication. As regards the 'superstructural' Marxist interpretations (Lukács, Korsch, etc.), it is important to see that they only partially break with economism because although they reject the epiphenomenalist concept of ideology, class reductionism is none the less still present. Finally, it must be realised that the third moment is only just beginning and that the superseding of both aspects of economism is a theoretical task which for the most part still remains to be carried out.

Antonio Gramsci must surely be the first to have undertaken a complete and radical critique of economism, and it is here that his main contribution to the Marxist theory of ideology lies. It is the object of this chapter, therefore, to analyse Gramsci's contribution within this perspective. First, however, it is important to recognise the particular difficulties that such a reading would involve. Some of these are inherent in any attempt at what is called a 'symptomatic reading', while others stem from the particular nature of Gramsci's writings and their fragmentary character. The main pitfall to be avoided at all costs, is an instrumental reading of Gramsci, one which takes advantage of the unsystematic nature of his work to extrapolate passages in an arbitrary fashion in order to back up a thesis bearing little relation to his thought. If symptomatic readings involve *practising a problematic* it is vital to make the latter explicit in order to avoid transferring to the text in question the contradictions of the conceptual system upon which the analysis is based. In addition one should not lose sight of the fact that the problematic underlying the analysis of the text is *external* to it, and that the unity of the text is often established along quite separate lines from the problematic itself. To avoid any ambiguity I shall start by defining the fundamental principles of the anti-reductionist problematic which is the basis of this reading of Gramsci. It should then be possible to judge whether the hypothesis with which I intend to proceed, which consists in attributing to Gramsci the merit of having laid the foundations of such a conception, can be accepted or not.

Principles of a non-reductionist conception of ideology

The non-reductionist conception of ideology which constitutes the theoretical foundation of this symptomatic reading of Gramsci is based on the following principles:

1   The notion of the concrete as overdetermination of contradictions. Faced with a Hegelian-type conception which reduces each conjuncture to a process of the auto-development of a single contradiction, which as a result reduces the present to an *abstract* and *necessary* moment of a linear and predetermined development, I accept Althusser's conception which establishes the primacy of the notion of conjuncture in the analysis of the concrete, and considers every conjuncture as an overdetermination of contradictions, each one of which can be thought *abstractly* in conceptual independence from the others. This con-stitutes the basis of a non-reductionist conception of the political and the ideological, given the fact that reductionism stems precisely from Marxism's adoption of a Hegelian historicist model. This leads to a consideration of all contradictions as moments in the development of a single contradiction – the class contradiction – which as a consequence leads one to attribute a class character to all political and ideological elements. The central problem of contemporary Marxism lies in the elaboration of a non-reductionist theory of ideology and of politics which will account for the determination in the last instance by the economic.

2   How is this need for a conception which is both Marxist and non-reductionist expressed in the concrete case of the theory of ideology? Following Althusser on this point, I understand by ideology a practice producing subjects (Althusser 1971, pp. 160–65). The subject is not the originating source of consciousness, the expression of the irruption of a subjective principle into objective historical processes, but the *product* of a specific practice operating through the mechanism of interpellation. If, according to Althusser's conception, social agents are not the constitutive principle of their acts, but supports of the structures, their sub-jective principles of identity constitute an additional structural element resulting from specific historical practices. In this case, how are the principles of over-determination and of the determination in the last instance by the economic combined? Let us first take overdetermination.

The social agent possesses several principles of ideological determination, not just one: he is hailed (interpellated) as the member of either sex, of a family, of a social class, of a nation, of a race or as an aesthetic onlooker, etc., and he lives these different subjectivities in which he is constituted in a relation of mutual implication. The problem consists in determining the *objective* relation between these subjective principles or ideological elements. In a reductionist perspective each of these has a necessary class-belonging. But if, on the contrary, we accept the principle of overdetermination, we must conclude that there can exist no necessary relation between them, and that it is consequently impossible to attribute a necessary class-belonging to them. However, it is here that the second principle – the determination in the last instance by the economic – intervenes. To stress determination in the last instance by the economic is equivalent to saying determination in the last instance by the social classes inasmuch as we define classes as constituting antagonistic poles in the dominant relations of production. This brings us, therefore, to the following assertion: if the ideological elements referred to do not *express* social classes, but if nevertheless classes do, in the last instance, determine ideology, then we must thereby conclude that this determination can only be the result of the establishing of an articulating principle of these ideological elements, one which must result in actually *conferring upon them* a class character. This point, however, leaves a whole series of questions unresolved, and it is in this area that the elaboration of the anti-reductionist conception of ideology still remains to be done. In effect the assertion that the class character of an ideology is conferred upon it by its own articulating principle suggests the area in which the solution is to be found, but this in itself does not provide the theoretical answer to the problem.

The two points above have dealt with the theoretical bases of a nonreductionist conception of ideology, and the ground still to be covered in order to achieve a rigorous formulation of this conception has been indicated. The central concern of this chapter is to determine the ways in which these problems were recognised as such by Gramsci and to see what kind of solutions he proposed. I will attempt to show how the Gramscian conception of *hegemony* involved, *in the practical state*, the operation of an anti-reductionist problematic of ideology. I shall go even further and maintain that it is this whole anti-reductionist conception of ideology which is the actual condition of *intelligibility* of Gramsci's conception of hegemony, and that the difficulties encountered in the interpretation of this conception stem from the fact that this anti-reductionist problematic has not so far been stressed.

Before going on to analyse Gramsci's conception, it will first be necessary to take a detour via the Second International. In effect, economism did not present itself to Gramsci as an abstract or academic problem since it was on the contrary deeply embedded in the political practice of the Second International and was the root cause of the massive defeats suffered by the German and Italian working-class movements in the decade following the First World War. It is within this context that Gramsci's thought gains its significance and is to be understood.

The Second International and economism

The Second International's theory of the collapse of capitalism was based on an interpretation of Marx's thought whereby the proletarian revolution was the necessary and inevitable consequence of the development of the economic contradictions of the capitalist mode of production. Ideology did not have any autonomy since the development of socialist consciousness was the corollary of the numerical growth of the proletariat as a class, and of the exacerbation of economic contradictions. On the other hand, socialist consciousness was identified with the consciousness of the social agents, and the latter's principle of identity was to be found in the class to which they belonged. The two forms of economism were therefore combined: that is to say the epiphenomenonist conception of the role of ideology and the reductionist conception of its nature. This type of interpretation of Marxism had its epistemological foundations in a positivist conception of science which viewed historical materialism in terms of a model of scientificity then prevalent in the physical sciences.[2] This gave rise to the assumption that the validity of Marx's theory depended on the empirical proof of the three laws considered to constitute the basis of his analysis of the capitalist mode of production: increasing concentration, overproduction, and proletarianisation. The conviction that these laws would be enacted and that they would automatically bring about the proletarian revolution led the defenders of the catastrophe theory to assert the inevitable nature of socialism. As Kautsky wrote in his commentary on the Erfurt Programme:

> We believe that the collapse of the existing society is inevitable because we know that economic development naturally and necessarily produces contradictions which oblige the exploited to combat private property. We know that it increases the numbers and strength of the exploiters whose interests lie in the maintenance of the existing order, and that it finally brings about unbearable contradictions for the mass of the population which is left only with the choice between brutalisation and inertia or the overturning of the existing system of ownership.
>
> (Kautsky 1892, p. 106)[3]

The Second International was strongly reductionist from an ideological point of view, and since it considered that all ideological elements had a necessary class-belonging, it concluded from this that all elements belonging to the discourse of the bourgeoisie had to be decisively rejected by the working class whose aim had to be to cultivate pure proletarian values and to guard against all external contamination. This is how democracy came to be considered the typical ideological expression of the bourgeoisie.

In order to understand how such an interpretation of Marxism was able to come into being, it is important to recapture the historical climate of those years. On the one hand, there was a strong bourgeoisie which had succeeded in extending its hold over the whole of society and in articulating the democratic demands to its class discourse. On the other hand, there was the working class organised into powerful unions and mass parties, which made it possible to achieve success in its struggle for economic demands. This situation caused a twofold tension in socialist thought between (a) the need to establish a radical break between socialist ideology and bourgeois ideology, which was the only way to ensure the independence of the socialist movement at a time when the bourgeoisie still exercised a considerable power of attraction, and (b) the need to establish a point of contact between the revolutionary objectives of the workers' movement and its growing success in the field of reforms within the capitalist system. Kautsky's economism constituted a full reply to these two needs. Since the bourgeoisie had succeeded in assimilating popular and democratic ideology to its discourse, Kautskyism concluded that democracy was necessarily a bourgeois ideology. Democracy therefore ceased to be seen, as in the young Marx, as the terrain of a permanent revolution begun by the bourgeoisie but concluded by the proletariat, and became instead a class ideology. The class criterion began to become the fundamental criterion at all levels and this is how one of the fundamental characteristics of economism originated, that is to say, class reductionism. On the other hand, if the working class was to take no part in the direction of other social forces and was to limit itself to the defence of its own interests, then revolution could not be the result of the conscious intervention of the working class presenting itself as a political alternative for all the exploited, but had instead to represent the unfolding of the possibilities inherent in the economic contradictions. From this ensues the theory of the collapse of capitalism. However, since this collapse was seen as merely the result of the play of economic forces, the latter were considered to contain all the elements necessary to explain the historical process. As a consequence, political and ideological factors simply became epiphenomena, which constitute the second characteristic of Kautsky's economism.

This mechanistic conception was to undergo a crisis on several points at the beginning of the twentieth century. But the development of the critique of Kautskyan dogmatism had its own particular characteristics: in its most diverse and even antagonistic forms, the critique indicated the contradictions and inconsistencies of Kautskyism without, however, abandoning its presuppositions. What is more, these critiques constituted both a negation of Kautskyism as a system and a development of the various potentialities present in its ideological presuppositions. This tendency is particularly clear in the case of Bernstein and in the debate on revisionism. As a result of the nonrealisation of predictions based on the theory of the collapse of capitalism and also of certain glaring contradictions in the theory of the spontaneous determination of the socialist consciousness of the working class – as in the case of the British working class – Bernstein was driven to reject Marxism which he declared incapable of understanding real historical developments. Bernstein was to replace the Marxist vision of scientific socialism with a view of socialism as an 'ethical ideal', as a type of society towards which humanity should voluntarily orientate itself by virtue of moral principles.

Bernstein had understood that in view of the new conditions in which capitalism was developing, the theory of catastrophe could no longer be upheld and that in advanced capitalist countries the superstructures played an increasingly important part. This is why, unlike Kautsky, he saw the importance of the working-class struggle being extended to the political and ideological fields. It was, therefore, this recognition of the need to pose the problem of ideology in a radically different way which led Bernstein to challenge the economistic version of Marxism. However, since he identified Marx's doctrine with the theory of catastrophe, his critique of economism led him to reject Marxism outright. In effect, he considered that the attribution of an active role to ideologies had necessarily to contradict the Marxist theory of history. Thus Bernstein's break with Marxism is to be located within the theoretical domain constituted by the ideological presuppositions of the Second International which were never seriously challenged. If, on the one hand, he identified Marxism and the theory of catastrophe, on the other, he identified democracy and bourgeois parliamentarianism. This is why it is impossible to use Bernstein's revisionism as a basis for a theory of the autonomy of the political and the ideological as *specific objective levels*. For him objectivity meant determination, and the only form of determination with which he was acquainted was mechanical economic determinism. As a result, although he did intuit the fact that class reductionism and economic determinism had prevented Marxism from understanding the specific problems of the age of monopoly capital, the only alternative intellectual expression open to him lay in the opposite extreme, in a flight from objectivity, an irruption of subjectivity – the ethical ideal – into history. This gave rise to his recourse to Kantian ethics. From Sorel to Croce, all the tendencies which at the beginning of the century attempted to oppose the dominant positivist trend, did so in the name of voluntarism, of subjectivism or even of irrationalism. There was no other solution in an intellectual world where mechanical determination and objectivity had become synonymous.

Leninism and its consequences

If reductionism and epiphenomenalism had ended up by being inextricably linked in the thought of the Second International, then the historic experience of the Russian Revolution was to lay the basis for the breaking up of this unity. On the one hand, the revolution had triumphed in the European countries where it was least expected – in complete contradiction with the theory that revolution was the result of the mechanical unfolding of economic forces. It was obvious that this revolution had resulted from political intervention in a conjuncture which traditional Marxism had considered could never bring about a socialist outcome. As a result, this discredited the type of political reasoning which linked all historical changes to the relation between the forces of production and the relations of production, and it also called into question epiphenomenist presuppositions. On the other hand, Lenin's analysis of combined development, and the transformation of democratic slogans into socialist ones during the Russian Revolution, brought new prestige to the analyses made by the young Marx on the subject of the dialectic between democracy and classes, and it established a link between the Russian Revolution and the cycle of permanent revolutions which had been interrupted by the failure of the 1848 revolutions. In this way the reductionist presupposition was also seriously called into question.

Nevertheless, Lenin's analyses on this subject are on the one hand extremely succinct and on the other fairly ambiguous, since in various ways they did remain prisoner to the old problematic. In fact, it was Lenin's *political practice* rather than his actual thought which really proved to be a transforming force which shattered the narrow economistic confines of Western Marxist thought at the beginning of the century.

There were three possible attitudes which could further develop the new point of departure represented by Leninism. One of these was to see revolution as the result of the irruption of consciousness and will into history in opposition to fatalism and the determinism of economic forces. This represented the continuation of the voluntarist subjectivism of the pre-war period. The young Gramsci saw the Bolshevik triumph as the revolution against 'Capital'; Sorel saw it as the triumph of 'the method of liberating violence' and of the will. In the confusion of the post-war world in which an infinite variety of anti-*status quo* ideologies flourished and proliferated, Bolshevism had become for numerous sections of society the symbol of a revolutionary *élan* which spurned all restrictions and objective conditions.

Another possible attitude consisted in trying to make the primacy of consciousness and the autonomy of the political moment compatible with an objective class logic. This was possible as long as one defined classes by their position in the process of production while at the same time making class consciousness the highest moment in their process of self-development. It is this sort of conception which defines the parameters of Lukács' project in his *History and Class Consciousness* and this is why he only half succeeded in superseding economism. In effect, although by his insistence on the decisive function of class consciousness he was anti-economist because of the *efficacity* which he attributed to ideology, he was incapable of overcoming reductionism in his conception of the *nature* of ideology. For him, ideology was identified with class consciousness, and he therefore defined it as the 'imputed consciousness' of a social class which is determined by the place which it occupies in the relations of production. This means that Lukács broke with the Second International's epiphenomenalism but not with class reductionism. He used the heritage of Leninism in a one-sided fashion and only continued one of the two potential lines of development which this had opened up.

The third attitude was that of trying to extract all the theoretical consequences from Lenin's political practice, and this led to a complete and radical questioning of all aspects of the economistic problematic. Unfortunately, the extremely active period of theoretical elaboration of the 1920s was followed by the sterile silence of the Stalinist era which effectively blocked the development of Marxism for several decades. And yet, at that time there was one solitary effort made in this third direction. During his long years of captivity, in his reflections on the causes for the defeat of the working-class movement and the victory of fascism, alone in the isolation of his cell, Antonio Gramsci arrived at the source of all the errors: the lack of understanding of the nature and role of politics and ideology. In his *Prison Notebooks* this was to lead him to rethink all the problems central to Marxism in a radically anti-economistic perspective, and hence to develop all the potentialities present in Leninism.

Gramsci and hegemony

Having sketched in broad outline the Marxist problematic which provided the background against which Gramsci's thought developed, we must now return to the central problem of this chapter, that is, Gramsci's contribution to the Marxist theory of ideology. Let us first restate our main argument: this consists in showing that a radically anti-economistic problematic of ideology is operating *in the practical state* in Gramsci's conception of hegemony and that it constitutes its actual condition of *intelligibility*. I shall therefore begin by analysing the texts where Gramsci presents the concept of hegemony, in order to define its meaning and to study its evolution. I shall then discuss the implications which it has for the Marxist theory of ideology.

   The concept of hegemony first appeared in Gramsci's work in 1926 in 'Notes on the Southern Question'. It was introduced in the following way:

> The Turin communists posed concretely the question of the hegemony of the proletariat: i.e. of the social basis of the proletarian dictatorship and the workers' State. The proletariat can become the leading (*dirigente*) and the dominant class to the extent that it succeeds in creating a system of alliances which allows it to mobilise the majority of the working population against capitalism and the bourgeois State. In Italy, in the real class relations which exist there, this means to the extent that it succeeds in gaining the consent of the broad peasant masses.
>
> (Gramsci 1978, p. 443)[4]

This work marked a step forward in Gramsci's thought. Naturally he had understood the importance of an alliance with the peasantry before 1926, since already in 1919, in an article entitled 'Workers and Peasants', he had insisted on the role which the peasants had to play in the proletarian revolution. It was in his 'Notes on the Southern Question', however, that he was to put the question of this alliance in terms of hegemony for the first time and to stress the political, moral and intellectual conditions which were necessary to bring this about. Hence he insisted, for example, on the fact that the working class had to free itself entirely of corporatism in order to be capable of winning over the Southern intellectuals to its cause, since it was through them that it would be able to influence the mass of the peasantry. The existence of an intellectual and moral dimension in the question of hegemony was already something typical of Gramsci and was later to take on its own importance. However, we are still at the stage of the Leninist conception of hegemony seen as the leadership of the proletariat over the peasantry, that is to say, that it was political leadership which constituted the essential element of this conception in view of the fact that hegemony was thought of in terms of a *class alliance*. It is only later in the *Prison Notebooks* that hegemony in its typically Gramscian sense is to be found, and here it becomes the indissoluble union of political leadership and intellectual and moral leadership, which clearly goes beyond the idea of a simple class alliance.

The problematic of hegemony is to be found right from the first of the *Prison Notebooks*, but with an important innovation: Gramsci no longer applies it only to the *strategy* of the proletariat, but uses it to think of the practices of the ruling classes in general:

> The following historical and political criterion is the one on which research must be based: a class is dominant in two ways, that is to say it is dominant and ruling. It rules the allied classes and dominates the opposing classes.
>
> (Gramsci 1975, vol. 1; English trans. Gramsci 1971, p. 57)

There is no doubt that in mentioning the direction of the allied classes Gramsci is referring here to hegemony, and there are innumerable statements to this effect throughout the *Prison Notebooks*. For example, a few pages further on in the same *Notebook I*, in his examination of the role of the Jacobins in the French Revolution, he declares:

> Not only did they organise a bourgeois government, i.e., make the bourgeoisie the dominant class – they did more. They created the bourgeois State, made the bourgeoisie into the leading, hegemonic class of the nation, in other words gave the new State a permanent basis and created the compact modern French nation.
>
> (Gramsci 1975, vol. 1, p. 51; Gramsci 1971, p. 79)[5]

He indicates that it was by forcing the bourgeoisie to overcome its corporatist nature that the Jacobins managed to make it a hegemonic class. They in fact forced it to widen its class interests and to discover those interests which it had in common with the popular sectors, and it was on this basis that they were able to put themselves in command and to lead those sectors into the struggle. Here, therefore, we find once more the opposition between corporatist and hegemonic classes encountered in 'Notes on the Southern Question', but this time it is applied to the bourgeoisie. Gramsci had in fact begun to understand that the bourgeoisie had also needed to ensure itself popular support and that the political struggle was far more complex than had ever been thought by reductionist tendencies, since it did not consist in a simple confrontation between antagonistic classes but always involved complex relations of forces.

Gramsci analyses the relations of forces in all societies and studies the transition from a corporate to a hegemonic stage in a fundamental passage in *Notebook 4* (Gramsci 1975, vol. 1, pp. 457–59; Gramsci 1971, pp. 180–83).[6] He begins by distinguishing three principal levels at which the relations of forces exist:

1   the relation of social forces linked to the structure and dependent on the degree of development of the material forces of production;
2   the relation of political forces, that is to say the degree of consciousness and organisation within the different social groups;
3   the relation of military forces which is always, according to Gramsci, the decisive moment.

In his analysis of the different moments of political consciousness he distinguished three more degrees:

a   the *primitive economic* moment in which the consciousness of a group's own professional interests are expressed but not as yet their interests as a social class;
b   the *political economic* moment which is the one in which the consciousness of class interests is expressed, but only at an economic level;
c   the third moment is that of *hegemony*, 'in which one becomes aware that one's own corporate interests, in their present and future development, transcend the corporate limits of the purely economic class, and can and must become the interests of other subordinate groups too'.
                    (Gramsci 1975, vol. 1, pp. 457–59; Gramsci 1971, pp. 180–83)

For Gramsci, this is where the specifically political moment is situated, and it is characterised by ideological struggle which attempts to forge unity between economic, political and intellectual objectives, 'placing all the questions around which the struggle rages on a "universal", not a corporate level, thereby creating the hegemony of a fundamental social group over a series of subordinate ones'.
                    (Gramsci 1975, vol. 1, pp. 457–59; Gramsci 1971, pp. 180–83)

This text (which was to be reworked by Gramsci into its definitive form two years later in *Notebook 13*) is, I believe, one of the key texts for an understanding of the Gramscian conception of hegemony and it is surprising that until now little importance has been attached to it.[7] It is here in fact that Gramsci sets out a very different conception of hegemony from the one found in 'Notes on the Southern Question', since here it is no longer a question of a simple political alliance but of a complete fusion of economic, political, intellectual and moral objectives which will be brought about by one fundamental group and groups allied to it *through the intermediary of ideology* when an ideology manages to 'spread throughout the whole of society determining not only united economic and political objectives but also intellectual and moral unity' (Gramsci 1975, vol. 3, p. 1584; Gramsci 1971, pp. 180–85). From *Notebook 4* the Leninist conception of hegemony is doubly enriched: first, its extension to the bourgeoisie and then the addition of a new and fundamental dimension (since it is through this that unity at the political level will be realised), that of intellectual and moral direction. It was only later that Gramsci was to develop all the implications of this enrichment, but from *Notebook 4* onwards hegemony does assume its specifically Gramscian dimension. It is therefore already possible, on the basis of what has so far been discussed, to advance a tentative initial definition of a *hegemonic class*: it is a class which has been able to articulate the interests of other social groups to its own by means of ideological struggle. This, according to Gramsci, is only possible if this class renounces a strictly corporatist conception, since in order to exercise leadership, it must genuinely concern itself with the interests of those social groups over which it wishes to exercise hegemony – 'obviously the fact of hegemony presupposes that one takes into account the interests and the tendencies of the groups over which hegemony will be exercised, and it also presupposes a certain equilibrium, that is to say that the hegemonic groups will make some sacrifices of a corporate nature' (Gramsci 1975, vol. 1, p. 461). This conception of hegemony has certain very important consequences in relation to the way in which Gramsci envisaged the nature and the role of the state (Gramsci 1975, vol. 3, p. 1584; Gramsci 1971, p. 182):

> It is true that the State is seen as the organ of one particular group, destined to create favourable conditions for the latter's maximum expansion. But the development and expansion of the particular group are conceived of, and presented, as being the motor force of a universal expansion, of a development of all the 'national' energies. In other words the dominant group is coordinated concretely with the general interests of the subordinate groups, and the life of the State is conceived of as a continuous process of formation and superseding of unstable equilibria (on the juridical plane) between the interests of the fundamental group and those of the subordinate groups – equilibria in which the interests of the dominant group prevail, but only up to a certain point, i.e. stopping short of narrowly corporate economic interest.

It is, therefore, the problematic of hegemony which is at the root of this 'enlarging of the state' whose importance has quite rightly been stressed by Christine Buci-Glucksmann.[8] This was to permit Gramsci to break with the economistic conception of the state, only envisaged as a coercive bureaucratic apparatus in the hands of the dominant class, and to formulate the notion of the *integral state* which consisted of 'dictatorship + hegemony'. This is not the place to analyse Gramsci's contribution to the Marxist theory of the state (which is also of the utmost importance), so I shall limit myself to pointing out that this enlargement of the state works on two levels: first, it involves the enlarging of the social base of the state and the complex relations established between the state, the hegemonic class and its mass base; second, it also involves the enlarging of the state's functions, since the notion of the integral state implies the incorporation of the apparatuses of hegemony, of civil society, to the state.

Concerning the methods by which a class can become hegemonic, Gramsci distinguishes two principal routes: the first is that of transformism, and the second is that of expansive hegemony. Let us first take *transformism*. This is the method by which the Moderate Party during the Risorgimento managed to secure its hegemony over the forces fighting for unification. Here what was involved was 'the gradual but continuous absorption, achieved by methods which varied in their effectiveness, of the active elements produced by allied groups – and even those which came from the antagonistic groups … ' (Gramsci 1975, vol. 3, p. 2011; Gramsci 1971, p. 161). This naturally was only a bastard form of hegemony and the consensus obtained with these methods was merely a 'passive consensus'. In fact, the process whereby power was taken was termed a 'passive revolution' by Gramsci, since the masses were integrated through a system of absorption and neutralisation of their interests in such a way as to prevent them from opposing those of the hegemonic class. Gramsci contrasted this type of hegemony through absorption by what he called successful hegemony, that is to say, *expansive hegemony*. This had to consist in the creation of an active, direct consensus resulting from the genuine adoption of the interests of the popular classes by the hegemonic class, which would give rise to the creation of a genuine 'national-popular will'. Unlike the passive revolution, in fact, where vast sectors of the popular classes are excluded from the hegemonic system, in an expansive hegemony the whole society must advance. This distinction of two methods of hegemony makes it possible to specify further the tentative definition of hegemony already put forward. In fact, if hegemony is defined as the ability of one class to articulate the interest of other social groups to its own, it is now possible to see that this can be done in two very different ways: the interests of these groups can either be articulated so as to neutralise them and hence to prevent the development of their own specific demands, or else they can be articulated in such a way as to promote their full development leading to the final resolution of the contradictions which they express.

These texts prompt a series of further observations. First, only a fundamental class (that is to say one which occupies one of the two poles in the relations of production of a determinate mode of production) can become hegemonic, as Gramsci unequivocally states: 'though hegemony is ethico–political, it must also be economic, must necessarily be based on the decisive function exercised by the leading group in the decisive nucleus of economic activity' (Gramsci 1975, vol. 1, p. 461; Gramsci 1971, p. 161). This condition not only restricts the possible number of hegemonic classes, it also indicates the possible limitations of any forms of hegemony. If in fact the exercise of hegemony involves economic and corporate sacrifices on the part of the aspiring leading class, the latter cannot, however, go so far as to jeopardise its basic interests. Sooner or later, therefore, the bourgeoisie comes up against the limitations of its hegemony, as it is an exploiting class, since its class interests must, at a certain level, necessarily clash with those of the popular classes. This, says Gramsci, is a sign that it has exhausted its function and that from then on 'the ideological bloc tends to crumble away; then "spontaneity" may be replaced by "constraint" in ever less disguised and indirect forms, culminating in outright police measures and *coups d'état* (Gramsci 1975, vol. 3, p. 2012; Gramsci 1971, pp. 60–1). Thus only the working class, whose interests coincide with the limitation of all exploitation, can be capable of successfully bringing about an expansive hegemony.

The most important aspect of Gramsci's hegemony still remains to be studied. This is the aspect of *intellectual and moral leadership* and the way in which this is achieved. In fact, all the points which have been raised could be entirely compatible with a conception of hegemony seen as alliance of classes. However, if Gramsci's hegemony were limited to political leadership, it would only differ from Lenin's concept in that Gramsci does not restrict its use to the strategy of the proletariat, but also applies it to the bourgeoisie. Now it has been pointed out that the conception of hegemony is doubly enriched with respect to Lenin, as it also involves the addition of a new dimension which is inextricably linked to political direction, and that is intellectual and moral leadership. As a result, the establishing of hegemony became a phenomenon which went far beyond a simple class alliance. In fact, for Gramsci – and it is this which constitutes his originality – hegemony is not to be found in a purely instrumental alliance between classes through which the *class demands* of the allied classes are articulated to those of the fundamental class, with each group maintaining its own individuality within the alliance as well as its own ideology. According to him, hegemony involves the creation of a *higher synthesis*, so that all its elements fuse in a 'collective will' which becomes the new protagonist of political action which will function as the protagonist of political action during that hegemony's entire duration. It is through ideology that this collective will is formed since its very existence depends on the creation of ideological unity which will serve as 'cement' (Gramsci 1975, vol. 2, p. 1380). This is the key to the indissoluble unity of the two aspects of Gramscian hegemony, since the formation of the collective will and the exercise of political leadership depend on the very existence of intellectual and moral leadership. To account for these two aspects and the way in which they are articulated undoubtedly constitutes the major difficulty to be faced in any study of the conception of hegemony in Gramsci's thought. It is this, moreover, which explains why a comprehensive definition of hegemony has not been established so far despite the abundant literature existing on this subject. In fact, most interpretations unilaterally stress one or the other aspect, which gives rise to widely differing and often opposing interpretations, according to whether political direction or moral and intellectual direction is stressed.[9] The few interpretations which do try to account for both aspects at once do so on the basis of an erroneous conception of one or the other of the two, or else of the link between them.[10]

If, therefore, we wish finally to manage to establish a comprehensive definition of Gramsci's conception of hegemony which accounts for its specificity and does not ignore any of its potentialities, it is important to be able to think theoretically of the kind of relation established between its two components, that is, the secret of their unity, and to see what are the main characteristics resulting from this. To do this, the following question needs to be answered: how can one forge genuine ideological unity between different social groups in such a way as to make them unite into a single political subject? To answer this problem it is of course necessary to discuss the conception of ideology which is present – both explicitly and implicitly – in Gramsci's work. It will then be shown how it is impossible to give a coherent account of the specificity of Gramsci's conception from the perspective of an economistic problematic of ideology.

Hegemony and ideology

The best point of departure for an analysis of the conception of ideology operating in the Gramscian problematic of hegemony is to study the way in which he envisaged the process of the formation of a new hegemony. The notes referring to how a new collective will must be formed through moral and intellectual reform which will be the work of the 'Modern Prince' are, therefore, the most revealing on this subject.[11] But first the few texts in which Gramsci explicitly sets out his conception of ideology must be discussed.

The problematic of ideology

Gramsci immediately places himself on entirely different ground from those viewing ideology as false consciousness or as a system of ideas, and he rebels against all epiphenomenalist conceptions which reduce it to mere appearances with no efficacy.

> The claim, presented as an essential postulate of historical materialism, that every fluctuation of politics and ideology can be presented and expounded as an immediate expression of the structure, must be contested in theory as primitive infantilism, and combated in practice with the authentic testimony of Marx, the author of concrete political and historical works.
> (Gramsci 1975, vol. 2, p. 871; Gramsci 1971, p. 407)

According to Gramsci, the starting point of all research on ideology must be Marx's assertion that 'men gain consciousness of their tasks on the ideological terrain of the superstructures' (Gramsci 1975, vol. 1, p. 437; Gramsci 1971, p. 365). So that the latter, he declares, must be considered 'operating realities which possess efficacy' (Gramsci 1975, vol. 2, p. 869; Gramsci 1971, p. 377), and if Marx sometimes terms them illusions, it is only in a polemical sense in order to clearly specify their historical arid transitory nature. Gramsci was to formulate his own definition of ideology as the terrain 'on which men move, acquire consciousness of their position, struggle' (Gramsci 1975, vol. 1, p. 337; Gramsci 1971, p. 377). Ideology, he declares, must be seen as a battlefield, as a continuous struggle, since men's acquisition of consciousness through ideology will not come individually but always through the intermediary of the ideological terrain where two 'hegemonic principles' confront each other (Gramsci 1975, vol. 2, p. 1236). The self's acquisition of consciousness is in effect only possible through an ideological formation constituted not only of discursive elements, but also of non-discursive elements which Gramsci designates by the rather vague term 'conformism'. His intention becomes clear, however, when he indicates that the acquisition of this necessary consciousness through conformism results in the fact 'that one is always mass-man or collective-man' (Gramsci 1975, vol. 2, p. 1376; Gramsci 1971, p. 324). One finds here, in fact, the idea that the subjects are not originally given but are always produced by ideology through a socially determined ideological field, so that subjectivity is always the product of social practice. This implies that ideology has a material existence, and that far from consisting in an ensemble of spiritual realities, it is always materialised in practices. The nature of ideology as practice is further reinforced by the identification Gramsci establishes between ideology and religion (in the Crocean sense of a world-view with its corresponding norms of action) – as it serves to stress that ideology organises action. In effect Gramsci considers that a world-view is manifest in all action and that this expresses itself in a very elaborate form and at a high level of abstraction – as is the case with philosophy – or else it is expressed in much simpler forms as the expression of 'common sense' which presents itself as the spontaneous philosophy of the man in the street, but which is the popular expression of 'higher' philosophies (Gramsci 1975, vol. 2, p. 1063; Gramsci 1971, pp. 323–26). These world-views are never individual facts but the expression of the 'communal life of a social bloc', which is why Gramsci calls them 'organic ideologies' (Gramsci 1975, vol. 2, p. 868; Gramsci 1971, p. 376). It is these which 'organise the human masses' and which serve as the informative principle of all individual and collective activities, since it is through these that men acquire all their forms of consciousness (Gramsci 1975, vol. 2, p. 1492). But if it is through organic ideologies that men acquire all their forms of consciousness, and if these organic ideologies are world-views of determinate social blocs, this means that all forms of consciousness are necessarily political. This enables Gramsci to make the following equation: philosophy = ideology = politics. This identification has generally been misunderstood, and it is this which underlies all the misinterpretations of Gramsci's historicism which present it as a Hegelian reading of Marxism.[12] In fact, what Gramsci was trying to do was to think the role of subjectivity, but so as not to present it as the irruption of the individual consciousness into history. To achieve this, he posits consciousness not as originally given but as the effect of the system of ideological relations into which the individual is inserted. Thus, it is ideology which creates subjects and makes them act.

Ideology as a practice producing subjects is what appears to be the real idea implicit in Gramsci's thoughts on the operative and active nature of ideology and its identification with politics. However, he did not have the necessary theoretical tools at his disposal to express this intuition adequately, and he had to content himself with making allusions to it using very ambiguous formulas strongly influenced by Crocean historicism. Let us take, for example, the definition of ideology as 'a conception of the world implicitly manifest in art, in law, in economic activity, in all individual and collective manifestations of life' (Gramsci 1975, vol. 2, p. 1380; Gramsci 1971, p. 328). If this definition is examined in the light of the one in which ideology is seen as a world-view with its corresponding norms of action and Gramsci's repeated insistence on the fact that ideology is the terrain on which men acquire all their forms of consciousness, then it becomes plain that this definition (far from having to be interpreted as showing that Gramsci is dealing with a Hegelian problematic of expressive totality in which ideology plays the central role), must be understood as an allusion to the fact that it is through ideology that all possible types of 'subjects' are created.

Another very new aspect of the Gramscian problematic of ideology is the importance which he attributes to the *material and institutional nature of ideological practice*. In effect, Gramsci insists on the fact that this practice possesses its own agents, that is to say, the *intellectuals*. They are the ones in charge of elaborating and spreading organic ideologies (Gramsci 1975, vol. 3, p. 1518; Gramsci 1971, p. 12), and they are the ones who will have to realise moral and intellectual reform (Gramsci 1975, vol. 2, p. 1407; Gramsci 1971, pp. 60–1). Gramsci classes the intellectuals into two main categories depending on whether they are linked to one of the two fundamental classes (organic intellectuals), or to classes expressing previous modes of production (traditional intellectuals). Apart from stressing the role of the intellectuals, Gramsci insists on the importance of the material and institutional structure for the elaboration and spreading of ideology. This is made up of different *hegemonic apparatuses*: schools, churches, the entire media and even architecture and the names of the streets (Gramsci 1975, vol. 1, p. 332). This ensemble of apparatuses is termed the *ideological structure* of a dominant class by Gramsci, and the level of the superstructure where ideology is produced and diffused is called *civil society*. This constitutes the ensemble of 'private' bodies through which the political and social hegemony of a social group is exercised (Gramsci 1975, vol. 1, p. 476; Gramsci 1971, p. 12).

It is now obvious that we are far from the economistic problematic of ideology and that Gramsci is clearly situated on a different terrain. What is quite new in him is the awareness of the material nature of ideology and of the fact that it constitutes a practice inscribed in apparatuses which plays an indispensable practical-social role in all societies. He intuited the fact that this practice consists in the production of subjects, but he did not quite manage to formulate this theoretically. Besides, one should never forget that all these new ideas are expressed by Gramsci in an ambiguous form which is now outdated. Since, as has already been indicated, the only intellectual tradition available to assist in the elaboration of an anti-economistic problematic was Croce's historicism. In any case, Gramsci never set out to elaborate a theory of ideology and his thought is not presented in a systematic way. Having said all this, however, it does nevertheless seem possible to assert that Gramsci's problematic anticipated Althusser in several respects: the material nature of ideology, its existence as the necessary level of all social formations, and its function as the producer of subjects are all implicit in Gramsci, although it was Althusser who was to be the first to formulate his conception in a rigorous fashion.

A non-reductionist conception

Gramsci's contribution to the Marxist theory of ideologies, however, is not limited to his having shown that they were objective and operative realities, as real as the economy itself, and that they played a crucial role in all social formations. Such a conception, however, only definitively supersedes the first facet of economism and still leaves room for the possible existence of complicated forms of reductionism. Now Gramsci was not simply content to criticise the epiphenomenal conception as he went much further and queried the reductionist conception which made ideology a function of the class position of the subjects. There can be no doubt that it is here that the most important and original aspect of his contribution is to be found. Unfortunately, it is also the least understood aspect, and this explains why all the potentialities which this opened out to Marxist analysis have virtually remained undeveloped.

It must be admitted here that this is a much more difficult area, since Gramsci never presented the anti-reductionist problematic in an explicit fashion, although it does exist *in the practical state* in the way in which he conceived hegemony. This problematic must, therefore, be clearly brought out, and it must be shown that it provides the *actual condition of intelligibility* of Gramsci's hegemony. However, before embarking on a study of texts which will serve as points of reference, it is worth briefly recapitulating the three principles underlying the reductionist problematic of ideology, since this will make it easier to bring out the difference between Gramsci's conception and this one. The three principles are as follows:

1 All subjects are class subjects.
2 Social classes have their own paradigmatic ideologies.
3 All ideological elements have a necessary class belonging.

Gramsci's opposition to the first principle emerges clearly at once. According to him, the subjects of political action cannot be identified with social classes. As has already been seen, they are 'collective wills' which obey specifically formed laws in view of the fact that they constitute the political expression of hegemonic systems created through ideology. Therefore, the subjects (the social classes) which exist at the economic level, are not duplicated at the political level; instead, different 'inter-class' subjects are created. This constitutes Gramsci's break with the first principle of reductionism and provides him with the necessary theoretical basis to enable him to think of hegemony beyond a simple class alliance as the creation of a superior unity where there will be a fusion of the participant elements of the hegemonic bloc. We know that this fusion will be realised through ideology, but the question remains, how and on what basis? We have now, in effect, reached the point of having to answer our previously formulated question: how can genuine ideological unity between different social groups be created?

There are two possible solutions to the problem. The first is the only one which can be formulated within a reductionist problematic of ideology (as exemplified by principles 2 and 3). It consists in viewing this ideological unity as the imposition of the class ideology of the main group upon the allied groups. This leads one to define a hegemonic class as one which has been capable of creating ideological consensus with other groups on the basis of the role played by its own ideology as the dominant one, and to reduce the problematic of ideology to a mere phenomenon of ideological inculcation. This, for example, is the kind of solution underlying Nicos Poulantzas's (1973) interpretation of Gramsci's conception of hegemony. According to him, in so far as hegemony in Gramsci refers to a situation in which class domination involves a function of direction by means of which active consent of the dominated class is created, then this is similar to Lukács' notion of class consciousness world-view, and hence to the Hegelian problematic of the subject. He declares that if this kind of problematic is transposed to Marxism, then it leads to the conception that class is the subject of history, the genetic totalising principle of the instances of a social formation. In this context it is the ideology consciousness world-view of the class viewed as the subject of history, that is of the hegemonic class, which founds the unity of a formation, in so far as it determines the adhesion of the dominated classes within a determinate system of domination (ibid., p. 138).

Such an interpretation of Gramsci's thought is only possible if one identifies hegemony with the imposition of the dominant ideology (understood here in the Lukácsian form of the dominant class's world-view class consciousness). I think that what has so far been demonstrated is already sufficient to show that this is a completely incorrect interpretation of Gramsci's thought. This does, in fact, prevent Poulantzas from grasping the full extent of Gramsci's conception of hegemony, and it leads him to find some incoherent elements in it, especially as regards the extension of this conception to the strategy of the proletariat. Poulantzas declares this extension unacceptable since it implies 'that a class imposes its own world-view on a formation and therefore actually conquers the place of the dominant ideology before the conquest of political power' (ibid., p. 204). Now, not only does Gramsci indicate the possibility of a class becoming hegemonic before the seizure of power, but he insists on the *necessity* of its doing so. Can one really talk of incoherence on his part? If so, then it must seriously affect the whole of his work in view of the importance which this conception plays in his thought. On the other hand, could this not rather indicate a way of understanding hegemony which differs from the one which Poulantzas attributes to him; that is to say a conception which assumes that the problem of the creation of an ideological unity is tackled on the basis of a non-reductionist conception of ideology? In fact, this is the case, and it is this which explains why this fundamental aspect of Gramsci's thought remained for a long time completely unnoticed, since it was absolutely *unthinkable* within the reductionist problematic dominating Marxist thought.[13]

So we must now present the second solution – the one to be found in Gramsci – to the problem of the possibility of forming ideological unity between different social groups. It is a solution which, of course, does not consist in the imposition of the class ideology of one of the groups over the others. An analysis of the way in which Gramsci visualises the process leading to the constitution of a new hegemony through *intellectual and moral reform* will throw light on the subject.

As already previously mentioned, the importance of intellectual and moral reform lies in the fact that the hegemony of a fundamental class consists in the creation of a 'collective will' (on the basis of a common world-view which will serve as a unifying principle) in which this class and its allies will fuse to form a 'collective man':

> From this one can deduce the importance of the 'cultural aspect', even in practical (collective) activity. An historical act can only be performed by 'collective man', and this presupposes the attainment of a 'cultural-social' unity through which a multiplicity of dispersed wills, with heterogeneous aims, are welded together with a single aim, on the basis of an equal and common conception of the world.
>
> (Gramsci 1975, vol. 2, p. 1330; Gramsci 1971, p. 349)

The creation of a new hegemony, therefore, implies the transformation of the previous ideological terrain and the creation of a new world-view which will serve as a unifying principle for a new collective will. This is the process of ideological transformation which Gramsci designates with the term 'intellectual and moral reform'. What is important now is to see how this process is envisaged by Gramsci. The two following passages are extremely significant in this context:

> What matters is the criticism to which such an ideological complex is subjected by the first representatives of the new historical phase. This criticism makes possible a process of differentiation and change in the relative weight that the elements of the old ideologies used to possess. What was previously secondary and subordinate, or even incidental, is now taken to be primary – becomes the nucleus of a new ideological and theoretical complex. The old collective will dissolve into its contradictory elements since the subordinate ones develop socially ...
>
> (Gramsci 1975, vol. 2, p. 1058; Gramsci 1971, p. 195)

> How, on the other hand should this historical consciousness, proposed as autonomous consciousness, be formed? How should everyone choose and combine the elements for the constitution of such an autonomous consciousness? Will each element imposed have to be repudiated *a priori*? It will have to be repudiated inasmuch as it is imposed, but not in itself, that is to say that it will be necessary to give it a new form which is specific to the given group.
>
> (Gramsci 1975, vol. 3, p. 1875)

Here Gramsci indicates extremely clearly that intellectual and moral reform does not consist in making a clean sweep of the existing world-view and in replacing it with a completely new and already formulated one. Rather, it consists in a process of transformation (aimed at producing a new form) and of rearticulation of existing ideological elements. According to him, an ideological system consists in a particular type of articulation of ideological elements to which a certain 'relative weight' is attributed. The objective of ideological struggle is not to reject the system and all its elements but to rearticulate it, to break it down to its basic elements and then to sift through past conceptions to see which ones, with some changes of content, can serve to express the new situation (Gramsci 1975, vol. 2, p. 1322). Once this is done, the chosen elements are finally rearticulated into another system.

It is obvious that, viewed in this way, moral and intellectual reform is incomprehensible within a reductionist problematic which postulates the existence of paradigmatic ideologies for each social class, and the necessary class-belonging of all ideological elements. If, in effect, one does accept the reductionist hypothesis, moral and intellectual reform can only amount to replacing one class ideology by another. In the case of the hegemony of the working class, therefore, the latter would have to extricate the social groups which it required as allies from the influence of bourgeois ideology and impose its own ideology upon them. In order to do this, it would have to combat bourgeois ideology by totally rejecting all its elements since these would be intrinsically and irremediably bourgeois, and since the presence of one of these elements within socialist discourse would prove that working-class ideology had been contaminated by bourgeois ideology; in this event, ideological struggle would always be reduced to the confrontation of two closed and previously determined systems. This, of course, is not Gramsci's conception, and the information so far available already makes it possible to assert that his conception of ideology *cannot be reductionist* since in that case the way in which he visualises moral and intellectual reform would be totally incomprehensible.

What, then, is the conception of ideology developed in Gramsci's theory of hegemony? In order to clarify this, it is first necessary to determine what kind of answers Gramsci gives to the following questions:

1 What constitutes the unifying principle of an ideological system?
2 How can one determine the class character of an ideology or of an ideological element?

This brings us to one of the least developed aspects of Gramsci's thought and we will have to be content with a few rather imprecise indications which will need to undergo the test of a symptomatic reading. To begin with, let us recall the elements of the problem which have already been analysed. We know that, according to Gramsci, hegemony (which is only possible for a fundamental class) consists in the latter exercising a political, intellectual and moral role of leadership within a hegemonic system which is cemented by a common world-view (organic ideology). We also know that intellectual and moral leadership exercised by the hegemonic class does not consist in the imposition of the class ideology upon the allied groups.

Time and time again Gramsci stresses the fact that every single hegemonic relation is necessarily 'pedagogic and occurs amongst the different forces of which it is composed' (Gramsci 1975, vol. 2, p. 1331; Gramsci 1971, p. 350). He also insists that in a hegemonic system there must exist democracy between the ruling group and the ruled groups (Gramsci 1975, vol. 2, p. 1056; Gramsci 1971, p. 56 n). This is also valid at the ideological level, of course, and it implies that this common world-view unifying the hegemonic bloc is really the organic expression of the whole bloc (and here we have the explanation of the chief meaning of the term 'organic ideology'). This world-view will therefore include ideological elements from varying sources, but its unity will stem from its articulating principle which will always be provided by the hegemonic class. Gramsci calls this articulating principle a *hegemonic principle*. He never defines this term very precisely, but it seems that it involves a system of values, the realisation of which depends on the central role played by the fundamental class at the level of the relations of production. Thus, the intellectual and moral direction exercised by a fundamental class in a hegemonic system consists in providing the articulating principle of the common world-view, the value system to which the ideological elements coming from the other groups will be articulated in order to form a unified ideological system, that is to say, an organic ideology. This will always be a complex ensemble whose contents can never be determined in advance since it depends on a whole series of historical and national factors and also on the relations of forces existing at a particular moment in the struggle for hegemony. It is, therefore, by their articulation to a hegemonic principle that the ideological elements acquire their class character which is not intrinsic to them. This explains the fact that they can be 'transformed' by their articulation to another hegemonic principle. Ideological struggle in fact consists of a process of *disarticulation-rearticulation* of given ideological elements in a struggle between two hegemonic principles to appropriate these elements; it does not consist of the confrontation of two already elaborated, closed world-views. Ideological ensembles existing at a given moment are, therefore, the result of the relations of forces between the rival hegemonic principles and they undergo a perpetual process of transformation (Gramsci 1975, vol. 3, p. 1863).

It is now possible to answer our two questions:

1   The unifying principle of an ideological system is constituted by the hegemonic principle which serves to articulate all the other ideological elements. It is always the expression of a fundamental class.
2   The class character of an ideology or of an ideological element stems from the hegemonic principle which serves as its articulating centre.

However, we are still a long way from having solved all the problems. There remains, for example, the problem of the nature of those ideological elements which do not have a necessary class character. It is not clear what they express, and Gramsci does not give us an answer. But, in spite of this, it is possible to find a few very significant definite pointers to a solution. In a passage where he reflects on what will determine the victory of one hegemonic principle over another, Gramsci declares that a hegemonic principle does not prevail by virtue of its intrinsic logical character but rather when it manages to become a 'popular religion' (Gramsci 1975, vol. 2, p. 1084).

What are we supposed to understand by this? Elsewhere Gramsci insists that a class wishing to become hegemonic has to 'nationalise itself' (Gramsci 1975, vol. 3, p. 1729; Gramsci 1971, p. 241), and further on he declares:

> the particular form in which the hegemonic ethico-political element presents itself in the life of the state and the country is 'patriotism' and 'nationalism', which is 'popular religion', that is to say it is the link by means of which the unity of leaders and led is effected.
>
> (Gramsci 1975, vol. 2, p. 1084)

In order to understand what Gramsci means, it is necessary to relate all these statements to his conception of the 'national-popular'. Although this conception is not fully formulated, it plays an important role in his thought. For Gramsci, everything which is the expression of the 'people-nation' is 'national-popular'.[14] A successful hegemony is one which manages to create a 'collective national-popular will', and, for this to happen, the dominant class must have been capable of articulating to its hegemonic principle all the national-popular ideological elements, since it is only if this happens that it (the class) appears as the representative of the general interest. This is why the ideological elements expressing the 'national-popular' are often at stake in the fierce struggle between classes fighting for hegemony. As regards all this, Gramsci points out some changes of meaning undergone by terms like 'nationalism' and 'patriotism' as they are appropriated by different fundamental classes and articulated to different hegemonic principles (Gramsci 1975, vol. 2, p. 1237). He also stresses the role which those terms play as a link leading to the creation of the union between leaders and led and in providing a base for a popular religion.

It is now possible to understand Gramsci's statement in which he declares that a hegemonic principle asserts itself when it manages to become a popular religion. What he means is that what has to be chiefly at stake in a class's struggle for hegemony is the attempt to articulate to its discourse all national-popular ideological elements. This is how it can 'nationalise itself'.[15]

The conception of ideology found in the practical state in Gramsci's problematic of hegemony consists therefore of a practice which transforms the class character of ideological elements by the latter's articulation to a hegemonic principle differing from the one to which they are at present articulated. This assumes that these elements do not in themselves express class interests, but that their class character is conferred upon them by the discourse to which they are articulated and by the type of subject thus created.

Hegemony and war of position

It is only now that the anti-reductionist problematic of ideology implied by Gramsci's hegemony has been made explicit that it is possible to really grasp the meaning and *full extent* of his concept of hegemony: a class is hegemonic when it has managed to articulate to its discourse the overwhelming majority of ideological elements characteristic of a given social formation, in particular the national-popular elements which allow it to become the class expressing the national interest. A class's hegemony is, therefore, a more complex phenomenon than simple political leadership: the latter, in effect, is the consequence of another aspect which is itself of prime importance. This is the creation of a unified coherent ideological discourse which will be the product of the articulation to its value system of the ideological elements existing within a determinate historical conjuncture of the society in question. These elements, which have no necessary class-belonging, rightly constitute for this reason the terrain of ideological struggle between the two classes confronting each other for hegemony. Therefore, if a class becomes hegemonic, it is not, as some interpretations of Gramsci would have it, because it has succeeded in imposing its class ideology upon society or in establishing mechanisms legitimising its class power. This kind of interpretation completely alters the nature of Gramsci's thought because it reduces his conception of ideology to the traditional Marxist conception of false consciousness which necessarily leads to presenting hegemony as a phenomenon of ideological inculcation. Now, it is precisely against this type of reductionism that Gramsci is rebelling when he proclaims that politics is not a "'*marché de dupes*'" (Gramsci 1975, vol. 3, p. 1595; Gramsci 1971, p. 164). For him, ideology is not the mystified-mystifying justification of an already constituted class power, it is the 'terrain on which men acquire consciousness of themselves', and hegemony cannot be reduced to a process of ideological domination.

Once the real meaning of Gramsci's hegemony has been understood, all the pseudo-incoherencies disappear from his thought. For example, the problem of knowing why Gramsci can use this conception both to designate the practices of the bourgeoisie and those of the working class becomes clear as does the reason for his envisaging the possibility of a class becoming hegemonic before the seizure of power. It is, in fact, the link which had been established between hegemony and ideological domination which made it impossible to grasp the internal coherence of Gramsci's thought and which made it appear full of discrepancies. Once, however, the problematic of ideology, which is operating in the practical state in Gramsci's conception of hegemony, has been established, all the other conceptions fall quite naturally into place in a perfectly structured ensemble and the underlying meaning of his thought is revealed in all its coherence. I shall only take one example, but it is a crucially important one since it is the conception upon which Gramsci bases his entire strategy of transition to socialism in the West: I am referring to the *war of position*.

Gramsci's thought on the strategy of the working class in its struggle for socialism is organised around the conception of hegemony. This thought has its starting point in the enlarging of the phenomenon of hegemony which Gramsci began to consider applicable to the bourgeoisie as well, since he understood that state power was not limited to the power of a single class and that the bourgeoisie had managed to ensure itself a 'historical base', a group of allies led by it through its hegemonic apparatuses. In this way it had created a 'collective man' which functioned as an autonomous political subject. From here, Gramsci reaches the conclusion that political struggle does not only take place between the two fundamental antagonistic classes, since the 'political subjects' are not social classes but 'collective wills' which are comprised of an ensemble of social groups fused around a fundamental class. If, therefore, the struggle between the antagonistic classes constitutes, in the final instance, the determining level of all political struggle, the struggle of all the other groups within a social formation must nevertheless be articulated to it. These other groups will provide the 'historical base' of a dominant class, and it is on this terrain that the struggle for hegemony – by means of which a fundamental class tries to win over the other social groups – takes place. The revolutionary process can, therefore, not be restricted to a movement organised on strict class lines which would tend to develop a pure proletarian consciousness detached from the rest of society. The road to hegemony in fact makes it imperative to take into account a double process: the self-awareness of oneself as an autonomous group, and the creation of a basis of consensus:

> A study of how these innovatory forces developed, from subaltern groups to hegemonic and dominant groups, must therefore seek out and identify the phases through which they acquired: i. autonomy *vis-à-vis* the enemies they had to defeat, and ii. support from the groups which actively or passively assisted them; for this entire process was historically necessary before they could unite in the form of the State. It is precisely by these two yardsticks that the level of historical and political consciousness which the innovatory forces progressively attained in the various phases can be measured – and not simply by the yardstick of their separation from the formerly dominant forces.
>
> (Gramsci 1975, vol. 3, p. 2289; Gramsci 1971, p. 53)

It is, therefore, vital for the working class not to isolate itself within a ghetto of proletarian purism. On the contrary, it must try to become a 'national class', representing the interests of the increasingly numerous social groups. In order to do this, it must cause the disintegration of the historical bases of the bourgeoisie's hegemony by disarticulating the ideological bloc by means of which the bourgeoisie's intellectual direction is expressed. It is, in fact, only on this condition that the working class will be able to rearticulate a new ideological system which will serve as a cement for the hegemonic bloc within which it will play the role of a leading force. This process of disarticulation-rearticulation constitutes in fact the famous 'war of position' which Gramsci conceives as the revolutionary strategy best adapted to countries where the bourgeoisie has managed to firmly establish its hegemony due to the development of civil society. Unless one has grasped the real meaning of Gramsci's concept of hegemony – which consists in the capacity of a fundamental class to articulate to its discourse the ideological elements characteristic of a given social formation – then it is impossible to understand the nature of the war of position. In effect, the war of position is the process of ideological struggle by means of which the two fundamental classes try to appropriate the non-class ideological elements in order to integrate them within the ideological system which articulates itself around their respective hegemonic principles. This is, therefore, only a stage in the struggle, the one in which the new hegemonic bloc cements itself, but it is a decisive moment since Gramsci states, 'in politics, once the war of position has been won, it has been won definitively' (Gramsci 1975, vol. 2, p. 802; Gramsci 1971, p. 239). It will in fact only be a question of time before the military relations of forces begin to lean towards the bloc of socialist forces as soon as all the popular forces rally to socialism and the bourgeoisie finds itself isolated. As a result, far from designating a reformist strategy as certain interpretations of Gramsci maintain,[16] the war of position represents the translation into political strategy of a non-reductionist conception of ideology and politics. This stresses the fundamental role of ideological struggle and the form of popular war which the struggle for socialism must assume: 'in politics the war of position is the conception of hegemony' (Gramsci 1975, vol. 2, p. 973; Gramsci 1971, p. 239). This statement of Gramsci's can only be understood in the light of the anti-reductionist problematic of ideology which has been presented as the very condition of intelligibility of his conception of hegemony. Only when this has been grasped can one glimpse all the political consequences involved. These are crystallised into a conception of socialist revolution seen not as a strictly proletarian one but as a complex process of political and ideological transformations in which the working class plays the leading role. The war of position understood as the struggle for hegemony within all the anti-capitalist sectors also explains Gramsci's insistence on the 'national' character of the struggle:

> The international situation should be considered in its national aspect. In reality, the internal relations of any nation are the result of a combination which is 'original' and (in a certain sense) unique; these relations must be understood and conceived in their originality and uniqueness if one wishes to dominate them and direct them. To be sure, the line of development is towards internationalism, but the point of departure is 'national' – and it is from this point of departure that one must begin.
>
> (Gramsci 1975, vol. 3, p. 1729)

Conclusion

In this chapter I have argued that in Gramsci's conception of hegemony one finds in the practical state a radically *anti-economistic* problematic of ideology and that it constitutes the condition of intelligibility of the specificity of his conception of hegemony. However, I am not claiming that all the problems of the Marxist theory of ideology are solved by Gramsci – even in the practical state. In any case, the conceptual tools which he had to use have been completely superseded, and nowadays we are equipped to deal with the problem of ideology in a far more rigorous fashion, thanks to the development of disciplines such as linguistics and pyschoanalysis. Nevertheless, Gramsci's contribution to the Marxist theory of ideology must be considered of crucial importance for several reasons:

1 Gramsci was the first to stress the material nature of ideology, its existence as a necessary level of all social formations, its inscription in practices and its materialisation into apparatuses.
2 Gramsci broke away radically from the conception of ideology as false consciousness, i.e. a distorted representation of reality because it is determined by the place occupied by the subject in the relations of production, and he anticipated the conception of ideology as a practice producing subjects.
3 Finally, Gramsci also queried the general principle of reductionism which attributes a necessary class-belonging to all ideological elements.

As regards the first two points, Gramsci's thought has been taken up and thoroughly developed by Louis Althusser – although the latter reached the same point of view in quite a different way – and so his ideas have spread through the Althusserian school. As regards his criticism of reductionism, however, it is unfortunate that his contribution has not been fully recognised, as it is in this area that the theoretical potentialities of his thought urgently need developing. This is particularly so since the Marxist theory of ideology has not yet managed to free itself entirely of the reductionist problematic and hence remains trapped by insidious forms of economism.

The topicality and importance which Gramsci's work has for Marxist researchers working in the field of ideology lie in the fact that Gramsci's conception points the way to a possible solution to the most serious problem of the Marxist theory of ideology. The problem consists in superseding economism while at the same time adhering to the problematic of historical materialism. In fact, once the elementary phase of ideology seen as an epiphenomenon has been superseded, Marxist theory still has to face the following difficulty: how to show to what extent ideological practice actually has real autonomy and efficacity while still upholding the principle of the determination in the last instance by the economic. This is a problem which Althusser himself has not yet been capable of solving satisfactorily, and it is why he has recently been accused of economism.[17] However, if his critics propose a solution which effectively resolves the problem of economism, this is done at the expense of abandoning historical materialism. In effect, by identifying economism with the thesis of the determination in the last instance by the economy, and by proposing the total autonomy of ideological practices as a solution, they call into question the basic tenets of historical materialism.

In Gramsci's work the outline of another kind of solution to the problem can be found, and it is worth analysing it before deciding whether the solution to the problem of economism is really impossible within the theoretical framework of Marxism. As presented here, the problematic of hegemony contains in the practical state the broad outlines of a possible articulation between the relative autonomy of ideology and the determination in the last instance by the economy. In fact, the conception of ideology brought out by Gramsci's conception of hegemony attributes real autonomy to it, since the ideological elements which ideological practice aims at transforming do not possess a necessary class-belonging and hence do not constitute the ideological representation of interests existing at the economic level. On the other hand, however, this autonomy is not incompatible with the determination in the last instance by economy, since the hegemonic principles serving to articulate these elements are always provided by the fundamental classes. Here, of course, I am only designating the area where a solution might be found, and if work is to be done in this direction, there are a large number of problems still to be solved before it will be possible to formulate a theoretical solution. It does nevertheless seem to be an area which ought to prove fruitful.

Finally, I wish to indicate another area in which Gramsci's conception of hegemony opens out extremely fruitful perspectives. This is to be found in his *conception of politics*. Gramsci was extremely aware of this since after all he declared that economism had to be combated 'not only in the theory of historiography but also – and more especially – in political practice and theory', and that 'in this area the struggle can and must be conducted by developing the concept of hegemony' (Gramsci 1975, vol. 3, p. 1596; Gramsci 1971, p. 165). The ways in which economism manifests itself in the field of politics are extremely varied and range from the 'wait-and-see' attitude of the Second International to the 'purism' of the extreme left. These are two apparently opposing forms and yet they do both express the same lack of understanding of the true nature of politics and its role in a social formation. The fundamental error of the economistic conception – its epiphenomenalist and reductionist conception of the superstructures – manifests itself in this domain by an *instrumental* conception of the state and of politics. In identifying the state with the repressive apparatus, it reduces the field of politics, since its vital relation with the ideological struggle is severed. Gramsci's 'enlarged' notion of the state, which is correlative to the role attributed to hegemony, recuperates this forgotten dimension of politics, and ideological struggle becomes a fundamental aspect of political struggle. Politics thereby ceases to be conceived as a separate specialist activity and becomes a dimension which is present in all fields of human activity. In effect, if no individual can become a subject except through his participation in a 'mass-man', there is not one aspect of human experience which escapes politics and this extends as far as 'common sense'.

This conception of politics should make it possible to devise a completely new approach to the problem of *power* which has generally not been satisfactorily treated by Marxists. Actually, once the hegemonic dimension of politics which expresses itself in Gramsci's notion of the 'integral state' has been re-established, and once it has been accepted that the supremacy of a class is not solely exercised by means of its domination over adversaries, but also by means of its role of leadership over allied groups, then one can begin to understand that, far from being localised in the repressive state apparatuses, power is exercised at all levels of society and that it is a 'strategy' – as Michel Foucault puts it. So this is yet another field of research opened up by Gramsci's non-reductionist conception of hegemony, and it is an extremely topical one.

It is in fact quite remarkable to see the extraordinary way in which some contemporary research – such as that of Foucault or Derrida which brings out a completely new conception of politics[18] – converges with Gramsci's thought, and having recognised the anti-reductionist character of his thought, I do not think it too hazardous to predict that the topicality of Gramsci's work and his influence will go on increasing in the future.

Notes

1 This chapter was translated into English by Denise Derôme.
2 For a thorough analysis of the epistemological foundations of the Marxism of the Second International as well as of Bernstein's revisionism, see Leonardo Paggi's excellent introduction to Max Adler (1974).
3 This is cited by Lucio Colletti in his introduction to Bernstein's book in Italian translation, *I presupposti del socialismo e i compiti della socialdemocrazia* (Bari: Laterza, 1974), p. xix.
4 Antonio Gramsci, 'Quelques Thèmes sur la Question Méridionale'. This is published in the appendix to Marie-Antonietta Macciochi, *Pour Gramsci* (Paris: Seuil, 1974), p. 316.
5 It is important to stress the fact that, for Gramsci, hegemony only refers to the moment of leadership and does not include the moment of domination, since several interpretations which declare that domination is part of hegemony reach conclusions which completely alter the character of Gramsci's thought. See, for example, Luciano Gruppi, *Il concetto di egemonia in Gramsci* (Rome: Editori Riuniti,1972), and Massimo Salvadori, 'Gramsci e il PCI: due concezioni dell "egemonia"', *Mondo Operaio*, vol. 2, November 1976, reprinted in Mouffe (1979), pp. 237–58.
6 This text was reworked by Gramsci two years later and is to be found in its definitive form in *Notebook 13*. See Gramsci (1975), vol. 3, pp. 1583–86.
7 These texts have not passed totally unnoticed. Several works on Gramsci (for example, Leonardo Paggi's article, 'Gramsci's General Theory of Marxism' in Mouffe 1979, pp. 113–67) do attribute some importance to them, but not as regards the conception of hegemony.
8 For an analysis of Gramsci's contribution to the Marxist theory of the state, see Buci-Glucksmann (1975).
9 If political leadership is exclusively stressed, this leads to the reduction of Gramsci's hegemony to the Leninist conception of hegemony as an alliance of classes. In his intervention at the Cagliari Congress in 1968 ('Gramsci e la concezione della società civile', translated in Mouffe (1979) as 'Gramsci and the Conception of Civil Society', pp. 21–47), Norberto Bobbio was the first to insist on the specificity of Gramsci's conception and on the importance which the latter attributed to moral and intellectual direction. However, the interpretation which Bobbio gave of this does not succeed in making clear its articulation to the economy and so leads to an excessively 'superstructural' interpretation of Gramsci's thought.
10 A typical example of this kind of interpretation consists in presenting hegemony as an alliance of classes in which one of the two imposes its class ideology on the other. This problem will be dealt with again in the third part of this chapter.
11 These are mainly to be found in *Notebook 13*, 'Noterelle sulla politica del Machiavelli' (Gramsci 1975, vol. 3, pp. 1555–652; Gramsci 1971, pp. 123–202).

12 Most authors who criticise Gramsci for this reason base themselves on the critique of historicism developed by Louis Althusser in *Lire le Capital*, where, wrongly in my view, he assimilates Gramsci's problematic to that of Lukács, cf. Althusser (1970), especially the chapter 'Marxism is not a Historicism'.

13 This is why even those writers who *intuited* the radical newness of Gramsci's conception of hegemony did not manage to think it. In my view, this is the case of Buci-Glucksmann (1975). As regards work on Gramsci in English, the dominating tendency has been to identify hegemony with ideological domination. For exceptions to this see, S. Hall, B. Lumley and G. McLennan, 'Politics and Ideology: Gramsci', *Cultural Studies* 10 (1977); Raymond Williams, *Marxism and Literature* (Oxford: Oxford University Press, 1977). The way in which these authors pose the problem of hegemony bears similarities in several respects to the way in which it is seen in this chapter.

14 This is a conception which Gramsci develops above all as regards its application to literature (1975, vol. 3, pp. 2113–20; Gramsci 1971, pp. 421 ff.), but he does indicate that all ideological or political manifestations can have a 'national-popular' character when there exists an organic link between the intellectuals and the people.

15 Gramsci's indications naturally do not provide a solution to the problem of the nature of the non-class ideological elements. They simply suggest the type of response which he could have had in mind. This problem does, however, require a rigorous theoretical solution. One possible line of research seems to have been developed by Ernesto Laclau in his book *Politics and Ideology in Marxist Theory* (London: New Left Books, 1977), where he deals with the specificity of the popular-democratic contradiction.

16 Perry Anderson supports this view in his article, 'The Antinomies of Antonio Gramsci', *New Left Review*, no. 100, 1977. His interpretation of Gramsci exemplifies the fact that the lack of understanding of the nature of Gramsci's hegemony and the anti-reductionist problematic of ideology which it implies makes it impossible to grasp either the specificity of Gramsci's thought or its coherence.

17 On this subject, see Paul Hirst, 'Althusser and the Theory of Ideology', *Economy and Society*, vol. 5, no. 4, 1976.

18 Foucault's recent work since *L'Ordre du Discours* has led him to stress increasingly the political function of intellectuals, and Derrida's work at GREPH (*Groupe pour la recherche de l'enseignement de la philosophie et de l'histoire*) has led him to uncover the political dimension of philosophical practice. Their research converges towards a new conception of politics and power which is anticipated on several points by Gramsci's thought.

References

Adler, Max. 1974. *Il socialismo egli intellettuali*. Bari: De Donato.

Althusser, Louis. 1970. *Reading Capital*. London: New Left Books.

——1971. *Lenin and Philosophy and Other Essays*. London: New Left Books.

Buci-Glucksmann, Christine. 1975. *Gramsci et l'État*. Paris: Fayard.

Gramsci, Antonio. 1971. *Selections from the Prison Notebooks*. Ed. and trans. Q. Hoare and G. Nowell Smith. London: Lawrence & Wishart.

——1975. *Quaderni dal carcere*, 4 vols. Ed. V. Gerratana. Turin: Einaudi.

——1978. *Selections from Political Writings, 1921–26*. Ed. and trans. Q. Hoare. London: Lawrence & Wishart.

Kautksy, Karl. 1892. *Das Erfurter Programm*. Stuttgart: Verlag von J.H.W. Diek.

Mouffe, Chantal (ed.). 1979. *Gramsci and Marxist Theory*. London: Routledge & Kegan Paul.

Poulantzas, Nicos. 1973. *Political Power and Social Classes*. London: New Left Books.

2

HEGEMONY AND NEW POLITICAL SUBJECTS

Toward a new concept of democracy (1988)[1]

> It is incomprehensible that equality should not ultimately penetrate the political world as it has elsewhere. That men should be eternally unequal among themselves in one single respect and equal in others is inconceivable; they will therefore one day attain equality in all respects.
>
> Alexis de Tocqueville, *Democracy in America*

Despite Tocqueville's remarkable insight into the potential implications of the 'democratic revolution,' it is unlikely that he could have imagined its leading, today, to our questioning the totality of social relationships. He believed, in fact, as his reflections on women's equality testify, that the ineluctable drive toward equality must take into account certain real differences grounded in nature. It is precisely the permanent alterity based on such a conception of natural essences that is contested today by an important segment of the feminist movement. It is not merely that the democratic revolution has proven to be more radical than Tocqueville foresaw; the revolution has taken forms that no one could have anticipated because it attacks forms of inequality that did not previously exist. Clearly, ecological, antinuclear, and antibureaucratic struggles, along with all the other commonly labeled 'new social movements' – I would prefer to call them 'new democratic struggles' – should be understood as resistances to new types of oppression emerging in advanced capitalist societies. This is the thesis my essay will develop, and I shall try to answer the following questions: (1) What kind of antagonism do the new social movements express? (2) What is their link with the development of capitalism? (3) How should they be positioned in a socialist strategy? (4) What are the implications of these struggles for our conception of democracy?

Theoretical positions

Within every society, each social agent is inscribed in a multiplicity of social relations – not only social relations of production but also the social relations, among others, of sex, race, nationality, and vicinity. All these social relations determine position-alities or subject positions, and every social agent is therefore the locus of many subject positions and cannot be reduced to only one. Thus, someone inscribed in the relations of production as a worker is also a man or a woman, white or black, Catholic or Protestant, French or German, and so on. A person's subjectivity is not constructed only on the basis of his or her position in the relations of production. Furthermore, each social position, each subject position, is itself the locus of mul-tiple possible constructions, according to the different discourses that can construct that position. Thus, the subjectivity of a given social agent is always precariously and provisionally fixed, or, to use the Lacanian term, sutured at the intersection of various discourses.

I am consequently opposed to the class reductionism of classical Marxism, in which all social subjects are necessarily class subjects (each social class having its own ideological paradigm, and every antagonism ultimately reducible to a class antagonism). I affirm, instead, the existence in each individual of multiple subject positions corresponding both to the different social relations in which the indivi-dual is inserted and to the discourses that constitute these relations. There is no reason to privilege, a priori, a 'class' position as the origin of the articulation of subjectivity. Furthermore, it is incorrect to attribute necessary paradigmatic forms to this class position. Consequently, a critique of the notion of 'fundamental interests' is required, because this notion entails fixing necessary political and ideological forms within determined positions in the production process. But interests never exist prior to the discourses in which they are articulated and constituted; they cannot be the expression of already existing positions on the economic level.

I am opposed to the economic view of social evolution as governed by a single economic logic, the view that conceives the unity of a social formation as the result of 'necessary effects' produced in ideological and political superstructures by the economic infrastructures. The distinction between infra- and superstructure needs to be questioned because it implies a conception of economy as a world of objects and relations that exist prior to any ideological and political conditions of existence. This view assumes that the economy is able to function on its own and follow its own logic, a logic absolutely independent of the relations it would allegedly determine. Instead, I shall defend a conception of society as a complex ensemble of heterogeneous social relations possessing their own dynamism. Not all such rela-tions are reducible to social relations of production or to their ideological and political conditions of reproduction. The unity of a social formation is the product of political articulations, which are, in turn, the result of the social practices that produce a hegemonic formation.

By 'hegemonic formation', I mean an ensemble of relatively stable social forms, the materialization of a social articulation in which different social relations react reciprocally either to provide each other with mutual conditions of existence, or at least to neutralize the potentially destructive effects of certain social relations on the reproduction of other such relations. A hegemonic formation is always centred around certain types of social relations. In capitalism, these are the relations of production, but this fact should not be explained as an effect of structure; it is, rather, that the centrality of production relations has been conferred by a hegemonic policy. However, hegemony is never established conclusively. A constant struggle must create the conditions necessary to validate capital and its accumulation. This implies a set of practices that are not merely economic, political and cultural as well. Thus, the development of capitalism is subject to an incessant political struggle, periodically modifying those social forms through which social relations of production are assured their centrality. In the history of capitalism we can see the rhythm of successive hegemonic formations.

All social relations can become the locus of antagonism insofar as they are constructed as relations of subordination. Many different forms of subordination can become the origin of conflict and struggle. There exists, therefore, in society a multiplicity of potential antagonisms, and class antagonism is only one among many. It is not possible to reduce all those forms of subordination and struggle to the expression of a single logic located in the economy. Nor can this reduction be avoided by positing a complex mediation between social antagonisms and the economy. There are multiple forms of power in society that cannot be reduced to or deduced from one origin or source.

New antagonisms and hegemonic formations

My thesis is that the new social movements express antagonisms that have emerged in response to the hegemonic formation that was *fully* installed in Western countries after the Second World War, a formation in crisis today. I say fully installed because the process did not begin at that time; these hegemonic forms were evolving, were being put into place since the beginning of this century. Thus, we also had social movements before the Second World War, but they really fully developed only after the war in response to a new social hegemonic formation.

The antagonisms that emerged after the war, however, have not derived from the imposition of forms of subordination that did not exist before. For instance, the struggles against racism and sexism resist forms of domination that existed not only before the new hegemonic formation but also before capitalism. We can see the emergence of those antagonisms in the context of the dissolution of all the social relations based on hierarchy, and that, of course, is linked to the development of capitalism, which destroys all those social relations and replaces them with commodity relations. So, it is with the development of capitalism that those forms of subordination can emerge as antagonisms. The relations may have existed previously, but they could not emerge as antagonisms before capitalism. Thus, we must be concerned with the structural transformations that have provided some of the objective conditions for the emergence of these new antagonisms. But you cannot automatically derive antagonism and struggle from the existence of these objective conditions – they are necessary but not sufficient – unless you assume people will necessarily struggle against subordination. Obviously I am against any such essentialist postulate. We need to ask under what conditions those relations of subordination could give birth to antagonisms, and what other conditions are needed for the emergence of struggles against these subordinations.

It is the hegemonic formation installed after the Second World War that, in fact, provides these conditions. We may characterize this formation as articulating: (a) a certain type of labour process based on the semi-automatic assembly line; (b) a certain type of state (the Keynesian interventionist state); and (c) new cultural forms that can be described as 'mediating culture'. The investiture of such a hegemonic formation involved a complex process, articulating a set of transformations, each of which derived from a different logic. It is impossible to derive any one of these from another in some automatic fashion, as in an economistic logic. In fact, the transformations of the labour process that led to Taylorization and finally to Fordism were governed by the need to destroy the autonomy that workers continued to exercise in the labour process and to end worker resistance to the valorization of capital. But the Fordist semi-automatic assembly line made possible a mass production for which, given the low salary level, there were insufficient outlets. Thus, the working class's mode of life had to change significantly in order to create the conditions necessary for accumulation to regain its ascendancy. However, the fact that certain conditions were necessary for the accumulation and reproduction of capitalist social relations to function in no way guaranteed that these conditions would come about. The solution was to use worker struggles, which were multiplying in response to the intensification of labour, to establish a connection between increased productivity and increased wages. But this required a state intervention with a double purpose: it was just as urgent to counter the capitalist's inclination to lower wages as it was to set up a political framework in which workers' demands could be made compatible with the reproduction of capitalism. This provides significant evidence that this new hegemonic formation resulted from a political intervention.

These changes in the labour process can also be defined as a transformation of an extensive regime of accumulation into an intensive regime of accumulation. The latter is characterized by the expansion of capitalist relations of production to the whole set of social activities, which are thereby subordinated to the logic of production for profit. A new mode of consumption has been created that expresses the domination of commodity relations over non-commodity relations. As a consequence, a profound transformation of the existing way of life has taken place. Western society has been transformed into a big marketplace where all the products of human labour have become commodities, where more and more needs must go through the market to be satisfied. Such a 'commodification of social life' has destroyed a series of previous social relations and replaced them with commodity relations. This is what we know as the consumer society.

Today, it is not only through the sale of their labour power that individuals are submitted to the domination of capital but also through their participation in many other social relations. So many spheres of social life are now penetrated by capitalist relations that it is almost impossible to escape them. Culture, leisure, death, sex, everything is now a field of profit for capital. The destruction of the environment, the transformation of people into mere consumers – these are the results of that subordination of social life to the accumulation of capital. Those new forms of domination, of course, have been studied by many authors, but there has been a tendency, especially at the beginning of the 1960s – you will remember Marcuse's *One-Dimensional Man* – to believe that the power of capital was so overwhelming that no struggle, no resistance, could take place. Yet a few years later it became clear that those new forms of domination would not go unchallenged; they have given rise to many new antagonisms, which explains the widening of all forms of social conflict since the middle of the 1960s. My thesis is that many of the new social movements are expressions of resistances against that commodification of social life and the new forms of subordination it has created.

But that is only one aspect of the problem; there is a second aspect that is extremely important. You remember that we have defined the hegemonic formation not only in terms of Fordism but also in terms of the Keynesian welfare state. The new hegemonic formation has been characterized by growing state intervention in all aspects of social life, which is a key characteristic of the Keynesian state. The intervention of the state led to a phenomenon of bureaucratization, which is also at the origin of new forms of subordination and resistance. It must be said that in many ways commodification and bureaucratization are articulated together, as when the state acts in favour of capital. Thus, while it might be difficult to distinguish between them, I think it is extremely important to do so and analyze them as different systems of domination. There may be cases in which the state acts against the interests of capital to produce what Claus Offe has called 'decommodification'. At the same time, such interventions, because of their bureaucratic character, may produce new forms of subordination. This is the case, for example, when the state provides services in fields of health, transportation, housing, and education.

A third aspect of the problem is that some new types of struggle must be seen as resistances to the growing uniformity of social life, a unity that is the result of the kind of mass culture imposed by the media. This imposition of a homogenized way of life, of a uniform cultural pattern, is being challenged by different groups that reaffirm their right to their difference, their specificity, be it through the exaltation of their regional identity or their specificity in the realm of fashion, music, or language.

The profound changes brought about by this construction of a hegemonic formation gave rise to the resistances expressed in the new social movements. However, as I have said, one should not blame new forms of inequality for all the antagonisms that emerged in the 1960s. Some, like the women's movement, concerned long-standing types of oppression that had not yet become antagonistic because they were located in a hierarchical society accepting certain inequalities as 'natural'.

Whether antagonism is produced by the commodification of all social needs, or by the intervention of state bureaucracy, or by cultural levelling and the destruction of traditional values (whether or not the latter are themselves oppressive) – what all these antagonisms have in common is that the problem is not caused by the individual's defined position in the production system; they are, therefore, not 'class antagonisms'. Obviously this does not mean that class antagonism has been eliminated. In fact, insofar as more and more areas of social life are converted into 'services' provided by capitalism, the number of individuals subordinated to capitalist production relations increases. If you take the term 'proletarian' in its strict sense, as a worker who sells his or her labour, it is quite legitimate to speak of a process of proletarianization. The fact that there are an increasing number of individuals who may suffer capitalist domination as a class does not signify a new form of subordination but rather the extension of an already existing one. What is new is the spread of social conflict to other areas and the politicization of all these social relations. When we recognize that we are dealing with resistances to forms of oppression developed by the post-war hegemonic formation, we begin to understand the importance of these struggles for a socialist programme.

It is wrong, then, to affirm, as some do, that these movements emerged because of the crisis of the welfare state. No doubt that crisis exacerbated antagonisms, but it did not cause them; they are the expression of a triumphant hegemonic formation. It is, on the contrary, reasonable to suppose that the crisis was in part provoked by the growing resistance to the domination of society by capital and the state. Neoconservative theoreticians are, therefore, not wrong to insist on the problem of the ungovernability of Western countries, a problem they would solve by slowing down what they call the 'democratic assault'. To propose the crisis as the origin of the new social movements is, in addition, politically dangerous: it leads to thinking of them as irrational manifestations, as phenomena of social pathology. Thus, it obscures the important lessons these struggles provide for a reformulation of socialism.

New antagonisms and democratic struggle

I have thus far limited my analysis to the transformations that have taken place in Western societies after World War II and to the resulting creation of new forms of subordination and inequality, which produced in turn the new social movements. But there is an entirely different aspect of the question that must now be developed. Pointing to the existence of inequalities is not sufficient to explain why they produce social unrest. If you reject, as I obviously do, the assumption that the essence of humankind is to struggle for equality and democracy, then there is an important problem to resolve. One must determine what conditions are necessary for specific forms of subordination to produce struggles that seek their abolition. As I have said, the subordination of women is a very old phenomenon, which became the target of feminist struggles only when the social model based on hierarchy had collapsed. It is here that my opening reference to de Tocqueville is pertinent, for he was the first to grasp the importance of the democratic revolution on the symbolic level. As long as equality has not yet acquired (with the democratic revolution) its place of central significance in the social imagination of Western societies, struggles for this equality cannot exist. As soon as the principle of equality is admitted in one domain, however, the eventual questioning of all possible forms of inequality is an ineluctable consequence. Once begun, the democratic revolution has had, necessarily, to undermine all forms of power and domination, whatever they might be.

I would like to elaborate on the relationship between antagonism and struggle and to begin with the following thesis: An antagonism can emerge when a collective subject – of course, here I am interested in political antagonism at the level of the collective subject – that has been constructed in a specific way, to certain existing discourses, finds its subjectivity negated by other discourses or practices. That negation can happen in two basic ways. First, subjects constructed on the basis of certain rights can find themselves in a position in which those rights are denied by some practices of discourses. At that point there is a negation of subjectivity or identification which can be the basis for an antagonism. I am not saying that this *necessarily* leads to an antagonism; it is a necessary but not sufficient condition. The second form in which antagonism emerges corresponds to that expressed by feminism and the black movement. It is a situation in which subjects constructed in subordination by a set of discourses are, at the same time, interpellated as equal by other discourses. Here we have a contradictory interpellation. Like the first form, it is a negation of a particular subject position, but, unlike the first, it is the subjectivity-in-subordination that is negated, which opens the possibility for its deconstruction and challenging.

For example, consider the case of the suffragist movement, or, more generally, the question of why it is that, although women's subordination has existed for so long, only at the end of the nineteenth century and the beginning of the twentieth century did subordination give rise to a feminist movement. That has led some Marxist feminists to say that there was no real women's subordination before; women's subordination is a consequence of capitalism and that is why feminism emerged under capitalism. I think this is wrong. Imagine the way women were constructed, as women, in the Middle Ages. All the possible discourses – the church, the family – constructed women as subordinate subjects. There was absolutely no possibility, no play, in those subject positions for women to call that subordination into question. But with the democratic revolutions of the nineteenth century the assertion that 'men are equal' appears for the first time. Obviously 'men' is ambiguous because it refers to both men and women, so women found themselves contradictorily interpellated. As citizens, women are equal, or at least interpellated as equal, but that equality is negated by their being women. (It is no coincidence that Mary Wollstonecraft, one of the important English feminists, was living with William Godwin, who was an important radical; this demonstrates the influence of radicalism on the emergence of the suffragist movement.) So that is what I understand by contradictory interpellation – the emergence of a section of equality at a point of new subjectivity, which contradicts the subordination in all other subject positions. That is what allows women to extend the democratic revolution, to question all their subordinate subject positions. The same analysis could be given for the emergence of the black liberation movement.

I should emphasize here the importance of actually existing discourse in the emergence and construction of antagonisms. Antagonisms are always discursively constructed; the forms they take depend on existing discourses and their hegemonic role at a given moment. Thus, different positions in sexual relations do not necessarily construct the concept of woman or femininity in different ways. It depends on the way the antagonism is constructed, and the enemy is defined by the existing discourses. We must also take into account the role of the democratic discourse that became predominant in the Western world with the 'democratic revolution'. I refer to the transformation, at the level of the symbolic, that deconstructed the theological-political-cosmological vision of the Middle Ages, a vision in which people were born into a specific place in a structured and hierarchical society for which the idea of equality did not exist.

People struggle for equality not because of some ontological postulate but because they have been constructed as subjects in a democratic tradition that puts those values at the centre of social life. We can see the widening of social conflict as the extension of the democratic revolution into more and more spheres of social life, into more social relations. All positions that have been constructed as relations of domination/subordination will be deconstructed because of the subversive character of democratic discourse. Democratic discourse extends its field of influence from a starting point, the equality of citizens in a political democracy, to socialism which extends equality to the level of the economy and then into other social relations, such as sexual, racial, generational, and regional. Democratic discourse questions all forms of inequality and subordination. That is why I propose to call those new social movements 'new democratic struggles', because they are extensions of the democratic revolution to new forms of subordination. Democracy is our most subversive idea because it interrupts all existing discourses and practices of subordination.

Now I want to make a distinction between democratic antagonism and democratic struggle. Democratic antagonisms do not necessarily lead to democratic struggles. Democratic antagonism refers to resistance to subordination and inequality; democratic struggle is directed toward a wide democratization of social life. I am hinting here at the possibility that democratic antagonism can be articulated into different kinds of discourse, even into right-wing discourse, because antagonisms are polysemic. There is no one paradigmatic form in which resistance against domination is expressed. Its articulation depends on the discourses and relations of forces in the present struggle for hegemony.

Stuart Hall's analysis of Thatcherism enables us to understand the way popular consciousness can be articulated to the Right. Indeed, any democratic antagonism can be articulated in many different ways. Consider the case of unemployment. A worker who loses his or her job is in a situation – the first one described above – in which, having been defined on the basis of the right to have a job, he or she now finds that right denied. This can be the locus of an antagonism, although there are ways of reacting to unemployment that do not lead to any kind of struggle. The worker can commit suicide, drink enormously, or batter his or her spouse; there are many ways people react against that negation of their subjectivity. But consider now the more political forms that reaction can take. There is no reason to believe the unemployed person is going to construct an antagonism in which Thatcherism or capitalism is the enemy. In England, for example, the discourse of Thatcherism says, 'You have lost your job because women are taking men's jobs.' It constructs an antagonism in which feminism is the enemy. Or it can say, 'You have lost your job because all those immigrants are taking the jobs of good English workers.' Or it can say, 'You have lost your job because the trade unions maintain such high wages that there are not enough jobs for the working class.' In all these cases, democratic antagonism is articulated to the Right rather than giving birth to democratic struggle.

Only if the struggle of the unemployed is articulated with the struggle of blacks, of women, of all the oppressed, can we speak of the creation of a democratic struggle. As I have said, the ground for new struggles has been the production of new inequalities attributable to the postwar hegemonic formation. That the objective of these struggles is autonomy and not power has often been remarked. It would, in fact, be wrong to oppose radically the struggles of workers to the struggles of the new social movements; both are efforts to obtain new rights or to defend endangered ones. Their common element is thus a fundamental one.

Once we have abandoned the idea of a paradigmatic form, which the worker's struggles would be obliged to express, we cannot affirm that the essential aim of these struggles is the conquest of political power. What is needed is an examination of the different forms that democratic struggles for equality may take, according to the type of adversary they oppose and the strategy they imply. In the case of resistances that seek to defend existing rights against growing state intervention, it is obvious that the matter of autonomy will be more important than for those resistances that seek to obtain state action in order to redress inequalities originating in civil society. This does not change the fact that they are of the same nature by virtue of their common aim: the reduction of inequalities and of various forms of subordination. That the vast extension of social conflict we are living through is the work of the democratic revolution is better understood by the New Right than by the Left. This is why the Right strives to halt the progress of equality. Starting from different viewpoints, both neo-liberal theoreticians of the market economy and those who are called, in the United States, 'neoconservatives' are variously seeking to transform dominant ideological parameters so as to reduce the central role played in these by the idea of democracy, or else to redefine democracy in a restrictive way to reduce its subversive power.

For neoliberals like Hayek, the idea of democracy is subordinated to the idea of individual liberty, so that a defence of economic liberty and private property replaces a defence of equality as the privileged value in a liberal society. Naturally, Hayek does not attack democratic values frontally, but he does make them into an arm for the defence of individual liberty. It is clear that, in his thinking, should a conflict arise between the two, democracy should be sacrificed.

Another way to stop the democratic revolution is offered by the neoconservatives, whose objective is to redefine the notion of democracy itself so that it no longer centrally implies the pursuit of equality and the importance of political participation. Democracy is thus emptied of all of its substance, on the pretext that it is being defended against its excesses, which have led it to the edge of the egalitarian abyss.

To this purpose, Brzezinski, when he was director of the Trilateral Commission, proposed a plan to 'increasingly separate the political systems from society and to begin to conceive of the two as separate entities'. The idea was to remove as many decisions as possible from political control and to give their responsibility exclusively to experts. Such a measure seeks to depoliticize the most fundamental decisions, not only in the economic but also in the social and political spheres, in order to achieve, in the words of Huntington, 'a greater degree of moderation in democracy'.

The attempt is to transform the predominant shared meanings in contemporary democratic liberal societies in order to rearticulate them in a conservative direction, justifying inequality. If it succeeds, if the New Right's project manages to prevail, a great step backward will have been taken in the movement of the democratic revolution. We shall witness the establishment of a dualistic society, deeply divided between a sector of the privileged, those in a strong position to defend their rights, and a sector of all those who are excluded from the dominant system, whose demands cannot be recognized as legitimate because they will be inadmissible by definition.

It is extremely important to recognize that, in their anti-egalitarian crusade, the various formations of the New Right are trying to take advantage of the new antagonisms born of commodification, bureaucratization and the uniformization of society. Margaret Thatcher's success in Great Britain and Ronald Reagan's in the United States are unmistakable signs: the populist Right has been able to articulate a whole set of resistances countering the increase in state intervention and the destruction of traditional values and to express them in the language of neoliberalism. It is thus possible for the Right to exploit struggles that express resistance to the new forms of subordination stemming from the hegemonic formation of the Keynesian welfare state.

This is why it is both dangerous and mistaken to see a 'privileged revolutionary subject' constituted in the new social movements, a subject who would take the place formerly occupied by the now fallen worker class. I think this is the current thinking represented by Alain Touraine in France and by some of the people linked with the peace movement in Germany. They tend to see new social movements in a much too simplistic way. Like those of the workers, these struggles are not necessarily socialist or even progressive. Their articulation depends on discourses existing at a given moment and on the type of subject the resistances construct. They can, therefore, be as easily assimilated by the discourses of the anti-status quo Right as by those of the Left, or be simply absorbed into the dominant system, which thereby neutralizes them or even utilizes them for its own modernization.

It is, in fact, evident that we must give up the whole problematic of the privileged revolutionary subject, which, thanks to this or that characteristic, granted *a priori* by virtue of its position in social relations, was presumed to have some universal status and the historical mission of liberating society. On the contrary, if every antagonism is necessarily specific and limited, and there is no single source for all social antagonisms, then the transition to socialism will come about only through political construction articulating all the struggles against different forms of inequality. If, in certain cases, a particular group plays a central role in this transition, it is for reasons that have to do with its political capacity to effect this articulation in specific historical conditions, not for *a priori* ontological reasons. We must move beyond the sterile dichotomy opposing the working class to the social movements, a dichotomy that cannot in any case correspond to sociological separation, since the workers cannot be reduced to their class position and are inserted into other types of social relations that form other subject positions. We must recognize that the development of capitalism and of increasing state intervention has enlarged the scope of the political struggle and extended the effect of the democratic revolution to the whole of social relations. This opens the possibility of a war for position at all levels of society, which may, therefore, open up the way for a radical transformation.

The new antagonisms and socialism

This war for position is already underway, and it has hitherto been waged more effectively by the Right than by the Left. Yet the success of the New Right's current offensive is not definitive. Everything depends on the Left's ability to set up a true hegemonic counteroffensive to integrate current struggles into an overall socialist transformation. It must create what Gramsci called an 'expansive hegemony', a chain of equivalences between all the democratic demands to produce the collective will of all those people struggling against subordination. It must create an 'organic ideology' that articulates all those movements together. Clearly, this project cannot limit itself to questioning the structural relations of capitalist production. It must also question the mode of development of those forces endemic to the rationale of capitalist production. Capitalism as a way of life is, in fact, responsible for the numerous forms of subordination and inequality attacked by new social movements.

The traditional socialist model, insofar as it accepts an assembly line productivity of the Fordist type, cannot provide an alternative within the current social crisis and must be profoundly modified. We need an alternative to the logic that promotes the maximum production of material goods and the consequent incessant creation of new material needs, leading in turn to the progressive destruction of natural resources and the environment. A socialist programme that does not include the ecological and antinuclear movements cannot hope to solve current problems. The same objection applies to a socialism tolerant of the disproportionate role given to the state. State intervention has, in fact, been proposed as a remedy for the capitalist anarchy. But with the triumph of the Keynesian state, the bourgeoisie has in large part realized this objective. Yet it is just this increase in state intervention that has given rise to the new struggles against the bureau-cratization of social life. A programme wishing to utilize this potential cannot, therefore, propose increased state intervention but must encourage increased self-determination and self-government for both individuals and citizens. This does not mean accepting the arguments of the New Right, or falling back into the trap of renewed privatization. The state ought to have charge of key sectors of the economy, including control of welfare services. But all these domains should be organized and controlled by workers and consumers rather than the bureaucratic apparatus. Otherwise, the potential of this anti-state resistance will simply be used by the Right for its own ends.

As for the women's movement, it is apparent that it needs an even more thoroughgoing transformation. Such a transformation is not utopian. We are beginning to see how a society in which the development of science and technology is directed toward the liberation of the individual rather than toward his or her servitude could also bring about a true equality of the sexes. The consequences of automation – the reduction of the workday and the change in the very notion of work that implies – make possible a far-reaching transformation of everyday life and of the sexual division of labour that plays such an important role in women's subordination. But for this to occur, the Left would have to abandon its con-servative attitude toward technological development and make an effort to bring these important changes under its control.

We hear, all too often, as a reaction to the apologists of postindustrial society, that we are still in a capitalist society and that nothing has changed. Though it is quite true that capitalism still prevails, many things have changed since Marx. We are, today, in the midst of an important restructuring. Whether the outcome will strengthen capitalism or move us ahead in the construction of a more democratic society depends on the ability of existing forces to articulate the struggles taking place for the creation of a new hegemonic formation.

What is specific to the present situation is the proliferation of democratic struggles. The struggle for equality is no longer limited to the political and economic arenas. Many new rights are being defined and demanded: those of women, of homo-sexuals, of various regional and ethnic minorities. All inequalities existing in our society are now at issue. To understand this profound transformation of the political field we must rethink and reformulate the notion of democracy itself, for the view we have inherited does not enable us to grasp the amplitude of the democratic revolution. To this end, it is not enough to improve upon the liberal parliamentary conception of democracy by creating a number of basic democratic forms through which citizens could participate in the management of public affairs, or workers in the management of industries. In addition to these traditional social subjects we must recognize the existence of others and their political characters: women and the various minorities also have a right to equality and to self-determination. If we wish to articulate all these democratic struggles, we must respect their specificity and their autonomy, which is to say that we must institutionalize a true pluralism, a *pluralism of subjects*.

A new conception of democracy also requires that we transcend a certain individualistic conception of rights and that we elaborate a central notion of *solidarity*. This can only be achieved if the rights of certain subjects are not defended to the detriment of the rights of other subjects. Now it is obvious that, in many cases, the rights of some entail the subordination of the rights of others. The defence of acquired rights is therefore a serious obstacle to the establishment of true equality for all. It is precisely here that one sees the line of demarcation separating the Left's articulation of the resistances of the new social movements from the utilization of these same by the New Right. Whereas the Left's programme seeks to set up a system of equivalences among the greatest possible number of democratic demands and thus strives to reduce all inequalities, the Right's solution, as a form of populism, satisfies the needs of certain groups by creating new inequalities. This is why the politics of the latter, instead of extending democracy, necessarily widens an already deep social split between the privileged and the nonprivileged.

The progressive character of a struggle does not depend on its place of origin – we have said that all workers' struggles are not progressive – but rather on its link to other struggles. The longer the chain of equivalences set up between the defence of the rights of one group and those of other groups, the deeper will be the democratization process and the more difficult it will be to neutralize certain struggles or make them serve the ends of the Right. The concept of solidarity can be used to form such a chain of democratic equivalences. It is urgent that we establish this new democratic theory, with the concept of solidarity playing the central role, to counter the New Right's offensive in the field of political philosophy.

Faced with an effort like Hayek's to redefine freedom individualistically, what the Left needs is a postindividualist concept of freedom, for it is still over questions of freedom and equality that the decisive ideological battles are being waged. What is at stake is the redefinition of those fundamental notions; and it is the nature of these relations that will determine the kinds of political subjects who will emerge and the new hegemonic bloc that will take shape.

To combine equality and liberty successfully in a new vision of democracy, one that recognizes the multiplicity of social relations and their corresponding subject positions, requires that we achieve a task conceived at the beginning of the democratic revolution, one that defines the kind of politics required for the advent of modernity. If to speak of socialism still means anything, it should be to designate an extension of the democratic revolution to the entirety of social relations and the attainment of a *radical, libertarian, and plural democracy*. Our objective, in other words, is none other than the goal Tocqueville perceived as that of democratic peoples, that ultimate point where freedom and equality meet and fuse, where people 'will be perfectly free because they are entirely equal, and where they will all be perfectly equal because they are entirely free'.

Note

1 This chapter was translated by Stanley Gray.

3

POST-MARXISM WITHOUT APOLOGIES (1987)

(With Ernesto Laclau)

Why should we rethink the socialist project today? In *Hegemony and Socialist Strategy* (Laclau and Mouffe, 1985) we pointed out some of the reasons. As participating actors in the history of our time, if we are actually to assume an interventionist role and not to do so blindly, we must attempt to wrest as much light as possible from the struggles in which we participate and from the changes which are taking place before our eyes. Thus, it is again necessary to temper 'the arms of critique'. The historical reality whereof the socialist project is reformulated today is very different from the one of only a few decades ago, and we will carry out our obligations as socialists and intellectuals only if we are fully conscious of the changes and persist in the effort of extracting all their consequences at the level of theory. The 'obstinate rigour' that Leonardo da Vinci proposed as a rule for intellectual work should be the only guideline in this task; and it leaves no space for complacent sleights of hand that seek only to safeguard an obsolete orthodoxy.

Since we have referred in our book to the most important of these historical transformations, we need do no more here than enumerate them: structural transformations of capitalism that have led to the decline of the classical working class in the post-industrial countries; the increasingly profound penetration of capitalist relations of production in areas of social life, whose dislocatory effects – concurrent with those deriving from the forms of bureaucratization which have characterized the Welfare State – have generated new forms of social protest; the emergence of mass mobilizations in Third World countries which do not follow the classical pattern of class struggle; the crisis and discrediting of the model of society put into effect in the countries of so-called 'actually existing socialism', including the exposure of new forms of domination established in the name of the dictatorship of the proletariat.

There is no room here for disappointment. The fact that any reformulation of socialism has to start today from a more diversified, complex and contradictory horizon of experiences than that of fifty years ago; not to mention 1914, 1871 or 1848 – is a challenge to the imagination and to political creativity. Hopelessness in this matter is only proper to those who, to borrow a phrase from J.B. Priestley, have lived for years in a fools' paradise and then abruptly move on to invent a fools' hell for themselves. We are living, on the contrary, one of the most exhilarating moments of the twentieth century: a moment in which new generations, without the prejudices of the past, without theories presenting themselves as 'absolute truths' of History, are constructing new emancipatory discourses, more human, diversified and democratic. The eschatological and epistemological ambitions are more modest, but the liberating aspirations are wider and deeper.

In our opinion, to rethink socialism in these new conditions compels us to undertake two steps. The first is to accept, in all their radical novelty, the transformations of the world in which we live – that is to say, neither to ignore them nor to distort them in order to make them compatible with outdated schemas so that we may continue inhabiting forms of thought which repeat the old formulae. The second is to start from this full insertion in the present – in its struggles, its challenges, its dangers – to interrogate the past: to search within it for the genealogy of the present situation; to recognize within it the presence – at first, marginal and blurred – of problems that are ours; and, consequently, to establish with that past a dialogue which is organized around continuities and discontinuities, identifications and ruptures. It is in this way, by making the past a transient and contingent reality rather than an absolute origin, that a *tradition* is given form.

In our book we attempted to make a contribution to this task, which today starts from different traditions and in different latitudes. In almost all cases we have received an important intellectual stimulus from our reviewers. Slavoj Žižek (1985), for example, has enriched our theory of social antagonisms, pointing out its relevance for various aspects of Lacanian theory. Andrew Ross (1986) has indicated the specificity of our line of argument in relation to several attempts in the United States to address similar problems, and has located it within the general framework of the debate about post-modernity. Alistair Davidson (1987) has characterized the new Marxist intellectual climate of which our book is part. Stanley Aronowitz (1986/87) has made some interesting and friendly criticisms from the standpoint of the intellectual tradition of the American Left. Philip Derbyshire (1985) has very correctly underlined the theoretical place of our text in the dissolution of essentialism, both political and philosophical. David Forgács (1985) has posed a set of important questions about the political implications of our book, which we hope to answer in future works.

However, there have also been attacks coming – as was to be expected from the fading epigones of Marxist orthodoxy. In this article we will answer the criticisms of one member of this tradition: Norman Geras (1987). The reason for our choice is that Geras – in an extremely unusual gesture for this type of literature – has done his homework: he has gone through our text thoroughly and has presented an exhaustive argument in reply. His merits, however, end there. Geras's essay is well rooted in the literary genre to which it belongs: the pamphlet of denunciation. His opinion about our book is unambiguous: it is 'profligate', 'dissolute', 'fatuous', 'without regard for normal considerations of logic, of evidence, or of due proportion'; it is 'shame-faced idealism', an 'intellectual vacuum', 'obscurantism', 'lacking all sense of reasonable constraint', 'lacking a proper sense of either measure or modesty'; it indulges in 'elaborate theoretical sophistries', in 'manipulating concepts' and in 'tendentious quotations'. After all this, he devotes forty pages (one third of the May–June 1987 issue of *New Left Review*) to a detailed analysis of such a worthless work. Furthermore, despite the fact that Geras does not know us personally, he is absolutely definite about the psychological motivations that led us to write the book – 'the pressure ... of age and professional status'; 'the pressures of the political time ... not very congenial, in the West at least, to the sustenance of revolutionary ideas'; 'the lure of intellectual fashion'; 'so-called realism, resignation or merely candid self-interest', etc. – conceding, however, that such perverse motivations are perhaps not 'consciously calculated for advantage'. (Thank you, Geras.) It is, of course, up to the reader to decide what to think about an author who opens an intellectual discussion by using such language and such an avalanche of *ad hominem* arguments. For our part, we will only say that we are not prepared to enter into a game of invective and counter-invective; we will therefore declare from the start that *we do not know* the psychological motivations behind Geras's inspiration to write what he does and that, not being his psychiatrists, we are quite uninterested in them. However, Geras also makes a series of substantive – though not substantial – criticisms of our book, and it is to these aspects of his piece that we shall refer. We shall first consider his critique of our theoretical approach and then move on to his points concerning the history of Marxism and the political issues that our book addresses. Let us start with the central category of our analysis: the concept of discourse.

Discourse

The number of absurdities and incoherencies that Geras has accumulated concerning this point is such that it is simply impossible to use his critical account as the framework for our reply. We will therefore briefly outline our conception of the social space as discursive, and then confront this statement with Geras's criticisms.

Let us suppose that I am building a wall with another bricklayer. At a certain moment I ask my workmate to pass me a brick and then I add it to the wall. The first act – asking for the brick – is linguistic; the second – adding the brick to the wall – is extralinguistic.[1] Do I exhaust the *reality* of both acts by drawing the distinction between them in terms of the linguistic/extralinguistic opposition? Evidently not, because, despite their differentiation in those terms, the two actions share something that allows them to be compared, namely the fact that they are both part of a total operation which is the building of the wall. So, then, how could we characterize this totality of which asking for a brick and positioning it are, both, partial moments? Obviously, if this totality includes both linguistic and non-linguistic elements, it cannot itself be either linguistic or extralinguistic; it has to be prior to this distinction. This totality which includes within itself the linguistic and the non-linguistic, is what we call *discourse*. In a moment we will justify this denomination; but what must be clear from the start is that *by discourse we do not mean a combination of speech and writing, but rather that speech and writing are themselves but internal components of discursive totalities.*

Now, turning to the term discourse itself, we use it to emphasize the fact that every social configuration is *meaningful*. If I kick a spherical object in the street or if I kick a ball in a football match, the *physical* fact is the same, but *its meaning* is different. The object is a football only to the extent that it establishes a system of relations with other objects, and these relations are not given by the mere referential materiality of the objects, but are, rather, socially constructed. This systematic set of relations is what we call discourse. The reader will no doubt see that, as we showed in our book, the discursive character of an object does not, by any means, imply putting its *existence* into question. The fact that a football is only a football as long as it is integrated within a system of socially constructed rules does not mean that it thereby ceases to be a physical object. A stone exists independently of any system of social relations, but it is, for instance, either a projectile or an object of aesthetic contemplation only within a specific discursive configuration. A diamond in the market or at the bottom of a mine is the same physical object; but, again, it is only a commodity within a determinate system of social relations. For that same reason it is the discourse which constitutes the subject position of the social agent, and not, therefore, the social agent which is the origin of discourse – the same system of rules that makes that spherical object into a football, makes me a player. The existence of objects is independent of their discursive articulation to such a point, that we could make of that mere existence – that is, existence extraneous to any meaning – the point of departure of social analysis. That is precisely what behaviourism, which is the opposite of our approach, does. Anyway, it is up to the reader to decide how we can better describe the building of a wall: whether by starting from the discursive totality of which each of the partial operation is a moment invested with a meaning, or by using such descriptions as: X emitted a series of sounds; Y gave a cubic object to X; X added this cubic object to a set of similar cubic objects; etc.

This, however, leaves two problems unsolved. The first is this: is it not necessary to establish here a distinction between meaning and action? Even if we accept that the meaning of an action depends on a discursive configuration, is not the action itself something different from that meaning? Let us consider the problem from two angles. Firstly, from the angle of meaning. Here the classical distinction is between semantics – dealing with the meaning of words; syntactics – dealing with word order and its consequences for meaning; and pragmatics – dealing with the way a word is actually used in certain speech contexts. The key point is to what extent a rigid separation can be established between semantics and pragmatics – that is, between meaning and use. From Wittgenstein onwards it is precisely this separation which has grown ever more blurred. It has become increasingly accepted that the meaning of a word is entirely context-dependent. As Hanna Fenichel Pitkin (1972, p. 84) points out:

> Wittgenstein argues that meaning and use are intimately, inextricably related, because use helps to determine meaning. Meaning is learned from, and shaped in, instances of use; so both its learning and its configuration depend on pragmatics ... Semantic meaning is compounded out of cases of a word's use, including all the many and varied language games that are played with it; so meaning is very much the product of pragmatics.
>
> (See also Cavell 1969, p. 9.)

The use of a term is an act – in that sense it forms part of pragmatics; on the other hand, the meaning is only constituted in the contexts of actual use of the term: in that sense its semantics is entirely dependent upon its pragmatics, from which it can be separated – if at all – only analytically. That is to say, in our terminology, every identity or discursive object is constituted in the context of an action. But, if we focus on the problem from the other angle, every non-linguistic action also has a meaning, and, therefore, we find within it the same entanglement of pragmatics and semantics that we find in the use of words. This leads us again to the conclusion that the distinction between linguistic and non-linguistic elements does not overlap with the distinction between 'meaningful' and 'not meaningful', since the former is a secondary distinction that takes place within meaningful totalities.

The other problem to be considered is the following: even if we assume that there is a strict equation between the social and the discursive, what can we say about the natural world, about the facts of physics, biology or astronomy that are not apparently integrated in meaningful totalities constructed by men? The answer is that natural facts are also discursive facts. And they are so for the simple reason that the idea of nature is not something that is already there, to be read from the appearances of things, but is itself the result of a slow and complex historical and social construction. To call something a natural object is a way of conceiving it that depends upon a classificatory system. Again, this does not put into question the fact that this entity which we call stone exists, in the sense of being present here and now, independently of my will; nevertheless the fact of its being a stone depends on a way of classifying objects that is historical and contingent. If there were no human beings on earth, those objects that we call stones would be there nonetheless; but they would not be 'stones', because there would be neither mineralogy nor a language capable of classifying them and distinguishing them from other objects. We need not stop for long on this point. The entire development of contemporary epistemology has established that there is no fact that allows its meaning to be read transparently. For instance, Popper's critique of verificationism showed that no fact can prove a theory, since there are no guarantees that the fact cannot be explained in a better way – therefore, determined in its meaning – by a later and more comprehensive theory. (This line of thought has gone far beyond the limits of Popperism; we could mention the advance represented by Kuhn's paradigms and by Feyerabend's epistemological anarchism.) And what is said of scientific theories can be applied to everyday languages that classify and organize objects.

Geras's four theses

We can now go to Geras's criticisms. They are structured around four basic theses: (1) that the distinction between the discursive and the extra-discursive coincides with the distinction between the fields of the spoken, written and thought, on the one hand, and the field of an external reality on the other; (2) that affirming the discursive character of an object means to deny the existence of the entity designated by that discursive object; (3) that denying the existence of extra-discursive points of reference is to fall in the bottomless abyss of relativism; (4) that affirming the discursive character of every object is to incur one of the most typical forms of idealism. Let us see.

We can treat the first two claims together. Geras writes:

> Every object is constituted as an object of discourse means all objects are given their being by, or are what they are by virtue of, discourse; which is to say (is it not?) that there is no pre-discursive objectivity or reality, that objects not spoken, written or thought about do not exist.
>
> (Geras 1987, p. 66)

To the question posed between brackets '(is it not?)', the answer is simply 'no, it is not'. The reader who has followed our text to this point will have no difficulty in understanding why. For – returning to our previous example – whether this stone is a projectile, or a hammer, or an object of aesthetic contemplation depends on its relations with me – it depends, therefore, on precise forms of discursive articulation – but the mere existence of the entity stone, the mere material and existential substratum does not. That is, Geras is making an elementary confusion between the being (*esse*) of an object, which is historical and changing, and the entity (*ens*) of that object which is not. Now, in our interchange with the world, objects are never given to us as mere existential entities; they are always given to us within discursive articulations. Wood will be raw material or part of a manufactured product, or an object for contemplation in a forest, or an obstacle that prevents us from advancing; the mountain will be protection from enemy attack, or a place for a touring trip, or the source for the extraction of minerals, etc. The mountain would not be any of these things if I were not here; but this does not mean that the mountain does not exist. It is because it exists that it can be all these things; but none of them follows necessarily from its mere existence. And as a member of a certain community, I will never encounter the object in its naked existence – such a notion is a mere abstraction; rather, that existence will always be given as articulated within discursive totalities. The second mistake Geras makes is that he reduces the discursive to a question of either speech, writing or thought, while our text explicitly affirms that, as long as every non-linguistic action is meaningful, it is also discursive. Thus, the criticism is totally absurd; it involves changing our concept of discourse midstream in the argument, and establishing an arbitrary identification between the being of an object and its existence. With these mis-representations it is very easy, evidently, to attribute imaginary inconsistencies to our text.

The third criticism – relativism – does not fare any better. Firstly, 'relativism' is, to a great extent, an invention of the fundamentalists. As Richard Rorty has pointed out:

> 'Relativism' is the view that every belief on a certain topic, or perhaps about *any* topic, is as good as every other. No one holds this view ... The philosophers who get *called* 'relativists' are those who say that the grounds for choosing between such opinions are less algorithmic than had been thought ... So the real issue is not between people who think one view as good as another and people who do not. It is between those who think our culture, or purpose, or intuitions cannot be supported except conversationally, and people who still hope for other sorts of support.
>
> (Rorty 1982, pp. 166–67)

Relativism is, actually, a false problem. A 'relativist' position would be one which affirmed that it is the same to think 'A is B' or 'A is not B'; that is to say, that it is a discussion linked to the being of the objects. As we have seen, however, outside of any discursive context objects *do not have* being; they have only *existence*. The accusation of the 'anti-relativist' is, therefore, meaningless, since it presupposes that there is a *being* of things as such, which the relativist is either indifferent to or proclaims to be inaccessible. But, as we have argued, things only have being within a certain discursive configuration, or 'language game', as Wittgenstein would call it. It would be absurd, of course, to ask oneself today if 'being a projectile' is part of the true being of the stone (although the question would have some legitimacy within Platonic metaphysics); the answer, obviously, would be: it depends on the way we use stones. For the same reason it would be absurd to ask oneself if, out-side all scientific theory, atomic structure is the 'true being' of matter – the answer will be that atomic theory is a way we have of classifying certain objects, but that these are open to different forms of conceptualization that may emerge in the future. In other words, the 'truth', factual or otherwise, about the being of objects is constituted within a theoretical and discursive context, and the idea of a truth outside all context is simply nonsensical.

Let us conclude this point by identifying the status of the concept of discourse. If the *being* – as distinct from existence – of any object is constituted within a discourse, it is not possible to differentiate the discursive, in terms of being, from any other area of reality. The discursive is not, therefore, an object among other objects (although, of course, concrete discourses are) but rather a theoretical *horizon*. Certain questions concerning the notion of discourse are, therefore, meaningless because they can be made only about objects within a horizon, not about the horizon itself. The following remark of Geras's must be included within this category:

> One could note again, for instance, how absolutely everything – subjects, experience, identities, struggles, movements – has discursive "conditions of possibility", while the question as to what may be the conditions of possibility of discourse itself, does not trouble the authors so much as to pause for thought.
>
> (Geras 1987, p. 69)

This is absurd. If the discursive is coterminous with the being of objects – the horizon, therefore, of the constitution of the being of every object – the question about the conditions of possibility of the being of discourse is meaningless. It is equivalent to asking a materialist for the conditions of possibility of matter, or a theist for the conditions of possibility of God.

Idealism and materialism

Geras's fourth criticism concerns the problem of idealism and we have to consider it in a more detailed way. The first condition for having a rational discussion, of course, is that the meaning of the terms one is using should be clear. Conceptual elucidation of the idealism/materialism opposition is particularly important in view not only of the widely differing contexts in which it has been used, but also of the fact that these contexts have often overlapped and so led to innumerable confusions. The idealism/materialism opposition has been used in attempts to refer to, roughly speaking, three different types of problem.

(1) The problem of the existence or non-existence of a world of objects external to thought. This is a very popular mistake which Geras incurs throughout his discussion. For the distinction here is not between idealism and materialism, but between idealism and realism. A philosophy such as Aristotle's, for example, which certainly is not materialist in any possible sense of the term, is clearly realist. The same can be said of the philosophy of Plato, since for him the Ideas *exist* in a heavenly place, where the mind contemplates them as something external to itself. In this sense, the whole of ancient philosophy was realist, since it did not put into question the existence of a world external to thought – it took it for granted. We have to reach the modern age with a philosophy such as Berkeley's, to find a total subordination of external reality to thought. However, it is important to realize that in this sense Hegel's absolute idealism, far from denying the reality of an external world, is its unequivocal affirmation. As Charles Taylor has asserted:

> This [absolute idealism] is paradoxically very different from all other forms of idealism, which tend to the denial of external reality, or material reality. In

the extreme form of Berkeley's philosophy, we have a denial of matter in favour of a radical dependence on the mind – of course God's, not ours. Hegel's idealism, far from being a denial of external material reality, is the strongest affirmation of it; it not only exists but necessarily exists.

(Taylor 1975, p. 109)

If this is the question at issue our position is, therefore, unequivocally realist, but this has little to do with the question of materialism.

(2) What actually distinguishes idealism from materialism is its affirmation of the ultimately conceptual character of the real; for example, in Hegel, the assertion that everything that is real is rational. Idealism, in its sense of opposition to materialism and not to realism, is the affirmation not that there do not *exist* objects external to the mind, but rather that the innermost nature of these objects is identical to that of mind that is to say, that it is ultimately *thought*. (Not thought of individual minds, of course; not even of a transcendent God, but *objective thought*.) Now, even if idealism in this second sense is only given in a fully coherent and developed form in Hegel, philosophers of antiquity are also predominantly idealist. Both Plato and Aristotle identified the ultimate reality of an object with its *form* – that is, with something 'universal', and hence conceptual. If I say that this object which is in front of me is rectangular, brown, a table, an object, etc., each of these determinants could also be applied to other objects – they are then 'universals', that is *form*. But what about the individual 'it' that receives all these determinations? Obviously, it is irrational and unknowable, since to know it would be to subsume it under a universal category. This last individual residue, which is irreducible to thought, is what the ancient philosophers called *matter*. And it was precisely this last residue which was eliminated by a consistent idealist philosophy such as Hegel's: it asserted the ultimate rationality of the real and thus became absolute idealism.

Thus, form is, at the same time, both the organizing principle of the mind and the ultimate reality of an object. As it has been pointed out:

[Form] cut[s] across the categories of epistemology and ontology for the being of the particular is itself exhaustively defined according to the requirements of knowledge ... Thought, word and thing are defined in relation to thinkable form, and thinkable form is itself in a relation of reciprocal definition with the concept of entity.

(Staten 1985, p. 6)

The true line of divide between idealism and materialism is, therefore, the affirmation or negation of the ultimate irreducibility of the real to the concept. (For example, a philosophy such as that of the early Wittgenstein, which presented a picture theory of language in which language shared the same 'logical form' as the thing, is entirely within the idealist field.)

It is important to note that, from this point of view, what has been traditionally called 'materialism' is *also* to a great extent idealist. Hegel knew this so well that in his *Greater Logic* materialism is presented as one of the first and crudest forms of idealism, since it assumes identity between knowledge and being (see *Greater Logic*, First Section, Chapter Two, final 'remark'.) Commenting on this passage, W.T. Stace points out:

> Atomism alleges that this *thing*, the atom, is the ultimate reality. Let it be so. But what is this thing? It is nothing but a congeries of universals, such perhaps as 'indestructible', 'indivisible', 'small', 'round', etc. All these are universals, or thoughts. 'Atom' itself is a concept. Hence even out of this materialism proceeds idealism.
>
> (Stace 1955, pp. 73–74)

Where, in all this, does Marx fit in? The answer cannot be unambiguous. In a sense, Marx clearly remains within the idealist field – that is to say, within the ultimate affirmation of the rationality of the real. The well known inversion of dialectics cannot but reproduce the latter's structure. To affirm that the ultimate law of motion of History is given not by the change of ideas in the minds of human beings but rather by the contradiction, in each stage, between the development of productive forces and the existing relations of production, does not modify things at all. For what is idealist is not the affirmation that the law of motion of History is the one rather than the other, but the very idea that there is an ultimate law of motion that can be conceptually grasped. To affirm the transparency of the real to the concept is equivalent to affirming that the real is 'form'. For this reason the most determinist tendencies within Marxism are also the most idealist, since they have to base their analyses and predictions on inexorable laws which are not immediately legible in the surface of historical life; they must base themselves on the internal logic of a closed conceptual model and transform that model into the (conceptual) essence of the real.

(3) This is not, however, the whole story. In a sense which we have to define more precisely, *there is* in Marx a definite movement away from idealism. But before we discuss this, we must characterize the structure and implications of any move away from idealism. As we have said, the essence of idealism is the reduction of the real to the concept (the affirmation of the rationality of the real or, in the terms of ancient philosophy, the affirmation that the reality of an object – as distinct from its existence – is *form*). This idealism can adopt the structure which we find in Plato and Aristotle – the reduction of the real to a hierarchical universe of static essences; or one can introduce movement into it, as Hegel does – on condition, of course, that it is movement *of the concept* and thus remains entirely within the realm of form. However, this clearly

indicates that any move away from idealism cannot but systematically weaken the claims of form to exhaust the reality of the object (i.e. the claims of what Heidegger and Derrida have called the 'metaphysics of presence'). But, this weakening cannot merely involve an affirmation of the thing's *existence* outside thought, since this 'realism' is perfectly compatible with idealism in our second sense. As has been pointed out,

> What is significant from a deconstructive viewpoint is that the sensible thing, even in a 'realist' like Aristotle, is itself unthinkable except in relation to intelligible form. Hence the crucial boundary for Aristotle, and for philosophy generally, does not pass between thought and thing *but within each of these, between form and formlessness or indefiniteness.*
>
> (Staten 1985, p. 7)

The instability of objects

Thus, it is not possible to abandon idealism by a simple appeal to the external object, since (1) this is compatible with the affirmation that the object is form and thus remains within the field of idealism and the most traditional metaphysics; and (2) if we take refuge in the object's mere 'existence', in the 'it' beyond all predication, we cannot say anything about it. But here another possibility opens up at once. We have seen that the 'being' of objects is different from their mere existence, and that objects are never given as mere 'existences' but are always articulated within discursive totalities. But in that case it is enough to show that no discursive totality is absolutely self-contained – that there will always be an outside which distorts it and prevents it from fully constituting itself – to see that the form and essence of objects are penetrated by a basic instability and precariousness, and that this is *their most essential possibility.* This is exactly the point at which the movement away from idealism starts.

Let us consider the problem more closely. Both Wittgenstein and Saussure broke with what can be called a referential theory of meaning i.e., the idea that language is a nomenclature which is in a one-to-one relation to objects. They showed that the word 'father', for instance, only means what it does because the words 'mother', 'son', etc. also exist. The totality of language is, therefore, a system of differences in which the identity of the elements is purely relational. Hence, every individual act of signification involves the totality of language (in Derridean terms, the presence of something always has the *traces* of something else which is absent). This purely relational or differential character is not, of course, exclusive to linguistic identities but holds for all signifying structures – that is to say, for all social structures. This does not mean that everything is language in the restricted sense of speech or writing, but rather that the relational or differential structure of language is the same for all signifying structures. So, if all identity is differential, it is enough that the system of differences is not closed, that it suffers the action of external discursive structures, for any identity (i.e., the *being*, not the *existence* of things) to be unstable. This is what shows the impossibility of attributing to the being of things the character of a fixed essence, and what makes possible the weakening of *form*, which constituted the cornerstone of traditional metaphysics. Human beings socially construct their world, and it is through this construction – always precarious and incomplete – that they give to a thing *its being*.[2] There is, then, a third meaning of the idealism/materialism opposition which is related neither to the problem of the external existence of objects, nor to a rigid counterposition of form and matter in which the latter is conceived as the 'individual existent'. In this third opposition, a world of fixed forms constituting the *ultimate* reality of the object (idealism) is challenged by the relational, historical and precarious character of the world of forms (materialism). For the latter, therefore, there is no possibility of eliminating the gap between 'reality' and 'existence'. Here, strictly speaking, there are two possible conceptual strategies: either to take 'idealism' and 'materialism' as two variants of 'essentialism'; or to consider that all essentialism, by subordinating the real to the concept, is idealism, and to see materialism as a variety of attempts to break with this subordination. Both strategies are, of course, perfectly legitimate.

Let us return at this point to Marx. There is in his work the beginning, but only the beginning, of a movement in the direction of materialism. His 'materialism' is linked to a *radical relationalism*: ideas do not constitute a closed and self-generated world, but are rooted in the ensemble of material conditions of society. However, his movement towards relationalism is weak and does not actually transcend the limits of Hegelianism (an inverted Hegelianism continues to be Hegelian). Let us look at these two moments:

(1) One possible way of understanding this embeddedness of ideas in the material conditions of society would be in terms of signifying totalities. The 'State' or the 'ideas' would not be self-constituted identities but rather 'differences' in the Saussurean sense, whose only identity is established relationally with other differences such as 'productive forces', 'relations of production', etc. The 'materialist' advance of Marx would be to have shown that the area of social differences which constitutes the signifying totalities is much wider and deeper than it had been supposed hitherto; that the material reproduction of society is part of the discursive totalities which determine the meaning of the most 'sublime' forms of political and intellectual life. This allows us to overcome the apparently insoluble problems concerning the base/superstructure relation: if State, ideas, relations of production, etc. have purely differential identities, the presence of each would involve the presence of the others – as the presence of 'father' involves the presence of 'son', 'mother', etc. In this sense, no *causal* theory about the efficacy of one element over another is necessary. This is the intuition that lies behind the Gramscian category of 'historical bloc': historical movement is explained not by laws of motion of History but by the organic link *between* base and superstructure.

(2) However, this radical relationalism of Marx is immediately translated into idealistic terms. 'It is not the consciousness of men that determines their

existence, but their social existence that determines their consciousness' (Marx 1971, p. 21). This could be read, of course, as a reintegration of consciousness with existence, but the expression could not be more unfortunate, since if social existence *determines* consciousness, then consciousness cannot be part of social existence.[3] And when we are told that the anatomy of civil society is political economy, this can only mean that there is a specific logic – the logic of the development of productive forces – which constitutes the *essence* of historical development. In other words, historical development can be rationally grasped and is therefore *form*. It is not surprising that the 'Preface' to the *Critique of Political Economy* depicts the outcome of the historical process exclusively in terms of the contradiction between productive forces and relations of production; nor is it surprising that class struggle is *entirely* absent from this account. All this is perfectly compatible with the basic premises of Hegelianism and metaphysical thought.

Let us now sum up our argument in this section. (1) The idealism/realism opposition is different from the idealism/materialism opposition. (2) Classical idealism and materialism are variants of an essentialism grounded on the reduction or the real to *form*. Hegel is, therefore, perfectly justified in regarding materialism as an imperfect and crude form of idealism. (3) A move away from idealism cannot be founded on the *existence* of the object, because nothing follows from this existence. (4) Such a move must, rather, be founded on a systematic weakening of form, which consists in showing the historical, contingent and constructed character of the *being* of objects; and in showing that this depends on the reinsertion of that being in the ensemble of relational conditions which constitute the life of a society as a whole. (5) In this process, Marx constitutes a transitional point: on the one hand, he showed that the meaning of any human reality is derived from a world of social relations much vaster than had previously been perceived; but on the other hand, he conceived the relational logic that links the various spheres in clearly essentialist or idealistic terms.

A first sense of our post-Marxism thus becomes clear. It consists in a deepening of that relational moment which Marx, thinking within a Hegelian and, in any case, nineteenth-century matrix, could only take so far. In an age when psychoanalysis has shown that the action of the unconscious makes all signification ambiguous; when the development of structural linguistics has enabled us to understand better the functioning of purely differential identities; when the transformation of thought – from Nietzsche to Heidegger, from pragmatism to Wittgenstein – has decisively undermined philosophical essentialism, we can reformulate the materialist programme in a much more radical way than was possible for Marx.

Either/or

At this point we should consider Geras's general methodological reproach that we have based our main theoretical conclusions on a false and rigid 'either/or' opposition; that is to say, that we have counterposed two polar and exclusive alternatives, without considering the possibility of intermediate solutions that avoid both extremes. Geras discusses this supposed theoretical mistake in relation to three points: our analysis of the concept of 'relative autonomy'; our treatment of Rosa Luxemburg's text on the mass strike; and our critique of the concept of 'objective' interest. As we will show, in all three cases Geras's criticism is based on a misrepresentation of our argument.

Firstly, *'relative autonomy'*. Geras quotes a passage of our book where we sustain, according to him, that

> *either* the basic determinants explain the nature, as well as the limits, of that which is supposed to be relatively autonomous, so that it is not really autonomous at all; *or* it is, flatly, *not* determined by them and they cannot be basic determinants … Laclau and Mouffe here deny to Marxism the option of a concept like relative autonomy. No wonder that it can only be for them the crudest sort of economism.
>
> (Geras 1987, p. 49)

Geras proposes, instead, the elimination of this 'inflexible alternative'. If, for example, his ankle is secured to a stout post by a chain he may not be able to attend a political meeting or play tennis, but he can still read and sing. Between total determination and partial limitation there is a whole range of intermediate possibilities. Now, it is not very difficult to realize that the example of the chain is perfectly irrelevant to what Geras intends to demonstrate, since it involves no more than a sleight of hand whereby a relation of determination is transformed into a relation of limitation. Our text does not assert that the State in capitalist society is not *relatively* autonomous, but rather, that we cannot conceptualize 'relative autonomy' by starting from a category such as 'determination in the last instance by the economy'. Geras's example is irrelevant because it is not an example of a relation of determination: the chain tied to his ankle does not *determine* that Geras reads or sings; it only limits his possible movements – and, presumably, this limitation has been imposed *against* Geras's will. Now, the base/superstructure model affirms that the base not only limits but *determines* the superstructure, in the same way that the movements of a hand determine the movements of its shadow on a wall. When the Marxist tradition affirms that a State is 'capitalist', or that an ideology is 'bourgeois', what is being asserted is not simply that they are in chains or prisoners of a type of economy or a class position, but rather that they *express or represent* the latter at a different level. Lenin, who, unlike Geras, *knew* what a relation of determination is, had an instrumentalist theory of the State. His vision is, no doubt, a simplistic one, but it has a considerably higher degree of realism than the chain of Geras, the latter seeming to suggest that the capitalist state is a prisoner limited by the mode of production in what otherwise would have been its spontaneous movements.

What our book asserts is not that the autonomy of the State is absolute, or that the economy does not have any limiting effect *vis-à-vis* the State's action, but rather that the *concepts* of 'determination in the last instance' and 'relative autonomy' are *logically* incompatible. And, when we *are* dealing with logical matters, alternatives are of the either/or type. This is what we have to show. In order to do so let us put ourselves in a situation most favourable to Geras: we will take as an example not a 'vulgar' Marxism but a 'distinguished' Marxism, one that avoids crude economists and introduces all imaginable sophistication in thinking the base/ superstructure relation. What conceptual instruments does such Marxism have to construct the concept of 'relative autonomy' starting from the concept of 'determination in the last instance'? We can only think of two types of attempt:

(1) It might be argued that the base determines the superstructure not in a direct way but through a complex system of *mediations*. Does this allow us to think the concept of 'relative autonomy'? By no means. 'Mediation' is a dialectical category; even more: it is the category out of which *dialectics* is constituted, and belongs, therefore, to the internal movement of the concept. Two entities that are related (and constituted) via mediations are not, strictly speaking, separate entities: each is an internal moment in the self-unfolding of the other. We can extend the field of mediations as much as we want: in this way we would give a less simplistic vision of social relations, but we would not advance a single step in the construction of the concept of relative autonomy. This is because autonomy – relative or not – means *self-determination*; but if the identity of the supposedly autonomous entity is constituted by its location within a totality, and this totality has an *ultimate* determination, the entity in question *cannot* be autonomous. According to Lukács, for instance, facts only acquire meaning as moments or determinations of a totality; it is within this totality – which could be as rich in mediations as we want – that the meaning of any identity is established. The exteriority that a relation of autonomy would require is therefore absent.

(2) So, let us abandon this attempt to use the concept of mediation and try instead a second line of defence of the logical compatibility of the two concepts. Could we, perhaps, assert that the superstructural entity is *effectively* autonomous – that is to say, that no system of mediations links it to the base – and that determination in the last instance by the economy is reduced to the fact that the latter *always* fixes the limits of autonomy (i.e., that the possibility of Geras's hair growing like Samson's to the point that he would be able to break the chain, is excluded)? Have we made any advance with this new solution? No, we are at exactly the same point as before. The *essence* of something is the ensemble of necessary characteristics which constitute its identity. Thus, if it is an *a priori* truth that the limits of autonomy are always fixed by the economy, then such limitation is not external to that entity but is part of its essence. The autonomous entity is an internal moment of the same totality in which the determination in the last instance is constituted and

hence there is no autonomy. (All this reasoning is, actually, unnecessary. To affirm *at the same time* that the intelligibility of the social whole proceeds from an ultimate determination, and that there are internal entities to that totality which escape that determination, was inconsistent from the beginning.)

Autonomy and determination

What happens if, instead, we abandon the concept of 'determination in the last instance by the economy'? It does not follow either that the autonomy is absolute, or that the 'economy' in a capitalist society does not impose fundamental structural limits on what can be done in other spheres. What *does* follow is (a) that the limitation and interaction between spheres cannot be thought in terms of the category of 'determination'; and (b) that there is no *last* instance on the basis of which society can be reconstructed as a rational and intelligible structure, but rather that the relative efficacy of each sphere depends on an unstable relation of antagonistic forces which entirely penetrates the social. For example, the structure of capitalist relations of production in a certain moment will impose limits on income distribution and access to consumer goods; but conversely, factors such as working-class struggles or the degree of union organization will also have a limiting effect on the rate of profit that can be obtained in a political and economic conjuncture. In our book we made reference to something that has been shown by numerous recent studies: namely, that the transition from absolute to relative surplus value, far from being the simple outcome of the internal logic of capital accumulation, is, to a large extent, the result of the efficacy of working-class struggles. That is to say, the economic space itself is structured as a political space, and the 'war of position' is not the superstructural consequence of laws of motion constituted outside it. Rather, such laws penetrate the very field of what was traditionally called the 'base' or 'infrastructure'. *If determination* was a *last* instance, it would be incompatible with autonomy, because it would be a relation of omnipotence. But, on the other hand, an *absolutely* autonomous entity would be one which did not establish an antagonistic relation with anything external to it, since for an antagonism to be possible, a partial efficacy of the two opposing forces is a prerequisite. The autonomy which both of them enjoy will therefore *always* be relative.

Our book states this clearly in the same paragraph which Geras quotes:

> If … we renounce the hypothesis of a final closure of the social, it is necessary to start from a plurality of political and social spaces which do not refer to any ultimate unitarian basis. Plurality is not the phenomenon to be explained, but the starting point of the analysis. But if, as we have seen, the identity of these spaces is always precarious, it is not possible simply to affirm the equation between autonomy and dispersion. *Neither total autonomy nor total subordination is, consequently, a plausible solution.*

> (Laclau and Mouffe 1985, p. 140)

The suggestion that we have set up a rigid alternative between total autonomy and absolute subordination is, therefore, simply an invention by Geras. All our analyses try, on the contrary, to overcome that 'either/or' alternative – see, for instance, our critique of the symmetrical essentialisms of the totality and the elements (pp. 103–5), or our discussion of the concept of representation (pp. 119–22). In order to overcome the alternative, however, it is necessary to construct a new terrain that goes beyond its two terms, and this implies a break with metaphysical categories such as the 'last instance' of the social. Geras also tries, apparently, to overcome this alternative, but he only proceeds by the trick of affirming determination in the last instance *theoretically* whilst eliminating it in the concrete example that he gives (the one of the chain). His overcoming of the alternative is, therefore, wishful thinking, and his discourse is lodged in permanent incoherence.

Geras's other two examples of our 'either/or' reductionism can be discussed briefly, since they repeat the same argumentative strategy and the same mistakes. Firstly, the case of Rosa Luxemburg. Geras quotes a fragment of our book where, *according to him*, we affirm that Marxism rests upon a well-known alternative:

> either capitalism leads through its necessary laws to proletarianization and crisis; or else these necessary laws do not function as expected, in which case … the fragmentation between different subject positions ceases to be an 'artificial product' of the capitalist state and becomes a permanent reality.

On which Geras comments: 'It is another stark antithesis. *Either* pure economic necessity bears the full weight of unifying the working class; *or* we simply have fragmentation' (Geras 1987, p. 50). This time, however, Geras has omitted a 'small' detail in his quotation; and his misquotation is so flagrant that he puts us – this time for sure – before the 'either/or' alternative of having to conclude that he is intellectually either irresponsible or dishonest. The 'detail' is that our text poses this alternative, not in respect of Marxism in general, but in respect of what would be, by *reductio ad absurdum*, their extreme reductionist or essentialist versions. The quotation comes from a passage where, after having pointed out the presence of a double historical logic in the text of Rosa Luxemburg – the logic of structural determinism and the logic of spontaneism – we proceeded to what we called an 'experiment of frontiers'. That is to say, we tried to see what logical consequences would follow from an imaginary extension of the operative area of either determinism or spontaneism. Thus we pointed out that it is *only* if Marxist discourse becomes *exclusively* determinist (that is, only in the imaginary case of our experiment) that the iron alternative to which Geras refers is posed. Our book presented the history of Marxism, on the contrary, as a sustained effort to escape the 'either/or' logic of determinism. It is exactly in these terms that we refer to the increasing centrality and area of operativity of the concept of 'hegemony'. In fact, the second step of our experiment – the moving of frontiers in a direction that expands the logic of spontaneism – is conducive to the political alternatives which our text suggests, and which are very different from those possible within a determinist model.

Misquotations apart, it is interesting to see how Geras himself attempts to escape the 'either/or' alternative. As in the case of relative autonomy, his solution is a mixture of journalistic impressionism and theoretical inconsistency. (It is significant that, despite his insulting and aggressive tone, Geras is suspiciously defensive and moderate when it comes to presenting his own political and theoretical proposals.) He asks:

> Why may we not think that between this devil and that blue sea there is something else: notwithstanding the wide diversity, a common structural situation, of exploitation, and some common features, like lack of autonomy and interest at work, not to speak of sheer unpleasantness and drudgery, and some pervasive economic tendencies, proletarianizing ones among them, and such also as create widespread insecurity of employment; all this providing a solid, objective *basis* – no more, but equally no less – for a unifying socialist politics? Why may we not?
>
> (Geras 1987, p. 50)

Why may we not indeed? All these things happen under capitalism, in addition to some more things that Geras omits to mention: imperialist exploitation, increasing marginalization of vast sectors of the population in the Third World and in the decaying inner cities of the post-industrial metropolis, ecological struggles against pollution of the environment, struggles against different forms of racial and sexual discrimination, etc. If it is a matter of *enumerating* the unpleasant features of the societies in which we live, which are the basis for the emergence of numerous antagonisms and contesting collective identities, the enumeration has to be complete. But if it is a matter, on the contrary, of answering such fragmentation with a theory of the necessary *class* nature of anti-capitalist agents, no mere descriptive enumeration will do the trick. Geras's 'classist' alternative is constituted only by means of interrupting at a certain point his enumeration of the collective antagonisms generated by late capitalism. The vacuity of this exercise is obvious. If Geras wants to found 'classism' on something other than the determinism of 'necessary laws of history', he has to propose a *theoretical alternative* of which there is not the slightest sign in his article.

Finally, the question of 'objective interests'. Ours is a criticism not of the notion of 'interests' but of their supposedly *objective* character: that is to say, of the idea that social agents have interests of which they are not conscious. To construct an 'interest' is a slow historical process, which takes place through complex ideological, discursive and institutional practices. Only to the extent that social agents participate in collective totalities are their identities constructed in a way that makes them capable of calculating and negotiating with other forces. 'Interests', then, are a social product and do not exist independently of the consciousness of the agents who are their bearers. The idea of an '*objective* interest' presupposes, instead, that social agents, far from being part of a process in which interests are constructed, merely *recognize* them – that is to say, that those interests are inscribed in their nature as a gift from Heaven. How it is possible to make this vision compatible with a non-essentialist conception of the social, only God and Geras know. Again, we are not dealing with an 'either/or' alternative. *There are* interests, but these are precarious historical products which are always subjected to processes of dissolution and redefinition. What there are not, however, are *objective* interests, in the sense in which they are postulated in the 'false consciousness' approach.

The history of Marxism

Let us move now to Geras's criticisms of our analysis of the history of Marxism. The centrality we give to the category of 'discourse' derives from our attempt to emphasize the purely historical and contingent character of the being of objects. This is not a fortuitous discovery which could have been made at any point in time; it is, rather, deeply rooted in the history of modern capitalism. In societies which have a low technological level of development, where the reproduction of material life is carried out by means of fundamentally repetitive practices, the 'language games' or discursive sequences which organize social life are predominantly stable. This situation gives rise to the illusion that the being of objects, which is a purely social construction, belongs to things themselves. The idea of a world organized through a stable ensemble of essential forms is the central presupposition in the philosophies of Plato and Aristotle. The basic illusion of metaphysical thought resides precisely in this unawareness of the historicity of being. It is only in the contemporary world, when technological change and the dislocating rhythm of capitalist transformation constantly alter the discursive sequences which construct the reality of objects, that the merely historical character of being becomes fully visible. In this sense, contemporary thought as a whole is, to a large extent, an attempt to cope with this increasing realization, and the consequent moving away from essentialism. In Anglo-American thought we could refer to the pragmatist turn and the anti-essentialist critique of post-analytic philosophy, starting from the work of the later Wittgenstein; in continental philosophy, to Heidegger's radicalization of phenomenology and to the critique of the theory of the sign in post-structuralism. The crisis of normative epistemologies, and the growing awareness of the non-algorithmic character of the transition from one scientific paradigm to another, point in the same direction.

What our book seeks to show is that this history of contemporary thought is *also* a history internal to Marxism; that Marxist thought has also been a persistent effort to adapt to the reality of the contemporary world and progressively to distance itself from essentialism; that, therefore, our present theoretical and political efforts have a genealogy which is internal to Marxism itself. In this sense we thought that we were contributing to the revitalization of an intellectual tradition. But the difficulties here are of a particular type which is worth discussing. The article by Geras is a good example. We learn from it, with amazement, that Bernstein and Sorel 'abandoned' Marxism – and in Geras this has the unmistakable connotation of betrayal. What can we think about this ridiculous story of 'betrayal' and 'abandonment'? What would one make of a history of philosophy which claimed that Aristotle betrayed Plato, that Kant betrayed Leibnitz, that Marx betrayed Hegel? Obviously, we would think that for the writer who reconstructs history in that way, the betrayed doctrine is an object of *worship*. And if we are dealing with a religious object, any dissidence or attempt to transform or to contribute to the evolution of that theory would be considered as apostasy. Most supporters of Marxism affirm its 'scientific' character. Science appears as separated by an absolute abyss from what mortal men think and do – it coincides with the distinction between the sacred and the profane. At a time when the philosophy of science is tending to narrow the epistemological gap between scientific and everyday languages, it seems deplorable that certain sectors of Marxism remain anchored to an image of science which is more appropriate to popular manuals from the age of positivism.

But this line of argument does not end here. Within this perspective the work of Marx becomes an *origin* – that is to say, something which contains within itself the seed of all future development. Thus, any attempt to go beyond it *must* be conceptualized as 'abandonment'. We know the story very well: Bernstein betrayed Marx; European social democracy betrayed the working class; the Soviet bureaucracy betrayed the revolution; the Western European Communist parties betrayed their revolutionary vocation; thus, the only trustees of 'Revolution' and 'Science' are the small sects belonging to imaginary Internationals which, as they suffer from what Freud called the 'narcissism of small differences', are permanently splitting. The bearers of Truth thus become fewer and fewer.

The history of Marxism that our book outlines is very different and is based on the following points. (1) Classical Marxism – that of the Second International – grounded its political strategy on the increasing centrality of the working class, this being the result of the simplification of social structure under capitalism. (2) From the beginning this prediction was shown to be false, and within the bosom of the Second International three attempts were made to respond to that situation: the Orthodox Marxists affirmed that the tendencies of capitalism which were at odds with the originary Marxist predictions were transitory, and that the postulated general line of capitalist development would eventually assert itself; the Revisionists argued that, on the contrary, those tendencies were permanent and that Social Democrats should therefore cease to organize as a revolutionary party and become a party of social reforms; finally revolutionary syndicalism, though sharing the reformist interpretation of the evolution of capitalism, attempted to reaffirm the radical perspective on the basis of a revolutionary reconstruction of class around the myth of the general strike. (3) The dislocations proper to uneven and combined development obliged the agents of socialist change – fundamentally the working class – to assume democratic tasks which had not been foreseen in the classical strategy, and it was precisely this taking up of new tasks which was denominated 'hegemony'. (4) From the Leninist concept of class alliances to the Gramscian concept of 'intellectual and moral' leadership, there is an increasing extension of hegemonic tasks, to the extent that for Gramsci social agents are not classes but 'collective wills'. (5) There is, then, an internal movement of Marxist thought from extreme essentialist forms – those of Plekhanov, for example – to Gramsci's conception of social practices as hegemonic and articulatory, which virtually places us in the field, explored in contemporary thought, of 'language games' and the 'logic of the signifier'.

As we can see, the axis of our argument is that, at the same time that essentialism disintegrated within the field of classical Marxism, new political logics and arguments started to replace it. If this process could not go further, it was largely due to the political conditions in which it took place: under the empire of Communist parties which regarded themselves as rigid champions of orthodoxy and repressed all intellectual creativity. If today we have to carry out the transition to post-Marxism by having recourse to a series of intellectual currents which are outside the Marxist tradition, it is to a large extent as a result of this process.

An atemporal critique

We will reply point by point to Geras's main criticisms of our analysis of the history of Marxism. First, he suggests that we have designed a very simple game, choosing at random a group of Marxist thinkers and separating the categories they inherited from classical Marxism from those other aspects of their work in which, confronted with a complex social reality, they were forced to move away from economic determinism. We are then alleged to have given medals to those who went furthest in this direction. This is, obviously, a caricature. In the first place, our main focus was not on economic determinism but on essentialism (it is possible to be absolutely 'superstructuralist' and nevertheless essentialist). In the second place, we did not consider 'any Marxist' at random but narrated an *intellectual history*: one of *progressive* disintegration within Marxism of the originary essentialism. Geras says nothing of this history. However, the image he describes fits his own vision well: for him there is no internal history of Marxism; Marxist categories have a validity which is atemporal, and it is only a question of complementing them here and there with a bit of empiricism and good sense.

Secondly, we are supposed to have contradicted ourselves by saying that Marxism is monist and dualist at the same time. But there is no contradiction here: what we asserted was that Marxism becomes dualist as a result of the failure of monism. A theory that starts by being pluralist would run no risk of becoming dualist.

Thirdly, Geras alleges that we have presented ourselves as the latest step in the long history of Marxism, and so fallen into the error, criticized by Althusser, of seeing in the past only a pre-announcement of oneself. Here, at least, Geras has posed a relevant intellectual question. Our answer is this: any history that deserves its name and is not a mere chronicle must proceed in the way we have proceeded – in Foucault's terms, history is always history of the present. If today I have the category 'income distribution', for instance, I can inquire about the distribution of income in ancient times or in the Middle Ages, even if that category did not exist then. It is by questioning the past from the perspective of the present that history is constructed. Historical reconstruction is impossible without *interrogating* the past. This means that there is not an *in-itself* of history, but rather a multiple refraction of it, depending on the traditions from which it is interrogated. It also means that our interpretations themselves are transitory, since future questions will result in very different images of the past. For this very reason, Althusser's critique of teleological conceptions of the past is not applicable in our case; we do not assert that we are the *culmination* of a process that was pre-announced, as in the transition from the 'in itself' to the 'for itself'. Although the present organizes the past, it can have no claim to have disclosed its 'essence'.

Finally, at several points Geras questions our treatment of texts by Trotsky and Rosa Luxemburg. In the case of Trotsky, we are said to have made use of 'tendentious quotations'. What we actually said was that: (1) Pokrovsky posed a *theoretical* question to Trotsky: namely, whether it is compatible with Marxism to attribute to the State such a degree of autonomy from classes as Trotsky does in the case of Russia; and (2) Trotsky, instead of answering *theoretically*, gave an account of Russian development and attempted to deal with the specific *theoretical* aspect of Pokrovsky's question only in terms of the contrast between the greenness of life and the greyness of theory ('Comrade Pokrovsky's thought is gripped in a vice of rigid social categories which he puts in place of live historical forces', etc.) (Trotsky 1971, p. 333). Thus the type of question that Pokrovsky's intervention implied – one referring to the degree of autonomy of the superstructure and its compatibility with Marxism – is not tackled by Trotsky at any point. The reader can check *all* the passages of Trotsky to which Geras refers and in *none* of them will s/he find a *theoretical* discussion concerning the relationship between base and superstructure. As for the idea that we demanded from Trotsky a theory of relative autonomy when we had affirmed its impossibility in another part of our book, we have already seen that this last point is a pure invention by Geras.

In the case of Rosa Luxemburg it is a question not of misquotations but of simplifications – that is, we are supposed to have reduced everything to the 'symbol'. Geras starts by enumerating five points, with which it would be difficult to disagree because they are simply a summary of Rosa Luxemburg's work on the mass strike. Our level of analysis is different, however, and does not contradict any of the five points in Geras's summary. The fifth point, for instance, reads: 'economic and political dimensions of the overall conflict interact, intersect, run together' (Geras 1987, p. 60). A further nine-point enumeration then explains what this interaction is, and we would not disagree with it either since it merely gives examples of such interaction. What our text asserts and what Geras apparently denies without presenting the slightest argument – is that through all these examples a specific social logic manifests itself, which is the logic of the symbol. A meaning is symbolic when it is a *second* meaning, added to the primary one ('rose', for example, can symbolize 'love'). In the Russian Revolution, 'peace', 'bread' and 'land' symbolized a variety of other social demands. For example, a strike for wage demands by any group of workers will, in an extremely repressive political context, also symbolize opposition to the system as a whole and encourage protest movements by very different groups; in this way an increasing relation of overdetermination and equivalence is created among multiple isolated demands. Our argument was that: (1) this is the mechanism described by Rosa Luxemburg in *The Mass Strike*; (2) it is, for her, the central element in the constitution of the unity between economic struggle and political class struggle; (3) her text is conceived as an intervention in the dispute between syndicalist and party theoreticians about the relative weight of economic and political struggle. Since Geras does not present any argument against these three theses, it makes little sense to prolong this discussion.[4]

Radical democracy

As is usual in sectarian literature, when it comes to talking about politics Geras has remarkably little to say. But we do need to deal with his assertion that it is an axiom that socialism should be democratic (Geras 1987, p. 79). The fact is that for any person who does not live on Mars, the relation between socialism and democracy is axiomatic only in Geras's mind. Has Geras ever heard of Stalinism, of the one-party system, of press censorship, of the Chinese Cultural Revolution, of the Polish *coup d'état*, of the entry of Soviet tanks into Prague and Budapest? And if the answer is that nothing of the kind is *true* socialism, we have to be clear what game we are playing. There are three possibilities. The first is that Geras is constructing an ideal model of society in the way that the utopian socialists did. Nothing, of course, prevents him from doing so and from declaring that in Gerasland collective ownership of the means of production and democracy go together; but in that case we should not claim to be speaking about the real world. The second possibility is to affirm that the authoritarian states of the Soviet bloc represent a transitory and necessary phase in the passage towards communism. This is the miserable excuse that 'progressive' intellectuals gave to support the worst excesses of Stalinism, from the Moscow trials onwards. The third possibility is to assert that these states are 'degenerate forms' of socialism. However, the very fact that such 'degeneration' is possible clearly indicates that the relation between socialism and democracy is far from being axiomatic.

For us the articulation between socialism and democracy, far from being an axiom, is a political project; that is, it is the result of a long and complex hegemonic construction, which is permanently under threat and thus needs to be continuously redefined. The first problem to be discussed, therefore, is the 'foundations' of a progressive politics. For Geras this presents the following difficulty: has not our critique of essentialism eliminated any possible basis for preferring one type of politics to another? Everything depends on what we understand by 'foundation'. If it is a question of a foundation that enables us to decide with apodictic certainty that one type of society is better than another, the answer is no, there cannot be such a foundation. However, it does not follow that there is no possibility of reasoning politically and of preferring, for a variety of reasons, certain political positions to others. (It is comical that a stern critic of 'either/or' solutions such as

Geras confronts us with exactly this type of alternative.) Even if we cannot decide algorithmically about many things, this does not mean that we are confined to total nihilism, since we can reason about the *verisimilitude* of the available alternatives. In that sense, Aristotle distinguishes between *phronesis* (prudence) and *theory* (purely speculative knowledge). An argument founded on the apodicticity of the conclusion is an argument which admits neither discussion nor any plurality of viewpoints; on the other hand, an argument which tries to found itself on the verisimilitude of its conclusions, is essentially pluralist, because it needs to make reference to other arguments, and since the process is essentially open, these can always be contested and refuted. The logic of verisimilitude is, in this sense, essentially *public and democratic*. Thus, the first condition of a radically democratic society is to accept the contingent and radically open character of all its values – and in that sense, to abandon the aspiration to a single foundation.

At this point we can refute a myth, the one which has it that our position is incompatible with humanism. What we have rejected is the idea that humanist values have the metaphysical status of an essence and that they are, therefore, prior to any concrete history and society. However, this is not to deny their validity; it only means that their validity is constructed by means of particular discursive and argumentative practices. The history of the production of 'Man' (in the sense of human beings who are bearers of rights in their exclusive human capacity) is a recent history – of the last three hundred years. Before then, all men were equal only in the face of God. This history of the production of 'Man' can be followed step by step and it has been one of the great achievements of our culture; to out- line this history would be to reconstruct the various discursive surfaces where it has taken place – the juridical, educational, economic and other institutions, in which differences based on status, social class or wealth were progressively eliminated. The 'human being', without qualification, is the overdetermined effect of this process of multiple construction. It is within this discursive plurality that 'humanist values' are constructed and expanded. And we know well that they are always threatened: racism, sexism, class discrimination, always limit the emergence and full validity of humanism. To deny to the 'human' the status of an essence is to draw attention to the historical conditions that have led to its emergence and to make possible, therefore, a wider degree of realism in the fight for the full realization of those values.

The transformation of political consciousness

Now, the 'humanization' of increasingly wider areas of social relations is linked to the fundamental process of transformation of political consciousness in Western societies during the last two hundred years, which is what, following Tocqueville, we have called the 'democratic revolution'. Our central argument is that socialism is an integral part of the 'democratic revolution' and has no meaning outside of it (which, as we will see, is very different from saying that socialism is axiomatically democratic). In order to explain our argument we will start from an analysis of the capitalist–worker relation. According to the classical Marxist thesis, the basic antagonism of capitalist society is constituted around the extraction of surplus-value by the capitalist from the worker. But it is important to see where the antagonism resides. A first possibility would be to affirm that the antagonism is inherent in the very form of the wage-labour–capital relation, to the extent that this form is based on the appropriation by capital of the worker's surplus labour. However, this solution is clearly incorrect: the capitalist–worker relation considered as form – that is to say, insofar as the worker is considered not as flesh and blood but only as the economic category of 'seller of labour power' – is not an antagonistic one. Only if the worker *resists* the extraction of his or her surplus-value by the capitalist does the relation become antagonistic, but such resistance cannot be logically deduced from the category 'seller of labour power'. It is only if we add a further assumption, such as the '*homo oeconomicus*' of classical political economy, that the relation becomes antagonistic, since it then becomes a zero-sum game between worker and capitalist. However, this idea that the worker is a profit-maximizer in the same way as the capitalist has been correctly rejected by all Marxist theorists.

Thus, there is only one solution left: that the antagonism is not intrinsic to the capitalist relation of production as such, but rather, that it is established *between* the relation of production and something external to it – for instance, the fact that below a certain level of wages the worker cannot live in a decent way, send his/her children to school, have access to certain forms of recreation, etc. The pattern and the intensity of the antagonism depend, therefore, to a large extent, on the way in which the social agent is constituted *outside the relations of production*. Now, the further we are from a mere subsistence level, the more the worker's expectations are bound up with a certain perception of his or her place in the world. This perception depends on the participation of workers in a variety of spheres and on a certain awareness of their rights; and the more democratic-egalitarian discourses have penetrated society, the less will workers accept as natural a limitation of their access to a set of social and cultural goods. *Thus, the possibility of deepening the anti-capitalist struggle itself depends on the extension of the democratic revolution. Even more: anti-capitalism is an internal moment of the democratic revolution.*[5]

However, if this is right, if antagonism is not intrinsic to the relation of production as such but is established between the relation of production and something external to it, then two consequences follow. The first is that there are no *a priori* privileged places in the anti-capitalist struggle. We should remember that for the Second International – for Kautsky, particularly – the idea of the centrality of the working class was linked to: (a) a vision of the collapse of capitalism as determined by the contradiction between forces and relations of production which would lead to increasing social misery – that is to say, to the contradiction *between* the capitalist system as a whole and the vast masses of the population; and (b) to the idea that capitalism would lead to proletarianization of the middle classes and the peasantry, as a result of which, when the crisis of the system came about, everything would be reduced to a simple showdown between capitalists and workers. However, as the second process has not taken place, there is no reason to assume that the working class has a privileged role in the *anti-capitalist* struggle. There are many points of antagonism between capitalism and various sections of the population (environmental pollution, property development in certain areas, the arms race, the flow of capital from one region to another, etc.), and this means that we will have a variety of anti-capitalist struggles. The second consequence is that the potential emergence of a radical anti-capitalist politics through the deepening of the democratic revolution, will result from global political decisions taken by vast sectors of the population and will not be linked to a particular position in the social structure. In this sense there are no *intrinsically* anti-capitalist struggles, although a set of struggles, within certain contexts, could *become* anti-capitalist.

Democratic revolution

If everything then depends on the extension and deepening of the democratic revolution, we should ask what the latter itself depends on and what it ultimately consists of. Marx correctly observed that capitalism only expands through permanent transformation of the means of production and the dislocation and progressive dissolution of traditional social relations. Such dislocation effects are manifest, on the one hand, in commodification, and on the other hand, in the set of phenomena linked to uneven and combined development. In these conditions, the radical instability and threat to social identities posed by capitalist expansion necessarily lead to new forms of collective imaginary which reconstruct those threatened identities in a fundamentally new way. Our thesis is that egalitarian discourses and discourses on rights play a fundamental role in the reconstruction of collective identities. At the beginning of this process in the French Revolution, the public space of citizenship was the exclusive domain of equality, while in the private sphere no questioning took place of existing social inequalities. However, as Tocqueville clearly understood, once human beings accept the legitimacy of the principle of equality in one sphere, they will attempt to extend it to every other sphere of life. Thus, once the dislocations generated by capitalist expansion became more general, more and more sectors constructed the legitimacy of their claims around the principles of equality and liberty. The development of workers' and anti-capitalist struggles during the nineteenth century was a crucial moment in this process, but it was not the only or the last one: the struggles of the so called 'new social movements' of the last few decades are a further phase in the deepening of the democratic revolution. Towards the end of the nineteenth century Bernstein clearly understood that future advances in the democratization of the State and of society would depend on autonomous initiatives starting from different points within the social fabric, since rising labour productivity and successful workers' struggles were having the combined effect that workers ceased to be 'proletarian' and became 'citizens', that is to say, they came to participate in an increasing variety of aspects of the life of their country. This was the start of the process that we have called the 'dispersion of subject positions'. Bernstein's view was, without any doubt, excessively simplistic and optimistic, but his predictions were fundamentally correct. However, it is important to see that from this plurality and dislocation there does not follow an increasing integration and adaptation to the system. The dislocatory effects that were mentioned above continue to influence all these dispersed subject positions, which is to say that the latter become the points which make possible a new radicalization, and with this, the process of the radical democratization of society acquires a new depth and a new impulse. The result of the process of dispersion and fragmentation, whose first phases Bernstein described, was not increasingly conformist and integrated societies: it was the great mobilizations of 1968.

There are two more points which require discussion. The first refers to liberalism. If the radical democratization of society emerges from a variety of autonomous struggles which are themselves overdetermined by forms of hegemonic articulation; if, in addition, everything depends on a proliferation of public spaces of argumentation and decision whereby social agents are increasingly capable of self-management, then it is clear that this process does not pass through a direct attack upon the State apparatuses but involves the consolidation and democratic reform of the liberal State. The ensemble of its constitutive principles – division of powers, universal suffrage, multi-party systems, civil rights, etc. – must be defended and consolidated. It is within the framework of these basic principles of the political community that it is possible to advance the full range of present-day democratic demands (from the rights of national, racial and sexual minorities to the anti-capitalist struggle itself).

The second point refers to totalitarianism. Here Geras introduces one of his usual confusions. In trying to present our critique of totalitarianism, he treats this critique as if it presupposed a fundamental identity between communism and fascism. Obviously this is not the case. Fascism and communism, as types of society, are totally different. The only possible comparison concerns the presence in both of a certain type of political logic by which they are societies with a *State Truth*. Hence, while the radical democratic imaginary presupposes openness and pluralism and processes of argumentation which never lead to an ultimate foundation, totalitarian societies are constituted through their claim to master the foundation. Evidently there is a strong danger of totalitarianism in the twentieth century, and the reasons are clear: insofar as dislocatory effects dominate and the old structures in which power was immanent dissolve, there is an increasing tendency to concentrate power in one point from which the attempt is made 'rationally' to reconstruct the ensemble of the social fabric. Radical democracy and totalitarianism are, therefore, entirely opposite in their attempts to deal with the problems deriving from dislocation and uneven development.

To conclude, we would like to indicate the three fundamental points on which we consider it necessary today to go beyond the theoretical and political horizon of Marxism. The first is a philosophical point which relates to the partial character of Marx's 'materialism', to its manifold dependence on crucial aspects of the categories of traditional metaphysics. In this respect, as we have tried to show, discourse theory is not just a simple theoretical or epistemological approach; it implies, by asserting the radical historicity of being and therefore the purely human nature of truth, the commitment to show the world for what it is: an entirely social construction of human beings which is not grounded on any metaphysical 'necessity' external to it – neither God, nor 'essential forms', nor the 'necessary laws of history'.

The second aspect refers to the social analyses of Marx. The greatest merit of Marxist theory has been to illuminate fundamental tendencies in the self-development of capitalism and the antagonisms that it generates. However, here again the analysis is incomplete and, in a certain sense, parochial – limited, to a great extent, to the European experience of the nineteenth century. Today we know that the dislocation effects which capitalism generates at the international level are much deeper than the ones foreseen by Marx. This obliges us to radicalize and to transform in a variety of directions Marx's conception of the social agent and of social antagonisms.

The third and final aspect is political. By locating socialism in the wider field of the democratic revolution, we have indicated that the political transformations which will eventually enable us to transcend capitalist society are founded on the plurality of social agents and of their struggles. Thus the field of social conflict is extended, rather than being concentrated in a 'privileged agent' of socialist change. This also means that the extension and radicalization of democratic struggles do not have a final point of arrival in the achievement of a fully liberated society. There will always be antagonisms, struggles, and partial opaqueness of the social; there will always be history. The myth of the transparent and homogeneous society – which implies the end of politics – must be resolutely abandoned.

We believe that, by clearly locating ourselves in a post-Marxist terrain, we not only help to clarify the meaning of contemporary social struggles but also give to Marxism its theoretical dignity, which can only proceed from recognition of its limitations and of its historicality. Only through such recognition will Marx's work remain present in our tradition and our political culture.

Notes

1 This example, as the reader will realize, is partly inspired by Wittgenstein.
2 In the same manner as reactionary theoreticians, Geras considers that he can fix the being of things once and for all. Thus, he says that to call an earthquake an expression of the wrath of God is a 'superstition', whilst calling it a 'natural phenomenon' is to state 'what it is'. The problem is not, of course, that it does not make perfect sense in our culture to call certain beliefs 'superstitions'. But, to counterpose 'superstitions' to 'what things *are*' implies: (1) that world-views can no longer change (that is to say, that our forms of thought concerning the idea of 'the natural' cannot be shown in the future to be contradictory, insufficient, and therefore 'superstitious'); (2) that, in contrast to men and women in the past, we have today a direct and transparent access to things, which is not mediated by any theory. With such reassurances, it is not surprising that Geras regards himself as a functionary of truth. It is said that at some point Mallarmé believed himself to be the individual mind which embodied the Absolute Spirit, and that he felt

overwhelmed. Geras makes the same assumption about himself far more naturally. It is perhaps worthwhile remarking that Geras's naive 'verificationism' will today hardly find defenders among philosophers *of any intellectual orientation*. W.V. Quine, for instance, who is well anchored in the mainstream tradition of Anglo-American analytic philosophy, writes:

> I do ... believe in physical objects and not in Homer's gods, and I consider it a scientific error to believe otherwise. But in point of epistemological footing the physical objects and the gods differ only in degree and not in kind. Both sorts of entities enter our conception only as cultural posits ... Moreover, the abstract entities which are the substance of mathematics – ultimately classes and classes of classes and so on up – are another posit in the same spirit. Epistemologically these are myths on the same footing with physical objects and gods, neither better nor worse except for differences in the degree to which they expedite our dealings with sense experiences.
>
> ('Two Dogmas of Empiricism', in *From a Logical
> Point of View* (New York, 1963), pp. 44–45)

3 Geras reasons in a similar way. Referring to a passage in our text where we write that 'the major consequence of a break with the discursive/extra-discursive dichotomy, is the abandonment of the thought/reality opposition', Geras believes that he is making a very smart materialist move by commencing: 'A world well and truly *external* to thought obviously has no meaning outside the thought/reality opposition' (1987, p. 67). What he does not realize is that in saying so he is asserting that thought is not part of reality and thus giving credence to a purely idealist conception of mind. In addition, he considers that to deny the thought/reality dichotomy is to assert that everything is thought, while what our text denies is the dichotomy as such, with precisely the intention of reintegrating thought to reality. (A deconstruction of the traditional concept of 'mind' can be found in Richard Rorty, *Philosophy and the Mirror of Nature*, Princeton, NJ: Princeton University Press, 1979.)

4 One further point concerning Rosa Luxemburg. Geras sustains (1987, fn., p. 62) that we deny that Rosa Luxemburg had a theory of the mechanical collapse of the capitalist system. This is not so. The point that we make is rather that nobody has pushed the metaphor of the mechanical collapse so far as to take it literally; and that, therefore, all Marxist writers of the period of the Second International combined, in different degrees, objective laws and conscious intervention of the class in their theorizations of the end of capitalism. A second point that we make in the passage in question – and here, yes, our interpretation clearly differs from Geras's – is that it is because the logic of spontaneism was not enough to ground the class nature of the social agents, that Luxemburg had to find a different grounding and was forced to appeal to a hardening of the objective laws of capitalist development. Fully to discuss this issue would obviously require far more space than we have here.

5 We would like to stress that, in our view, the various anti-capitalist struggles are an integral part of the democratic revolution, but this does not imply that socialism is *necessarily* democratic. The latter, as a form of economic organization based upon exclusion of private ownership of the means of production, can be the result, for example, of a bureaucratic imposition, as in the countries of Eastern Europe. In this sense, socialism *can be* entirely external to the democratic revolution. The compatibility of socialism with democracy, far from being an axiom, is therefore the result of a hegemonic struggle for the articulation of both.

References

Aronowitz, Stanley. 1986/87. 'Theory and Socialist Strategy', *Social Text*, Winter.
Cavell, Stanley. 1969. *Must We Mean What We Say?* New York.

Davidson, Alastair. 1987. In *Thesis Eleven* no. 16.

Derbyshire, Philip. 1985. In *City Limits*, 26 April.

Forgács, David. 1985. 'Dethroning the Working Class?', *Marxism Today*, May.

Geras, Norman. 1987. 'Post-Marxism?', *New Left Review* no. 163, May–June.

Laclau, Ernest and Mouffe, Chantal. 1985. *Hegemony and Socialist Strategy*. London: Verso.

Marx, Karl. 1971. *A Contribution to the Critique of Political Economy*. London.

Pitkin, Hanna Fenichel. 1972. *Wittgenstein and Justice*. Berkeley, CA: University of California Press.

Rorty, Richard. 1982. *Consequences of Pragmatism*. Minneapolis.

Ross, Andrew. 1986. In *m/f* no. 11/12.

Stace, W. T. 1955. *The Philosophy of Hegel*. New York.

Staten, Henry. 1985. *Wittgenstein and Derrida*. Oxford.

Taylor, Charles. 1975. *Hegel*. Cambridge.

Trotsky, Leon. 1971. *1905*. London.

Žižek, Slavoj. 1985. 'La société n'existe pas', *L'Ane*, October–December.

PART II
Radical Democracy
Pluralism, citizenship and identity

4

RADICAL DEMOCRACY

Modern or postmodern? (1988)[1]

What does it mean to be on the left today? In the twilight years of the twentieth century is it in any way meaningful to invoke the Enlightenment ideals that lay behind the project of the transformation of society? We are undoubtedly living through the crisis of the Jacobin imaginary, which has, in diverse ways, characterized the revolutionary politics of the last two hundred years. It is unlikely that Marxism will recover from the blows it has suffered; not only the discredit brought upon the Soviet model by the analysis of totalitarianism, but also the challenge to class reductionism posed by the emergence of new social movements. But the fraternal enemy, the social democratic movement, is not in any better shape. It has proved incapable of addressing the new demands of recent decades, and its central achievement, the welfare state, has held up badly under attack from the right, because it has not been able to mobilize those who should have interests in defending its achievements.

As for the ideal of socialism, what seems to be in question is the very idea of progress that is bound up with the project of modernity. In this respect, discussion of the postmodern, which until now had focused on culture, has taken a political turn. Alas, the debate all too quickly petrified around a set of simplistic and sterile positions. Whereas Habermas accuses of conservatism all those who criticize the universalist ideal of the Enlightenment (Habermas 1983), Lyotard declares with pathos that after Auschwitz the project of modernity has been eliminated (Lyotard 1985). Richard Rorty rightly remarks that one finds on both sides an illegitimate assimilation of the political project of the Enlightenment and its epistemological aspects. This is why Lyotard finds it necessary to abandon political liberalism in order to avoid a universalist philosophy, whereas Habermas, who wants to defend liberalism, holds on, despite all of its problems, to this universalist philosophy (Rorty 1985, pp. 161–75). Habermas indeed believes that the emergence of universalist forms of morality and law is the expression of an irreversible collective process of learning, and that to reject this implies a rejection of modernity, undermining the very foundations of democracy's existence. Rorty invites us to consider Blumenberg's distinction, in *The Legitimacy of the Modern Age*, between two aspects of the Enlightenment, that of 'self-assertion' (which can be identified with the political project) and that of 'self-foundation' (the epistemological project). Once we acknowledge that there is no necessary relation between these two aspects, we are in the position of being able to defend the political project while abandoning the notion that it must be based on a specific form of rationality.

Rorty's position, however, is problematic because of his identification of the political project of modernity with a vague concept of 'liberalism', which includes both capitalism and democracy. For, at the heart of the very concept of political modernity, it is important to distinguish two traditions, liberal and democratic, both of which, as MacPherson has shown, are articulated only in the nineteenth century and are thus not necessarily related in any way. Moreover, it would be a mistake to confuse this 'political modernity' with 'social modernity', the process of modernization carried out under the growing domination of relations of capitalist production. If one fails to draw this distinction between democracy and liberalism, between political liberalism and economic liberalism; if, as Rorty does, one conflates all these notions under the term *liberalism*, then one is driven, under the pretext of defending modernity, to a pure and simple apology for the 'institutions and practices of the rich North Atlantic democracies' (Rorty 1983, p. 585), which leaves no room for a critique (not even an immanent critique) that would enable us to transform them.

Confronted by this 'postmodernist bourgeois liberalism' that Rorty advocates, I would like to show how the project of a 'Radical and Plural Democracy', one that Ernesto Laclau and I (Laclau and Mouffe, 1985) have already sketched out in our book *Hegemony and Socialist Strategy: Towards a Radical Democratic Politics*, proposes a reformulation of the socialist project that avoids the twin pitfalls of Marxist socialism and social democracy, while providing the left with a new imaginary, an imaginary that speaks to the tradition of the great emancipatory struggles but that also takes into account recent theoretical contributions by psychoanalysis and philosophy. In effect, such a project could be defined as being both modern and postmodern. It pursues the 'unfulfilled project of modernity', but, unlike Habermas, we believe that there is no longer a role to be played in this project by the epistemological perspective of the Enlightenment. Although this perspective did play an important part in the emergence of democracy, it has become an obstacle in the path of understanding those new forms of politics, characteristic of our societies today, which demand to be approached from a nonessentialist perspective. Hence the necessity of using the theoretical tools elaborated by the different currents of what can be called the postmodern in philosophy and of appropriating their critique of rationalism and subjectivism.[2]

The democratic revolution

Different criteria have been suggested for defining modernity. They vary a great deal depending on the particular levels or features one wants to emphasize. I, for

one, think that modernity must be defined at the political level, for it is there that
social relations take shape and are symbolically ordered. Insofar as it inaugurates a
new type of society, modernity can be viewed as a decisive point of reference. In
this respect the fundamental characteristic of modernity is undoubtedly the advent
of the democratic revolution. As Claude Lefort has shown, this democratic
revolution is at the origin of a new kind of institution of the social, in which
power becomes an 'empty place'. For this reason, modern democratic society is
constituted as

> a society in which power, law and knowledge are exposed to a radical
> indetermination, a society that has become the theatre of an uncontrollable
> adventure, so that what is instituted never becomes established, the known
> remains undetermined by the unknown, the present proves to be undefinable.
>
> (Lefort 1986a, p. 305)

The absence of power embodied in the person of the prince and tied to a
transcendental authority preempts the existence of a final guarantee or source of
legitimation; society can no longer be defined as a substance having an organic
identity. What remains is a society without clearly defined outlines, a social structure that is impossible to describe from the perspective of a single, or universal,
point of view. It is in this way that democracy is characterized by the 'dissolution
of the landmarks of certainty' (Lefort 1986b, p. 29). I think that such an approach
is extremely suggestive and useful because it allows us to put many of the phenomena of modern societies in a new perspective. Thus, the effects of the democratic
revolution can be analyzed in the arts, theory, and all aspects of culture in general,
enabling one to formulate the question of the relation between modernity and
postmodernity in a new and more productive way. Indeed, if one sees the
democratic revolution as Lefort portrays it, as the distinctive feature of modernity,
it then becomes clear that what one means when one refers to postmodernity in
philosophy is to recognize the impossibility of any ultimate foundation or final
legitimation that is constitutive of the very advent of the democratic form of
society and thus of modernity itelf. This recognition comes after the failure of
several attempts to replace the traditional foundation that lay within God or Nature
with an alternative foundation lying in Man and his Reason. These attempts were
doomed to failure from the start because of the radical indeterminacy that is
characteristic of modern democracy. Nietzsche had already understood this
when he proclaimed that the death of God was inseparable from the crisis of
humanism.[3]

Therefore the challenge to rationalism and humanism does not imply the rejection of modernity but only the crisis of a particular project within modernity, the
Enlightenment project of self-foundation. Nor does it imply that we have to
abandon its political project, which is its achievement of equality and freedom for
all. In order to pursue and deepen this aspect of the democratic revolution, we
must ensure that the democratic project takes account of the full breadth and

specificity of the democratic struggles in our times. It is here that the contribution of the so-called postmodern critique comes into its own.

How, in effect, can we hope to understand the nature of these new antagonisms if we hold on to an image of the unitary subject as the ultimate source of intelligibility of its actions? How can we grasp the multiplicity of relations of subordination that can affect an individual if we envisage social agents as homogeneous and unified entities? What characterizes the struggles of these new social movements is precisely the multiplicity of subject-positions, which constitutes a single agent and the possibility for this multiplicity to become the site of an antagonism and thereby politicized. Thus the importance of the critique of the rationalist concept of a unitary subject, which one finds not only in poststructuralism but also in psychoanalysis, in the philosophy of language of the late Wittgenstein, and in Gadamer's hermeneutics.

To be capable of thinking politics today, and understanding the nature of these new struggles and the diversity of social relations that the democratic revolution has yet to encompass, it is indispensable to develop a theory of the subject as a decentred, detotalized agent, a subject constructed at the point of intersection of a multiplicity of subject-positions between which there exists no *a priori* or necessary relation and whose articulation is the result of hegemonic practices. Consequently, no identity is ever definitively established, there always being a certain degree of openness and ambiguity in the way the different subject-positions are articulated. What emerges are entirely new perspectives for political action, which neither liberalism – with its idea of the individual who only pursues his or her own interest – nor Marxism – with its reduction of all subject-positions to that of class – can sanction, let alone imagine.

It should be noted, then, that this new phase of the democratic revolution, while it is, in its own way, a result of the democratic universalism of the Enlightenment, also puts into question some of its assumptions. Many of these new struggles do in fact renounce any claim to universality. They show how in every assertion of universality there lies a disavowal of the particular and a refusal of specificity. Feminist criticism unmasks the particularism hiding behind those so called universal ideals which, in fact, have always been mechanisms of exclusion. Carole Pateman, for example, has shown how classical theories of democracy were based upon the exclusion of women:

> The idea of universal citizenship is specifically modern, and necessarily depends on the emergence of the view that all individuals are born free and equal, or are naturally free and equal to each other. No individual is naturally subordinate to another, and all must thus have public standing as citizens, that upholds their self-governing status. Individual freedom and equality also entails that government can arise only through agreement or consent. We are all taught that the 'individual' is a universal category that applies to anyone or everyone, but this is not the case. 'The individual' is a man.
>
> (Pateman 1986)

The reformulation of the democratic project in terms of radical democracy requires giving up the abstract Enlightenment universalism of an undifferentiated human nature. Even though the emergence of the first theories of modern democracy and of the individual as a bearer of rights was made possible by these very concepts, they have today become a major obstacle to the future extension of the democratic revolution. The new rights that are being claimed today are the expression of differences whose importance is only now being asserted, and they are no longer rights that can be universalized. Radical democracy demands that we acknowledge difference – the particular, the multiple, the heterogeneous – in effect, everything that had been excluded by the concept of Man in the abstract. Universalism is not rejected but particularized; what is needed is a new kind of articulation between the universal and the particular.

Practical reason: Aristotle versus Kant

This increasing dissatisfaction with the abstract universalism of the Enlightenment explains the rehabilitation of the Aristotelian concept of *phronesis*. This 'ethical knowledge,' distinct from knowledge specific to the sciences (*episteme*), is dependent on the ethos, the cultural and historical conditions current in the community, and implies a renunciation of all pretense to universality.[4] This is a kind of rationality proper to the study of human praxis, which excludes all possibility of a 'science' of practice but which demands the existence of a 'practical reason,' a region not characterized by apodictic statements, where the reasonable prevails over the demonstrable. Kant brought forth a very different notion of practical reason, one that required universality. As Ricoeur observes:

> By elevating to the rank of supreme principle the rule of universalisation, Kant inaugurated one of the most dangerous ideas which was to prevail from Fichte to Marx; that the practical sphere was to be subject to a scientific kind of knowledge comparable to the scientific knowledge required in the theoretical sphere.
>
> (Ricoeur 1986, pp. 248–51)

So, too, Gadamer criticizes Kant for having opened the way to positivism in the human sciences and considers the Aristotelian notion of *phronesis* to be much more adequate than the Kantian analysis of judgment to grasp the kind of relation existing between the universal and the particular in the sphere of human action (Gadamer 1984, pp. 33–39).

The development of the postempiricist philosophy of science converges with hermeneutics to challenge the positivistic model of rationality dominant in the sciences. Theorists such as Thomas Kuhn and Mary Hesse have contributed a great deal to this critique by pointing to the importance of rhetorical elements in the evolution of science. It is agreed today that we need to broaden the concept of rationality to make room for the 'reasonable' and the 'plausible' and to recognize the existence of multiple forms of rationality.

Such ideas are crucial to the concept of a radical democracy in which judgment plays a fundamental role that must be conceptualized appropriately so as to avoid the false dilemmas between, on the one hand, the existence of some universal criterion and, on the other, the rule of arbitrariness. That a question remains unanswerable by science or that it does not attain the status of a truth that can be demonstrated does not mean that a reasonable opinion cannot be formed about it or that it cannot be an opportunity for a rational choice. Hannah Arendt (1968) was absolutely right to insist that in the political sphere one finds oneself in the realm of opinion, or 'doxa,' and not in that of truth, and that each sphere has its own criteria of validity and legitimacy. There are those, of course, who will argue that such a position is haunted by the spectre of relativism. But such an accusation makes sense only if one remains in the thrall of a traditional problematic, which offers no alternative between objectivism and relativism.

Affirming that one cannot provide an ultimate rational foundation for any given system of values does not imply that one considers all views to be equal. As Rorty notes,

> The real issue is not between people who think one view as good as any other and people who do not. It is between people who think our culture, our purpose or institutions cannot be supported except conversationally and people who still hope for other sorts of support.
>
> (Rorty 1982, p. 167)

It is always possible to distinguish between the just and the unjust, the legitimate and the illegitimate, but this can only be done from within a given tradition, with the help of standards that this tradition provides; in fact, there is no point of view external to all tradition from which one can offer a universal judgment. Furthermore, to give up the distinction between logic and rhetoric to which the postmodern critique leads – and where it parts with Aristotle – does not mean that 'might makes right' or that one sinks into nihilism. To accept with Foucault that there cannot be an absolute separation between validity and power (since validity is always relative to a specific regime of truth, connected to power) does not mean that we cannot distinguish within a given regime of truth between those who respect the strategy of argumentation and its rules, and those who simply want to impose their power.

Finally, the absence of foundation 'leaves everything as it is,' as Wittgenstein would say, and obliges us to ask the same questions in a new way. Hence the error of a certain kind of apocalyptical postmodernism which would like us to believe that we are at the threshold of a radically new epoch, characterized by drift, dissemination, and by the uncontrollable play of significations. Such a view remains captive of a rationalistic problematic, which it attempts to criticize. As Searle has pointed out to Derrida:

The real mistake of the classical metaphysician was not the belief that there were metaphysical foundations, but rather the belief that somehow or other such foundations were necessary, the belief that unless there are foundations something is lost or threatened or undermined or just in question.

(Searle 1983, p. 78)

Tradition and democratic politics

Because of the importance it accords to the particular, to the existence of different forms of rationality, and to the role of tradition, the path of radical democracy paradoxically runs across some of the main currents of conservative thinking. One of the chief emphases of conservative thought does indeed lie in its critique of the Enlightenment's rationalism and universalism, a critique it shares with post-modernist thought; this proximity might explain why certain postmodernists have been branded as conservative by Habermas. In fact, the affinities can be found not on the level of the political but in the fact that, unlike liberalism and Marxism, both of which are doctrines of reconciliation and mastery, conservative philosophy is predicated upon human finitude, imperfection, and limits. This does not lead unavoidably to a defence of the *status quo* and to an antidemocratic vision, for it lends itself to various kinds of articulation.

The notion of tradition, for example, has to be distinguished from that of traditionalism. Tradition allows us to think our own insertion into historicity, the fact that we are constructed as subjects through a series of already existing discourses, and that it is through this tradition which forms us that the world is given to us and all political action made possible. A conception of politics like that of Michael Oakeshott, who attributes a central role to the existing 'traditions of behavior' and who sees political action as 'the pursuit of an intimation,' is very useful and productive for the formulation of radical democracy. Indeed, for Oakeshott,

> Politics is the activity of attending to the general arrangements of a collection of people who, in respect of their common recognition of a manner of attending to its arrangements, compose a single community … This activity, then, springs neither from instant desires, nor from general principles, but from the existing traditions of behavior themselves. And the form it takes, because it can take no other, is the amendment of existing arrangements by exploring and pursuing what is intimated in them.
>
> (Oakeshott 1967, p. 123)

If one considers the liberal democratic tradition to be the main tradition of behaviour in our societies, one can understand the extension of the democratic revolution and development of struggles for equality and liberty in every area of social life as being the pursuit of these 'intimations' present in the liberal democratic discourse. Oakeshott provides us with a good example, while unaware of the radical potential of his arguments. Discussing the legal status of women, he declares that:

the arrangements which constitute a society capable of political activity, whether these are customs or institutions or laws or diplomatic decisions, are at once coherent and incoherent; they compose a pattern and at the same time they intimate a sympathy for what does not fully appear. Political activity is the exploration of that sympathy; and consequently, relevant political reasoning will be convincing exposure of a sympathy, present but not yet followed up, and the convincing demonstration that now is the appropriate moment for recognizing it.

(ibid., p. 124)

He concludes that it is in this way that one is capable of recognizing the legal equality of women. It is immediately apparent how useful reasoning of this kind can be as a justification of the extension of democratic principles.

   This importance afforded to tradition is also one of the principal themes of Gadamer's philosophical hermeneutics, which offers us a number of important ways of thinking about the construction of the political subject. Following Heidegger, Gadamer asserts the existence of a fundamental unity between thought, language, and the world. It is through language that the horizon of our present is constituted; this language bears the mark of the past; it is the life of the past in the present and thus constitutes the movement of tradition. The error of the Enlightenment, according to Gadamer, was to discredit 'prejudices' and to propose an ideal of understanding which requires that one transcend one's present and free oneself from one's insertion into history. But it is precisely these prejudices that define our hermeneutical situation and constitute our condition of understanding and openness to the world. Gadamer also rejects the opposition drawn up by the Enlightenment between tradition and reason because for him:

tradition is constantly an element of freedom and of history itself. Even the most genuine and solid tradition does not persist by nature because of the inertia of what once existed. It needs to be affirmed, embraced, cultivated. It is, essentially, preservation such as is active in all historical change. But preservation is an act of reason, though an unconspicuous one. For this reason, only what is new, or what is planned, appears as the result of reason. But this is an illusion. Even where life changes violently, as in ages of revolution, far more of the old is preserved in the supposed transformation of everything than anyone knows, and combines with the new to create a new value.

(Gadamer 1984, p. 250)

This conception of tradition, as borne through language found in Gadamer, can be made more specific and complex if reformulated in terms of Wittgenstein's 'language games.' Seen in this light, tradition becomes the set of language games that make up a given community. Since for Wittgenstein language games are an indissoluble union between linguistic rules, objective situations, and forms of life (Wittgenstein 1953), tradition is the set of discourses and practices that form us as subjects. Thus we are able to think of politics as the pursuit of intimations, which in a Wittgensteinian perspective can be understood as the creation of new usages for the key terms of a given tradition, and of their use in new language games that make new forms of life possible.

To be able to think about the politics of radical democracy through the notion of tradition, it is important to emphasize the composite, heterogeneous, open, and ultimately indeterminate character of the democratic tradition. Several possible strategies are always available, not only in the sense of the different interpretations one can make of the same element, but also because of the way in which some parts or aspects of tradition can be played against others. This is what Gramsci, perhaps the only Marxist to have understood the role of tradition, saw as a process of disarticulation and rearticulation of elements characteristic of hegemonic practices.[5]

Recent attempts by neoliberals and neoconservatives to redefine concepts such as liberty and equality and to disarticulate the idea of liberty from that of democracy demonstrate how within the liberal democratic tradition different strategies can be pursued, making available different kinds of intimations. Confronted by this offensive on the part of those who want to put an end to the articulation that was established in the nineteenth century between liberalism and democracy and who want to redefine liberty as nothing more than an absence of coercion, the project of radical democracy must try to defend democracy and to expand its sphere of applicability to new social relations. It aims to create another kind of articulation between elements of the liberal democratic tradition, no longer viewing rights in an individualist framework but as 'democratic rights.' This will create a new hegemony, which will be the outcome of the articulation of the greatest possible number of democratic struggles.

What we need is a hegemony of democratic values, and this requires a multiplication of democratic practices, institutionalizing them into ever more diverse social relations, so that a multiplicity of subject-positions can be formed through a democratic matrix. It is in this way – and not by trying to provide it with a rational foundation – that we will be able not only to defend democracy but also to deepen it. Such a hegemony will never be complete, and anyway, it is not desirable for a society to be ruled by a single democratic logic. Relations of authority and power cannot completely disappear, and it is important to abandon the myth of a transparent society, reconciled with itself, for that kind of fantasy leads to totalitarianism. A project of radical and plural democracy, on the contrary, requires the existence of multiplicity, of plurality, and of conflict, and sees in them the *raison d'être* of politics.

Radical democracy, a new political philosophy

If the task of radical democracy is indeed to deepen the democratic revolution and to link together diverse democratic struggles, such a task requires the creation of new subject-positions that would allow the common articulation, for example, of antiracism, antisexism, and anticapitalism. These struggles do not spontaneously converge, and in order to establish democratic equivalences, a new 'common sense' is necessary, which would transform the identity of different groups so that the demands of each group could be articulated with those of others according to the principle of democratic equivalence. For it is not a matter of establishing a mere alliance between given interests but of actually modifying the very identity of these forces. In order that the defence of workers' interests is not pursued at the cost of the rights of women, immigrants, or consumers, it is necessary to establish an equivalence between these different struggles. It is only under these circumstances that struggles against power become truly democratic.

Political philosophy has a very important role to play in the emergence of this common sense and in the creation of these new subject positions, for it will shape the 'definition of reality' that will provide the form of political experience and serve as a matrix for the construction of a certain kind of subject. Some of the key concepts of liberalism, such as rights, liberty, and citizenship, are claimed today by the discourse of possessive individualism, which stands in the way of the establishment of a chain of democratic equivalences.

I have already referred to the necessity of a concept of democratic rights, rights which, while belonging to the individual, can only be exercised collectively and presuppose the existence of equal rights for others. But radical democracy also needs an idea of liberty that transcends the false dilemma between the liberty of the ancients and the moderns and allows us to think of individual liberty and political liberty together. On this issue, radical democracy shares the preoccupations of various writers who want to redeem the tradition of civic republicanism. This trend is quite heterogeneous, and it is therefore necessary to draw distinctions among the so-called communitarians who, while they all share a critique of liberal individualism's idea of a subject existing prior to the social relations that form it, have differing attitudes toward modernity. On the one hand, there are those like Michael Sandel and Alasdair Macintyre, inspired mainly by Aristotle, who reject liberal pluralism in the name of a politics of the common good; and, on the other hand, those like Charles Taylor and Michael Walzer, who, while they criticize the epistemological presuppositions of liberalism, try to incorporate its political contribution in the area of rights and pluralism.[6] The latter hold a perspective closer to that of radical democracy, whereas the former maintain an extremely ambiguous attitude toward the advent of democracy and tend to defend premodern conceptions of politics, drawing no distinctions between the ethical and the political which they understand as the expression of shared moral values.

It is probably in the work of Machiavelli that civic republicanism has the most to offer us, and in this respect the recent work of Quentin Skinner is of particular interest. Skinner shows that in Machiavelli one finds a conception of liberty that, although it does not postulate an objective notion of the good life (and therefore is, according to Isaiah Berlin, a 'negative' conception of liberty), nevertheless includes ideals of political participation and civic virtue (which, according to Berlin, are typical of a 'positive' conception of liberty). Skinner shows that the idea of liberty is portrayed in the *Discourses* as the capacity for individuals to pursue their own goals, their 'humours' (*humori*). This goes together with the affirmation that in order to ensure the necessary conditions for avoiding coercion and servitude, thereby rendering impossible the use of this liberty, it is indispensable for individuals to fulfil certain public functions and to cultivate required virtues. For Machiavelli, if one is to exercise civic virtue and serve the common good, it is in order to guarantee oneself a certain degree of personal liberty which permits one to pursue one's own ends (Skinner 1984). We encounter in this a very modern conception of individual liberty articulated onto an old conception of political liberty, which is fundamental for the development of a political philosophy of radical democracy.

But this appeal to a tradition of civic republicanism, even in the privileging of its Machiavellian branch, cannot wholly provide us with the political language needed for an articulation of the multiplicity of today's democratic struggles. The best it can do is provide us with elements to fight the negative aspects of liberal individualism while it remains inadequate to grasp the complexity of politics today. Our societies are confronted with the proliferation of political spaces which are radically new and different and which demand that we abandon the idea of a unique constitutive space of the constitution of the political, which is particular to both liberalism and civic republicanism. If the liberal conception of the 'unencumbered self' is deficient, the alternative presented by the communitarian defenders of civic republicanism is unsatisfactory as well. It is not a question of moving from a 'unitary unencumbered self' to a 'unitary situated self'; the problem is with the very idea of the unitary subject. Many communitarians seem to believe that we belong to only one community, defined empirically and even geographically, and that this community could be unified by a single idea of the common good. But we are in fact always multiple and contradictory subjects, inhabitants of a diversity of communities (as many, really, as the social relations in which we participate and the subject-positions they define), constructed by a variety of discourses and precariously and temporarily sutured at the intersection of those subject-positions. Thus the importance of the postmodern critique for developing a political philosophy aimed at making possible a new form of individuality that would be truly plural and democratic. A philosophy of this sort does not assume a rational foundation for democracy, nor does it provide answers, in the way of Leo Strauss, to questions concerning the nature of political matters and the best regime. On the contrary, it proposes to remain within the cave and, as Michael Walzer puts it, 'to interpret to one's fellow citizens the world of meanings that we share' (Walzer 1983, p. xiv). The liberal democratic tradition is open to many interpretations, and the politics of radical democracy is but one strategy among others. Nothing guarantees its success, but this project has set out to pursue and deepen the democratic project of modernity. Such a strategy requires us to abandon the abstract universalism of the Enlightenment, the essentialist conception of a social totality, and the myth of a unitary subject. In this respect, far from seeing the development of postmodern philosophy as a threat, radical democracy welcomes it as an indispensable instrument in the accomplishment of its goals.

Notes

1 Translated by Paul Holdengräber.
2 I am referring not only to post-structuralism but also to other trends like psychoanalysis, post-Heideggerian hermeneutics and the philosophy of language of the second Wittgenstein, which all converge in a critique of rationalism and subjectivism.
3 On this issue, see the insightful analysis of Gianni Vattimo, 'La crisi dell "umanismo,"' in *La fine della modernità* (Milan: Garzanti Editore, 1985), ch. 2.
4 Recent interpretations of Aristotle try to dissociate him from the tradition of natural law and to underline the differences between him and Plato on this issue. See, for instance, Hans-Georg Gadamer's remarks (1984, pp. 278–89).
5 On this issue, see my article 'Hegemony and Ideology in Gramsci,' in *Gramsci and Marxist Theory*, ed. Chantal Mouffe (London: Routledge & Kegan Paul, 1979), pp. 168–204.
6 I refer here to the following studies: Michael Sandel, *Liberalism and the Limits of Justice* (Cambridge: Cambridge University Press, 1982); Alasdair Macintyre, *After Virtue* (Notre Dame, IN: University of Notre Dame Press, 1984); Charles Taylor, *Philosophy and the Human Sciences*, Philosophical Papers, vol. 2 (Cambridge: Cambridge University Press, 1985); Walzer, (1983).

References

Arendt, Hannah. 1968. *Between Past and Future*. New York: Viking Press.
Gadamer, Hans-Georg. 1984. *Truth and Method*. New York: Crossroad.
Habermas, Jürgen. 1983. Modernity: An Incomplete Project. In *The Anti-Aesthetic: Essays on Postmodern Culture*, ed. Hal Foster. Port Townsend, WA: Bay Press.
Laclau, Ernesto, and Mouffe, Chantal. 1985. *Hegemony and Socialist Strategy: Towards a Radical Democratic Politics*. London: Verso.
Lefort, Claude. 1986a. *The Political Forms of Modern Society*. Oxford: Polity Press.
——1986b. *Essais sur le Politique*, Paris: Editions du Seuil.
Lyotard, Jean-François. 1985. *Immaterialität und Postmoderne*. Berlin.
Oakeshott, Michael. 1967. *Rationalism in Politics*. London: Methuen.
Pateman, Carole. 1986. Removing Obstacles to Democracy. Paper presented to the International Political Science Association meeting, Ottawa, Canada, October 1986 (mimeographed).
Ricoeur, Paul 1986. *Du texte a l'action*. Paris: Editions du Seuil.
Rorty, Richard. 1982. *Consequences of Pragmatism*. Minneapolis: University of Minnesota Press.
——1983. Postmodernist Bourgeois Liberalism. *Journal of Philosophy* 80 (October).
——1985. Habermas and Lyotard on Postmodernity. In *Habermas and Modernity*, ed. Richard J. Bernstein. Oxford: Polity Press.
Searle, John R. 1983. The Word Turned Upside Down. *New York Review of Books*, 27 October.
Skinner, Quentin. 1984. The Idea of Negative Liberty: Philosophical and Historical Perspectives. In *Philosophy in History*, eds. R. Rorty, J. B. Schneewind, and Q. Skinner. Cambridge: Cambridge University Press.
Walzer, Michael. 1983. *Spheres of Justice*. New York: Basic.
Wittgenstein, Ludwig. 1953. *Philosophical Investigations*. Trans. G.E.M. Anscombe. Oxford: Blackwell.

5

DEMOCRATIC CITIZENSHIP AND THE POLITICAL COMMUNITY (1992)

The themes of 'citizenship' and 'community' are being discussed in many quarters of the Left today. It is no doubt a consequence of the crisis of class politics and indicates the growing awareness of the need for a new form of identification around which to organize the forces struggling for a radicalization of democracy. I do indeed agree that the question of political identity is crucial and I consider that to attempt to construct 'citizens' identities should be one of the important tasks of democratic politics. But there are many different visions of citizenship and central issues are at stake in their contest. The way we define citizenship is intimately linked to the kind of society and political community we want.

How should we understand citizenship when our goal is a radical and plural democracy? Such a project requires the creation of a chain of equivalence among democratic struggles, and therefore the creation of a common political identity among democratic subjects. For the interpellation 'citizens' to be able to fulfil that role, what conditions must it meet?

These are the problems that I will address and I will argue that the key question is how to conceive of the nature of the political community under modern democratic conditions. I consider that we need to go beyond the conceptions of citizenship of both the liberal and the civic republican tradition while building on their respective strengths.

To situate my reflections in the context of the current discussions, I will begin by engaging with the debate between Kantian liberals and the so-called 'communitarians'. In this way I hope to bring to the fore the specificity of my approach both politically and theoretically.

Liberalism versus civic republicanism

What is really at stake between John Rawls and his communitarian critics is the issue of citizenship. Two different languages in which to articulate our identity as citizens are confronting each other. Rawls proposes representing the citizen of a constitutional democracy in terms of equal rights expressed by his two principles of justice. He affirms that once citizens see themselves as free and equal persons, they should recognize that to pursue their own different conceptions of the good, they need the same primary goods, i.e. the same basic rights, liberties and opportunities, as well as the same all-purpose means such as income and wealth and the same social bases of self-respect. This is why they should agree on a political conception of justice that states that 'all social primary goods – liberty and opportunity, income and wealth and the bases of self-respect – are to be distributed equally, unless an unequal distribution of any or all of these goods is to the advantage of the least favored' (Rawls 1971, pp. 302–3). According to that liberal view, citizenship is the capacity for each person to form, revise and rationally pursue his/her definition of the good. Citizens are seen as using their rights to promote their self interest within certain constraints imposed by the exigency to respect the rights of others. The communitarians object that it is an impoverished conception that precludes the notion of the citizen as one for whom it is natural to join with others to pursue common action in view of the common good. Michael Sandel has argued that Rawls's conception of the self is an 'unencumbered' one, which leaves no room for a 'constitutive' community, a community that would constitute the very identity of the individuals. It only allows for an 'instrumental' community, a community in which individuals with their previously defined interests and identity enter in view of furthering those interests (Sandel 1982).

For the communitarians the alternative to this flawed liberal approach is the revival of the civic republican view of politics that puts a strong emphasis on the notion of a public good, prior to and independent of individual desires and interests. Such a tradition has almost disappeared today because it has been displaced by liberalism, though it has a long history. It received its full expression in the Italian republics at the end of the Middle Ages but its origins go back to Greek and Roman thought. It was reformulated in England in the seventeenth century by James Harrington, John Milton and other republicans. Later it travelled to the New World through the work of the neo-Harringtonians, and recent studies have shown that it played a very important role during the American Revolution.[1]

There are indeed serious problems with the liberal conception of citizenship but we must be aware of the shortcomings of the civic republican solution, too. It does provide us with a view of citizenship much richer than the liberal one, and its conception of politics as the realm where we can recognize ourselves as participants in a political community has obvious appeal for the critics of liberal individualism. Nevertheless there is a real danger of coming back to a pre-modern view of politics, which does not acknowledge the novelty of modern democracy and the crucial contribution of liberalism. The defence of pluralism, the idea of individual liberty, the separation of church and state, the development of civil society, all these are constitutive of modern democratic politics. They require that a distinction be made between the private and the public domain, the realm of morality and the realm of politics. Contrary to what some communitarians propose, a modern democratic political community cannot be organized around a single substantive idea of the common good. The recovery of a strong participatory idea of citizenship should not be made at the cost of sacrificing individual liberty. This is the point where the communitarian critique of liberalism takes a dangerous conservative turn.

The problem, I believe, is not that of replacing one tradition by the other but drawing on both and trying to combine their insights in a new conception of citizenship adequate for a project of radical and plural democracy. While liberalism did certainly contribute to the formulation of the idea of a universal citizenship, based on the assertion that all individuals are born free and equal, it also reduced citizenship to a mere legal status, setting out the rights that the individual holds against the state. The way these rights are exercised is irrelevant as long as their holders do not break the law or interfere with the rights of others. Social cooperation aims only to enhance our productive capacities and facilitates the attainment of each person's individual prosperity. Ideas of public-mindedness, civic activity and political participation in a community of equals are alien to most liberal thinkers.

Civic republicanism, on the contrary, emphasizes the value of political partici-pation and attributes a central role to our insertion in a political community. But the problem arises with the exigency of conceiving the political community in a way that is compatible with modern democracy and liberal pluralism. In other words, we are faced with the old dilemma of how to reconcile the liberties of the ancients with the liberties of the moderns. The liberals argue that they are incom-patible and that today ideas about the 'common good' can only have totalitarian implications. According to them, it is impossible to combine democratic institu-tions with the sense of common purpose that pre-modern society enjoyed, and the ideals of 'republican virtue' are nostalgic relics which ought to be discarded. Active political participation, they say, is incompatible with the modern idea of liberty. Individual liberty can only be understood in a negative way as absence of coercion.

This argument, powerfully restated by Isaiah Berlin in 'Two Concepts of Liberty', is generally used to discredit any attempt to recapture the civic republican conception of politics. However, it has recently been challenged by Quentin Skinner, who shows that there is no basic necessary incompatibility between the classical repub-lican conception of citizenship and modern democracy (Skinner 1984). He finds in several forms of republican thought, particularly in Machiavelli, a way of conceiv-ing liberty which though negative – and therefore modern – includes political participation and civic virtue. It is negative because liberty is conceived as the absence of impediments to the realization of our chosen ends. But it also asserts that it is only as citizens of a 'free state', of a community whose members participate actively in the government, that such individual liberty can be guaranteed. To ensure our own liberty and avoid the servitude that would render its exercise impossible, we must cultivate civic virtues and devote ourselves to the common good. The idea of a common good above our private interest is a necessary condition for enjoying individual liberty. Skinner's argument is important because it refutes the liberals' claim that individual liberty and political participation can never be reconciled. This is crucial for a radical democratic project, but the kind of political community adequate for such an articulation between the rights of the individual and the political participation of the citizen then becomes the question to be addressed.

Modern democracy and political community

Another way to approach the debate between Kantian liberals like Rawls and the communitarians is via the question of the priority of the right over the good; this has a direct relevance to the issue of the modern democratic political community.

For Rawls such a priority indicates that individual rights cannot be sacrificed for the sake of the general welfare, as is the case with utilitarianism, and that the principles of justice impose restrictions on what are the permissible conceptions of the good that individuals are allowed to pursue. This is why he insists that the principles of justice must be derived independently of any particular conception of the good, since they need to respect the existence of a plurality of competing conceptions of the good in order to be accepted by all citizens. His aim here is to defend liberal pluralism which requires not imposing upon individuals any specific conception of well-being or particular plan of life. For liberals those are private questions bearing on individual morality, and they believe that the individual should be able to organize his/her life according to his/her own wishes, without unnecessary interventions. Hence the centrality of the concept of individual rights and the assertion that principles of justice must not privilege a particular conception of the good life.

I consider this an important principle, which needs defending because it is crucial for modern democratic societies. Indeed, modern democracy is precisely characterized by the absence of a substantive common good. This is the meaning of the democratic revolution as analysed by Claude Lefort (1986), who identifies it with the dissolution of landmarks of certainty. According to Lefort, modern democratic society is a society where power has become an empty space and is separated from law and knowledge. In such a society it is no longer possible to provide a final guarantee, a definite legitimation, because power is no longer incorporated in the person of the prince and associated to a transcendental instance. Power, law and knowledge are therefore exposed to a radical indeterminacy: in my terms, a substantive common good becomes impossible. This is also what Rawls indicates when he affirms that 'We must abandon the hope of a political community if by such a community we mean a political society united in affirming a general and comprehensive doctrine' (Rawls 1987, p. 10). If the priority of the right over the good were restricted to that, there would not be anything for me to disagree with. But Rawls wants to establish an absolute priority of the right over the good because he does not recognize that it can only exist in a certain type of society with specific institutions and that it is a consequence of the democratic revolution.

To that the communitarians reply, with reason, that such an absolute priority of the right cannot exist and that it is only through our participation in a community which defines the good in a certain way that we can acquire a sense of the right and a conception of justice. Charles Taylor correctly points out that the mistake with the liberal approach is that

> it fails to take account of the degree to which the free individual with his own goals and aspirations whose just rewards it is trying to protect, is himself only possible within a certain kind of civilization; that it took a long development of certain institutions and practices, of the rule of law, of rules of equal respect, of habits of common deliberation, of common association, of cultural development and so on, to produce the modern individual.
>
> (Taylor 1955, p. 200)

Where the communitarians lost their way is when some of them, such as Sandel, conclude that there can never be a priority of the right over the good, and that we should therefore reject liberal pluralism and return to a type of community organized around shared moral values and a substantive idea of the common good. We can fully agree with Rawls about the priority of justice as the principal virtue of social and political institutions and in defending pluralism and rights, while admitting that those principles are specific to a certain type of political association.

There is, however, another aspect of the communitarian critique of liberalism which we should not abandon but reformulate. The absence of a single substantive common good in modern democratic societies and the separation between the realm of morality and the realm of politics have, no doubt, signified an incontestable gain in individual freedom. But the consequences for politics have been very damaging. All normative concerns have increasingly been relegated to the field of private morality, to the domain of 'values', and politics has been stripped of its ethical components. An instrumentalist conception has become dominant, concerned exclusively with the compromise between already defined interests. On the other side, liberalism's exclusive concern with individuals and their rights has not provided content and guidance for the exercise of those rights. This has led to the devaluation of civic action, of common concern, which has caused an increasing lack of social cohesion in democratic societies. The communitarians are right to criticize such a situation and I agree with their attempt to revive some aspects of the classical conception of politics. We do need to re-establish the lost connection between ethics and politics, but this cannot be done by sacrificing the gains of the democratic revolution. We should not accept a false dichotomy between individual liberty and rights on one side and civic activity and political community on the other. Our only choice is not one between an aggregate of individuals without common public concern and a pre-modern community organized around a single substantive idea of the common good. Envisaging the modern democratic political community outside of this dichotomy is the crucial challenge.

I have already pointed out how Quentin Skinner indicates a possible form of articulation between individual freedom and civic participation. But we must also be able to formulate the ethical character of modern citizenship in a way that is compatible with moral pluralism and respects the priority of the right over the good. What we share and what makes us fellow citizens in a liberal democratic regime is not a substantive idea of the good but a set of political principles specific to such a tradition: the principles of freedom and equality for all. Those principles constitute what we can call, following Wittgenstein, a 'grammar' of political conduct. To be a citizen is to recognize the authority of those principles and the rules in which they are embodied; to have them informing our political judgement and our actions. To be associated in terms of the recognition of the liberal democratic principles, this is the meaning of citizenship that I want to put forward. It implies seeing citizenship not as a legal status but as a form of identification, a type of political identity: something to be constructed, not empirically given. Since there will always be competing interpretations of the democratic principles of equality and liberty, there will therefore be competing interpretations of democratic citizenship. I will inquire into the nature of a radical democratic citizenship, but before I do, I must return to the question of the political association or community.

The political community: *universitas* or *societas*?

As indicated previously, we need to conceive of a mode of political association, which, although it does not postulate the existence of a substantive common good, nevertheless implies the idea of commonality, of an ethico-political bond that creates a linkage among the participants in the association, allowing us to speak of a political 'community' even if it is not in the strong sense. In other words, what we are looking for is a way to accommodate the distinctions between public and private, morality and politics which have been the great contribution of liberalism to modern democracy, without renouncing the ethical nature of the political association.

I consider that, if we interpret them in a certain way, the reflections on civil association proposed by Michael Oakeshott (1975) in *On Human Conduct* can be very illuminating for such a purpose. Oakeshott shows that *societas* and *universitas*, which were understood in the late Middle Ages as two different modes of human association, can also represent two alternative interpretations of the modern state. *Universitas* indicates an engagement in an enterprise to pursue a common substantive purpose or to promote a common interest. It refers therefore to 'persons associated in a manner such as to constitute them a natural person, a partnership of persons which is itself a Person, or in some important respects like a person' (ibid., p. 203).

Contrary to that model of association of agents engaged in a common enterprise defined by a purpose, *societas* or 'civil association' designates a formal relationship in terms of rules, not a substantive relation in terms of common action.

> The idea *societa*s is that of agents who, by choice or circumstance, are related to one another so as to compose an identifiable association of a certain sort. The tie which joins them, and in respect of which each recognizes himself to be *socius*, is not that of an engagement in an enterprise to pursue a common substantive purpose or to promote a common interest, but that of loyalty to one another.
>
> (ibid., p. 201)

It is not a mode of relation, therefore, in terms of common action but a relation in which participants arc related to one another in the acknowledgement of the authority of certain conditions in acting.

Oakeshott insists that the participants in a *societas* or *cives* are not associated for a common enterprise nor with a view to facilitating the attainment of each person's individual prosperity; what links them is the recognition of the authority of the conditions specifying their common or 'public' concern, a 'practice of civility'. This public concern or consideration of *cives* Oakeshott calls *respublica*. It is a practice of civility specifying not performances, but conditions to be subscribed to in choosing performances. These consist in a complex of rules or rule-like prescriptions, which do not prescribe satisfactions to be sought or actions to be performed but 'moral considerations specifying conditions to be subscribed to in choosing performances' (ibid., p. 182).

It seems to me that Oakeshott's idea of the civil association as *societas* is adequate to define political association under modern democratic conditions. Indeed it is a mode of human association that recognizes the disappearance of a single substantive idea of the common good and makes room for individual liberty. It is a form of association that can be enjoyed among relative strangers belonging to many purposive associations and whose allegiances to specific communities are not seen as conflicting with their membership in the civil association. This would not be possible if such an association were conceived as *universitas*, as purposive association, because it would not allow for the existence of other genuine purposive associations in which individuals would be free to participate.

To belong to the political community what is required is that we accept a specific language of civil intercourse, the *respublica*. Those rules prescribe norms of conduct to be subscribed to in seeking self-chosen satisfactions and in performing self-chosen actions. The identification with those rules of civil intercourse creates a common political identity among persons otherwise engaged in many different enterprises. This modern form of political community is held together not by a substantive idea of the common good but by a common bond, a public concern. It is therefore a community without a definite shape or a definite identity and in continuous re-enactment.

Such a conception is clearly different from the pre-modern idea of the political community, but it is also different from the liberal idea of the political association. For liberalism also sees political association as a form of purposive association, of enterprise, except that in its case the aim is an instrumental one: the promotion of self-interest.

Oakeshott criticizes the liberal view of the state as a conciliator of interests, which he considers to be as remote from civil association as the idea of the state as promoter of an interest, and he declares 'it has been thought that the "Rule of Law" is enough to identify civil association whereas what is significant is the kind of law: "moral" or "instrumental"' (ibid., p. 318). His conception should therefore not be confounded with the liberal doctrine of the Rule of Law. He stresses the moral character of the *respublica* and affirms that political thought concerns the *respublica* in terms of *bonum civile*. He declares,

> Civility, then, denotes an order of moral (not instrumental) considerations, and the so-called neutrality of civil prescriptions is a half truth, which needs to be supplemented by the recognition of civil association as itself a moral and not a prudential condition.
>
> (ibid., p. 175)

By 'moral' he obviously refers not to a comprehensive view but to what I have proposed calling the 'ethico-political', since he asserts that what is civilly desirable cannot be inferred or derived from general moral principles and that political deliberation is concerned with moral considerations of its own.

> This *respublica* is the articulation of a common concern that the pursuit of all purposes and the promotion of all interests, the satisfaction of all wants and the propagation of all beliefs shall be in subscription to conditions formulated in rules indifferent to the merits of any interest or the truth or error of any belief and consequently not itself a substantive interest or doctrine.
>
> (ibid., p. 172)

We could say, using Rawls's vocabulary, that in a civil association or *societas* there exists a priority of the right over the good, but in Oakeshott's case, the principles that specify the right, the *respublica*, are conceived not in a Kantian manner as in Rawls, but in a Hegelian way, since for him, to be associated in terms of the recognition of the *respublica* is to enjoy a *sittlich* relation. What I find useful in this approach is that, while allowing for the recognition of pluralism and individual liberty, the notion of *societas* does not relinquish all normative aspects to the sphere of private morality. This mode of association, which Oakeshott traces back to Machiavelli, Montesquieu and Hegel, permits us to maintain a certain idea of the political community in the sense of a noninstrumental, an ethical, type of bond among *cives*, while severing it from the existence of a substantive common good.

I mentioned at the outset that to be useful to a radical democratic project Oakeshott's reflections needed to be interpreted in a certain way. I am, of course, perfectly aware of the conservative use he makes of the distinction between *societas* and *universitas*, but I believe that it is not the only and necessary one.[2] To be sure, Oakeshott's conservatism resides in the content he puts in the *respublica*, and that can obviously be solved by introducing more radical principles, as I will indicate later. But more fundamentally, it lies in his flawed idea of politics. For his conception of politics as a shared language of civility is only adequate for one aspect of politics: the point of view of the 'we', the friend's side. However, as Carl Schmitt has rightly pointed out, the criterion of the political is the friend/enemy relation. What is completely missing in Oakeshott is division and antagonism, that is, the aspect of the 'enemy'. It is an absence that must be remedied if we want to appropriate his notion of *societas*.

To introduce conflict and antagonism into Oakeshott's model, it is necessary to recognize that the *respublica* is the product of a given hegemony, the expression of power relations, and that it can be challenged. Politics is to a great extent about the rules of the *respublica* and its many possible interpretations, it is about the constitution of the political community, not something that takes place inside the political community as some communitarians would have it. Political life concerns collective, public action; it aims at the construction of a 'we' in a context of diversity and conflict. But to construct a 'we' it must be distinguished from the 'them' and that means establishing a frontier, defining an 'enemy'. Therefore, while politics aims at constructing a political community and creating a unity, a fully inclusive political community and a final unity can never be realized since there will permanently be a 'constitutive outside', an exterior to the community that makes its existence possible. Antagonistic forces will never disappear and politics is characterized by conflict and division. Forms of agreement can be reached but they are always partial and provisional since consensus is by necessity based on acts of exclusion. We are indeed very far from the language of civility dear to Oakeshott!

A radical democratic citizenship

What becomes of the idea of citizenship in such a perspective? If we understand citizenship as the political identity that is created through identification with the *respublica*, a new conception of the citizen becomes possible. First, we are now dealing with a type of political identity, a form of identification, no longer simply with a legal status. The citizen is not, as in liberalism, someone who is the passive recipient of specific rights and who enjoys the protection of the law. It is not that those elements become irrelevant but the definition of the citizen shifts because the emphasis is put on the identification with the *respublica*. It is a common political identity of persons who might be engaged in many different purposive enterprises and with differing conceptions of the good, but who accept submission to the rules prescribed by the *respublica* in seeking their satisfactions and in performing their actions. What binds them together is their common recognition of a set of ethico-political values. In this case, citizenship is not just one identity among others – as in liberalism – or the dominant identity that overrides all others – as in civic republicanism. It is an articulating principle that affects the different subject positions of the social agent (as I will show when I discuss the public/private distinction) while allowing for a plurality of specific allegiances and for the respect of individual liberty.

Since we are dealing with politics, however, there will be competing forms of identification linked to different interpretations of the *respublica*. In a liberal democratic regime we can conceive of the *respublica* as constituted by the political principles of such a regime: equality and liberty for all. If we put such a content in Oakeshott's notion of *respublica* we can affirm that the conditions to be subscribed to and taken into account in acting are to be understood as the exigency of treating the others as free and equal persons. This is clearly open to potentially very radical interpretations. For instance, a radical democratic interpretation will emphasize the numerous social relations where relations of domination exist and must be challenged if the principles of liberty and equality are to apply. It should lead to a common recognition among different groups struggling for an extension and radicalization of democracy that they have a common concern and that in choosing their actions they should subscribe to certain rules of conduct; in other words, it should construct a common political identity as radical democratic citizens.

The creation of political identities as radical democratic citizens depends therefore on a collective form of identification among the democratic demands found in a variety of movements: women, workers, black, gay, ecological, as well as in several other 'new social movements'. This is a conception of citizenship which, through a common identification with a radical democratic interpretation of the principles of liberty and equality, aims at constructing a 'we', a chain of equivalence among their demands so as to articulate them through the principle of democratic equivalence. For it is not a matter of establishing a mere alliance between given interests but of actually modifying the very identity of these forces. This is something that many pluralist liberals do not understand because they are blind to power relations. They agree on the need to extend the sphere of rights in order to include groups hitherto excluded but they see that process as a smooth one of progressive inclusion into citizenship. This is the typical story as told by T.H. Marshall in his celebrated article 'Citizenship and Social Class'. The problem with such an approach is that it ignores the limits imposed on the extension of pluralism by the fact that some existing rights have been constituted on the very exclusion or subordination of the rights of other categories. Those identities must first be deconstructed if several new rights are to be recognized.

To make possible a hegemony of the democratic forces, new identities are therefore required, and I am arguing here in favour of a common political identity as radical democratic citizens. By that, I understand a collective identification with a radical democratic interpretation of the principles of the liberal-democratic regime: liberty and equality. Such an interpretation presupposes that those principles are understood in a way that takes account of the different social relations and subject positions in which they are relevant: gender, class, race, ethnicity, sexual orientation, etc. Such an approach can only be adequately formulated within a problematic that conceives of the social agent not as a unitary subject but as the articulation of an ensemble of subject positions, constructed within specific discourses and always precariously and temporarily sutured at the intersection of those subject positions. Only with a non-essentialist conception of the subject which incorporates the psychoanalytic insight that all identities are forms of identification can we pose the question of political identity in a fruitful way. A non-essentialist perspective is also needed concerning the notions of *respublica, societas* and political community. For it is crucial to see them not as empirical referents but as discursive surfaces. Failure to do so would make the type of politics which is posited here completely incomprehensible.

On this point a radical democratic conception of citizenship connects with the current debates about 'postmodernity' and the critique of rationalism and universalism. The view of citizenship I am proposing rejects the idea of an abstract universalist definition of the public, opposed to a domain of the private seen as the realm of particularity and difference. It considers that, although the modern idea of the citizen was indeed crucial for the democratic revolution, it constitutes today an obstacle to its extension. As feminist theorists have argued, the public realm of modern citizenship has been based on the negation of women's participation.[3] This exclusion was seen as indispensable to postulate the generality and universality of the public sphere. The distinction public/private, central as it was for the assertion of individual liberty, also led to identifying the private with the domestic and played an important role in the subordination of women.

To the idea that the exercise of citizenship consists in adopting a universal point of view, made equivalent to Reason and reserved to men, I am opposing the idea that it consists in identifying with the ethico-political principles of modern democracy and that there can be as many forms of citizenship as there are interpretations of those principles.

In this view the public/private is not abandoned but reformulated. Here again Oakeshott can help us to find an alternative to the limitations of liberalism. *Societas* is, according to him, a civil condition in which every enterprise is 'private' while never immune from the 'public' conditions specified in *respublica*. In a *societas*,

> every situation is an encounter between 'private' and 'public', between an action or an utterance to procure an imagined and wished-for substantive satisfaction and the conditions of civility to be subscribed to in performing it; and no situation is the one to the exclusion of the other.
>
> (Oakeshott 1975, p. 183)

The wants, choices and decisions are private because they are the responsibility of each individual but the performances are public because they are required to subscribe to the conditions specified in *respublica*. Since the rules of the *respublica* do not enjoin, prohibit or warrant substantive actions or utterances, and do not tell agents what to do, this mode of association respects individual liberty. But the individual's belonging to the political community and identification with its ethico-political principles are manifested by her acceptance of the common concern expressed in the *respublica*. It provides the 'grammar' of the citizen's conduct.

In the case of a radical democratic citizen, such an approach allows us to visualize how a concern with equality and liberty should inform her actions in all areas of social life. No sphere is immune from those concerns, and relations of domination can be challenged everywhere. Nevertheless we are not dealing with a purposive kind of community affirming one single goal for all its members, and the freedom of the individual is preserved.

The distinction private (individual liberty)/public (*respublica*) is maintained as well as the distinction individual/citizen, but they do not correspond to discrete separate spheres. We cannot say: here end my duties as a citizen and begins my freedom as an individual. Those two identities exist in a permanent tension that can never be reconciled. But this is precisely the tension between liberty and equality that characterizes modern democracy. It is the very life of such a regime and any attempt to bring about a perfect harmony, to realize a 'true' democracy can only lead to its destruction. This is why a project of radical and plural democracy recognizes the impossibility of the complete realization of democracy and the final achievement of the political community. Its aim is to use the symbolic resources of the liberal democratic tradition to struggle for the deepening of the democratic revolution, knowing that it is a never-ending process. My thesis here has been that the ideal of citizenship could greatly contribute to such an extension of the principles of liberty and equality. By combining the ideal of rights and pluralism with the ideas of public spiritedness and ethico-political concern, a new modern democratic conception of citizenship could restore dignity to the political and provide the vehicle for the construction of a radical democratic hegemony.

Notes

1 For a general presentation of the debate, see my article 'American Liberalism and its Critics: Rawls, Taylor, Sandel and Walzer', *Praxis International* 8(2), July.
2 One of Oakeshott's targets is undoubtedly the idea of redistributive justice and the forms of state intervention that such an idea renders legitimate, but I do not believe that the distinction between *universitas* and *societas* necessarily commits us to reject state intervention as being inherently linked to a conception of the state as a purposive common enterprise. One can perfectly justify state intervention on the basis of a certain interpretation of the *respublica*.
3 See, for instance, Carole Pateman, *The Sexual Contract* (Stanford, CA: Stanford University Press, 1988); and Genevieve Fraisse, *Muse de la raison* (Aix-en-Provence 1989).

References

Berlin, Isaiah. 1969. Two Concepts of Liberty. In *Four Essays on Liberty*. Oxford: Oxford University Press.

Lefort, Claude. 1986. *The Political Forms of Modern Society*. Oxford: Polity Press.

Oakeshott, Michael. 1975. *On Human Conduct*. Oxford: Clarendon Press.

Rawls, John. 1971. *A Theory of Justice*. Oxford.

——1987. The Idea of an Overlapping Consensus. *Oxford Journal of Legal Studies* 7(1) Spring.

Sandel, Michael. 1982. *Liberalism and the Limits of Justice*. Cambridge: Cambridge University Press.

Skinner, Quentin. 1984. The Idea of Negative Liberty: Philosophical and Historical Perspective. In R. Rorty, J.B. Schneewind and Q. Skinner, eds., *Philosophy in History*. Cambridge.

Taylor, Charles, 1955. Philosophy and the Human Sciences, in *Philosophical Papers*, vol. 2. Cambridge: Cambridge University Press.

6

POLITICS AND THE LIMITS OF LIBERALISM (1993)

The much heralded 'triumph' of liberal democracy comes at a time when there are increasing disagreements concerning its nature. Some of these disagreements concern a central tenet of liberalism: the neutrality of the state. How is this to be understood? Is a liberal society one where the state is neutral and allows the coexistence of different ways of life and conceptions of the good? Or is it a society where the state promotes specific ideals like equality or personal autonomy? Several liberals, in an attempt to respond to the communitarian challenge, have recently argued that, far from neglecting ideas about the good, liberalism is the embodiment of a set of specific values.[1]

William Galston, for instance, maintains that the three most important advocates of the neutral state, Rawls, Dworkin and Ackerman, cannot avoid reference to a substantive theory of the good, which he calls 'rationalist humanism'. He claims that, without acknowledging it, they 'covertly rely on the same triadic theory of the good, which assumes the worth of human existence, the worth of human purposiveness and of fulfilment of human purposes, and the worth of rationality as the chief constraint on social principles and actions' (Galston 1991, p. 92). According to Galston, liberals should adopt a 'perfectionist' stance and state openly that liberalism promotes a specific conception of the good and is committed to the pursuit of the ends and virtues that are constitutive of the liberal polity.

While rejecting the solution of perfectionism, many liberals acknowledge the shortcomings of the neutrality thesis as it is usually formulated. This is the case with John Rawls, who, in his work subsequent to *A Theory of Justice*, has clearly distanced himself from the 'priority of the right over the good' type of interpretation which his communitarian critics imputed to him. He now insists that 'Justice as fairness is not procedurally neutral. Clearly its principles of justice are substantive and express far more than procedural values, and so do its political conception of person and society, which are represented in the original position' (Rawls 1993, p. 192).

Ronald Dworkin, for his part, never accepted the idea of an absolute neutrality. In his view, at the very heart of liberalism lies a certain conception of equality. It is because it must treat all its members as equal that the liberal state must be neutral. Thus he asserts that, 'Since the citizens of a society differ in their conceptions [of the good life], the government does not treat them as equals if it prefers one conception to another, either because the officials believe that one is intrinsically superior, or because one is held by the more numerous or more powerful groups' (Dworkin 1978, p. 127). For him, liberalism is based on a constitutive morality and not on scepticism. A liberal state must, he says, treat human beings as equals 'not because there is no right or wrong in political morality, but because that is what is right' (ibid., p. 142).

Of the three authors singled out by Galston, Bruce Ackerman is the only true 'neutralist', for he believes that what is constitutive of liberalism is a commitment to neutral dialogue and that the commitment to equality should be constrained by the conditions imposed by such a dialogue. Moreover, his conception of neutral dialogue leaves no space for philosophical inquiry into conceptions of the good and he defends the idea that liberalism should be based on scepticism since, according to him, 'there are no moral meanings hidden in the bowels of the universe' (Ackerman 1989, p. 368).

Political liberalism

I submit that what is really at stake in the debate about neutrality is the nature of pluralism and its place in liberal democracy. The way the liberal state is envisaged has far-reaching consequences for democratic politics. Indeed, it determines how to tackle crucial issues like that of 'multiculturalism'. My intention here is to examine what is currently the most influential position: namely, 'political liberalism', which aims at maintaining the idea of neutrality while reformulating it.

Political liberals like John Rawls and Charles Larmore[2] start from what they characterize as the 'fact' of pluralism, that is, the multiplicity of conceptions of the good that exist in modern democratic society. This leads to the 'liberal problem' of how to organize coexistence among people with different conceptions of the good. It is worth noting that they do not advocate pluralism because they believe diversity is particularly valuable, but rather because they consider it could not be eradicated without the use of state coercion. Theirs is a Lockean kind of thinking, based more on the reasons why pluralism should not be interfered with, than on recognition of its value. Take Rawls, for instance. He defines the modern predicament as constituted by '(i) the fact of pluralism and (ii) the fact of its permanence, as well as (iii) the fact that this pluralism can be overcome only by the oppressive use of state power (which presupposes a control of the state no group possesses)' (Rawls 1987, p. 22). Neutrality, then, is defined as non-interference with substantive views, and pluralism is identified with the toleration of different ways of life irrespective of their intrinsic value.

The critics of neutrality, on the other hand, assert that pluralism should be envisaged as an axiological principle, expressing the recognition that there are many different and incompatible ways of life that are nevertheless valuable. This is the meaning of the 'value pluralism' defended by Joseph Raz, who establishes a connection between pluralism and the ideal of personal autonomy. According to Raz, autonomy presupposes moral pluralism because it is only if a person has a variety of morally acceptable options to choose from that she can live an autonomous life. He states: 'To put it more precisely, if autonomy is an ideal then we are committed to such a view of morality: valuing autonomy leads to the endorsement of moral pluralism' (Raz 1986, p. 399).

Contrary to Rawls, who believes that pluralism requires the rejection of perfectionism, Raz sees a necessary link between the kind of perfectionism to which he is committed and the existence of pluralism. This allows him to conceive pluralism not merely as a 'fact' that we have grudgingly to accept, but as something to be celebrated and valued because it is the condition for personal autonomy. We can see why, from such a perspective, one more akin to John Stuart Mill than to Locke, the fostering of pluralism cannot be theorized in terms of neutrality.

'Political liberalism' claims to provide a better framework than perfectionism for accommodating the plurality of interests and visions of the good that exist in modern democratic societies. In the view of its champions, conceptions of liberalism that make reference to the good life are inadequate for that task because 'They have themselves become simply another part of the problem' (Larmore 1990, p. 345). How convincing is their case? Do they really offer the best perspective for envisaging the nature of a liberal democratic consensus? As I have indicated, the central concern of such conceptions is the possibility of social unity under modern conditions in which there is a multiplicity of conflicting conceptions of the good life. Rawls formulates this question in the following way: 'How is it possible that there may exist over time a stable and just society of free and equal citizens profoundly divided by reasonable though incompatible religious, philosophical and moral doctrines?' (Rawls 1993, p. xviii). It is as a solution to that problem that both Rawls and Larmore defend a liberalism that is strictly 'political' in the sense that it does not rely on any comprehensive moral ideal, on any philosophy of man of the type put forward by liberal philosophers like Kant or Mill. Their argument is that, if they are to be accepted by people who disagree about the nature of the good life, liberal institutions cannot be justified on grounds which are bound to be controversial, like ideals of Kantian autonomy or Millian individuality.

Political liberals concede to the perfectionists that the liberal state must necessarily make reference to some idea of the common good and that it cannot be neutral with respect to morality. Nevertheless – while granting that they cannot do without a theory of the good – they claim that theirs is a minimal theory. It should be distinguished from comprehensive views since it is a common morality which is restricted to principles that can be accepted by people who have different and conflicting ideals of the good life. According to Larmore, the proper meaning of the notion of 'neutrality' is as follows: 'Neutral principles are ones that we can justify without appealing to the controversial views of the good life to which we happen to be committed' (Larmore 1990, p. 341). And Rawls states that his theory of justice is a 'political' not a 'metaphysical' one, whose aim is

> to articulate a public basis of justification for the basic structure of a constitutional regime working from fundamental intuitive ideas implicit in the public political culture and abstracting from comprehensive religious, philosophical and moral doctrines. It seeks common ground – or, if one prefers, neutral ground – given the fact of pluralism.
>
> (Rawls 1993, p. 192)

Liberalism can, of course, offer other solutions to the problem of social unity. Some liberals consider that a Hobbesian *modus vivendi* should be enough to provide the type of consensus required by a pluralistic society. Others believe that a constitutional consensus on established legal procedures fulfils that role as effectively as would a consensus on justice. But 'political liberalism' finds those solutions wanting and proclaims the need for a moral type of consensus in which values and ideals play an authoritative role.

Explaining the objective of the political liberals, Larmore declares that they want to avoid appealing to controversial views of the good life, but also to scepticism, which is itself a matter of reasonable disagreement. Moreover, they are not satisfied with a type of justification based merely on strategic considerations, a Hobbesian one grounded on purely prudential motives. In Larmore's view, 'Only by finding a mean between these two extremes can liberalism work as a minimal moral conception' (Larmore 1990, p. 346).

In fact the ambition of 'political liberalism' is to formulate a definitive list of rights, principles and institutional arrangements that are unassailable and will create the basis of a consensus that is both moral and neutral. To that effect, these liberal thinkers propose to leave aside 'disputed' religious, philosophical and metaphysical issues and limit themselves to a strictly 'political' understanding of liberalism. This, they believe, could constitute the common ground that can still be obtained when there is no more possibility of a common good. One of their main tenets is that in a liberal society, people should not be made to accept institutions and arrangements on grounds that they could reasonably reject. Political discussion needs therefore to be constrained by rules that determine the type of convictions that can be appealed to in argumentation. Their enterprise consists in defining such a framework and hoping that it will create the conditions necessary to deliver indisputable results.

In the case of Larmore, the solution is a form of justification that relies on the two norms of rational dialogue and equal respect. For him, legitimate political principles are those which are arrived at through a rational dialogue in which the parties are moved by the norm of equal respect. This demands that we stand aside from disputed views of the good life and that we respect political neutrality when we devise principles for the political order. It implies that 'when disagreement arises, those wishing to continue the conversation should withdraw to neutral ground, in order either to resolve the dispute or, if that cannot be done rationally, to bypass it' (Larmore 1987, p. 59). Rawls, for his part, sees the solution in the creation of an overlapping consensus on a political conception of justice. By practising a method of 'avoidance' and ignoring philosophical and moral controversies, he hopes that a free agreement can be reached through public reason on principles of justice that 'specify a point of view from which all citizens can examine before one another whether or not their political institutions are just' (Rawls 1987, p. 5).

Liberalism and the negation of the political

The success of political liberalism hinges on the possibility of establishing the conditions for a type of argumentation that reconciles morality with neutrality. I will argue in a moment that its attempt to find a principle of social unity in a form of neutrality grounded on rationality cannot succeed. But first I want to show how the very formulation of such a project depends on evacuating the dimension of the political and conceiving the well-ordered society as one exempt from politics.

When we look at the argument closely, we see that it consists in relegating pluralism and dissent to the private sphere in order to secure consensus in the public realm. All controversial issues are taken off the agenda in order to create the conditions for a 'rational' consensus. As a result, the realm of politics becomes merely the terrain where individuals, stripped of their 'disruptive' passions and beliefs and understood as rational agents in search of self-advantage – within the constraints of morality, of course – submit to procedures for adjudicating between their claims that they consider 'fair'. This is a conception of politics in which one readily recognizes a typical case of the liberal negation of the political, such as Carl Schmitt has criticized, for whom 'liberal concepts typically move between ethics (intellectuality) and economics (trade). From that polarity they attempt to annihilate the political as a domain of conquering power and repression' (Schmitt 1976, p. 71).

To envisage politics as a rational process of negotiation among individuals is to obliterate the whole dimension of power and antagonism – what I call 'the political' – and thereby completely miss its nature. It is also to neglect the predominant role of passions as moving forces of human conduct. Furthermore, in the field of politics, it is groups and collective identities that we encounter, not isolated individuals, and its dynamics cannot be apprehended by reducing it to individual calculations. This has devastating consequences for the liberal approach since, as Freud has taught us, while self-advantage may in certain circumstances be an important motivation for the isolated individual, it very seldom determines the conduct of groups. It is not necessary to endorse entirely Schmitt's conception of the political in order to concede the strength of his point when he exposes the shortcomings of a view that presents politics as a neutral domain insulated from all the divisive issues that exist in the private realm. The liberal claim that a universal rational consensus could be produced by an undistorted dialogue, and that free public reason could guarantee the impartiality of the state, is only possible at the cost of denying the irreducible antagonistic element present in social relations, and this can have disastrous consequences for the defence of democratic institutions. To negate the political does not make it disappear; it only leads to bewilderment in the face of its manifestations and to impotence in dealing with them.

Liberalism, insofar as it is formulated within a rationalistic and individualistic framework, is bound to be blind to the existence of the political and to delude itself with regard to the nature of politics. Indeed, it eliminates from the outset the *differentia specifica* of politics, its handling of collective action and attempt to establish unity in a field crisscrossed with antagonisms. Liberalism overlooks the fact that it concerns the construction of collective identities and the creation of a 'we' as opposed to a 'them'. Politics, as the attempt to domesticate the political, to keep at bay the forces of destruction and to establish order, always has to do with conflicts and antagonisms. It requires an understanding that every consensus is, by necessity, based on acts of exclusion and that there can never be a fully inclusive 'rational' consensus.

This is a crucial point which the notion of the 'constitutive outside', borrowed from Derrida, can help us to elucidate. One of Derrida's central ideas is that the constitution of an identity is always based on excluding something and establishing a violent hierarchy between the resultant two poles – form/matter, essence/accident, black/white, man/woman, and so on. This reveals that there is no identity that is self-present to itself and not constructed as difference, and that any social objectivity is constituted through acts of power. It means that any social objectivity is ultimately political and has to show traces of the exclusion which governs its constitution, what we can call its 'constitutive outside'. As a consequence, all systems of social relations imply to a certain extent relations of power, since the construction of a social identity is an act of power.

Power, as Ernesto Laclau indicates, should not be conceived as an external relation taking place between two preconstituted identities, because it is power that constitutes the identities themselves. According to him,

> systems of social organization can be seen as attempts to reduce the margin of undecidability, to make way for actions and decisions that are as coherent as possible. But by the simple fact of the presence of negativity and given the primary and constitutive character of any antagonism, the hiding of the 'ultimate' undecidability of any decision will never be complete and social coherence will only be achieved at the cost of repressing something that negates it. It is in this sense that any consensus, that any objective and differential system of rules implies, as its most essential possibility, a dimension of coercion.
>
> (Laclau 1990, p. 172)

Rationality and neutrality

Now, it is precisely this dimension of undecidability and coercion that 'political liberalism' is at pains to eliminate. It offers us a picture of the well-ordered society as one from which antagonism, violence, power and repression have disappeared. But, in fact, this is only because they have been made invisible through a clever stratagem.

Political liberals are, of course, perfectly aware that the pluralism they defend cannot be total and that some views will have to be excluded. Nevertheless, they justify those exclusions by declaring that they are the product of the 'free exercise of practical reason' that establishes the limits of possible consensus. It is, according to them, necessary to distinguish between 'simple' and 'reasonable pluralism'.[3] When a point of view is excluded it is because this is required by the exercise of reason. Once exclusions are presented as arising from a free agreement resulting from rational procedures ('veil of ignorance' or rational dialogue), they appear as immune from relations of power. In that way rationality is the key to solving the 'paradox of liberalism': how to eliminate its adversaries while remaining neutral.

This strategy can be seen in Larmore's project to formulate a 'neutral justification of the neutrality of the state'. He starts by identifying neutrality with a minimal moral conception: a common ground that is neutral with respect to controversial views of the good life. Next, in order to specify that common ground in a neutral way, he resorts to shared norms of equal respect and rational dialogue. According to Larmore, because the norms of equal respect and rational dialogue have been central to Western culture, it should be possible to convince the romantic critics of modern individualism that they can support a liberal political order without having to renounce their cherished values of tradition and belonging. While acknowledging the debt that his conception of 'ideal conditions of rational argument' owes to Habermas's idea of an 'ideal speech situation', he claims that his approach is more contextualist than Habermas's because his ideal conditions of justification never depart entirely from our historical circumstances and are a function of our general view of the world (Larmore 1987). What Larmore has in mind, like Rawls, is the creation of an 'overlapping consensus' based on norms widely accepted in modern Western societies.

Larmore believes that, thanks to his device, he has reached principles that should be accepted by rational people interested in designing principles of political association, and that he has provided a justification for the neutrality of the state that does not depend on any controversial doctrine. But, as Galston has pointed out, besides the irony of attempting to resolve the dispute between the heirs of Kant and Mill and the neo-romantics by appealing to the Kantian conception of equal respect, Larmore's solution leaves out the increasing number of religious believers whose opposition to liberalism constitutes a much more real challenge than do the romantic critics of individualism (Galston 1991, p. 299).

Larmore would probably reply that disagreements of such a kind cannot be accepted as 'reasonable'. But who decides what is and what is not 'reasonable'? In politics the very distinction between 'reasonable' and 'unreasonable' is already the drawing of a frontier; it has a political character and is always the expression of a given hegemony. What is at a given moment deemed 'rational' or 'reasonable' in a community is what corresponds to the dominant language games and the 'common sense' that they construe. It is the result of a process of 'sedimentation' of an ensemble of discourses and practices whose political character has been elided. If it is perfectly legitimate to make a distinction between the reasonable and the unreasonable, such an opposition has implications that must be acknowledged. Otherwise a specific configuration of practices and arrangements becomes naturalized and is put out of reach of critical inquiry. In a modern democracy, we should be able to question the very frontiers of reason and to put under scrutiny the claims to universality made in the name of rationality. As Judith Butler reminds us, 'To establish a set of norms that are beyond power or force is itself a powerful and forceful conceptual practice that sublimates, disguises and extends its own power play through recourse to tropes of normative universality' (Butler 1992, p. 7).

The same effort to eliminate undecidability and power can be found in Rawls. Justice as fairness is presented as an acceptable basis for consensus in a pluralistic society because it is non-partisan and transcends the different comprehensive views. To be sure, Rawls now acknowledges that his theory is not transhistorical but is the answer to a specific question: namely, 'Which conception of justice is most appropriate for realizing the value of liberty and equality in basic institutions?' This of course implies that the discussion is going to be constrained by the premise that the values of liberty and equality are the ones to be taken into account. For him, this requirement simply indicates that we start from the fundamental intuitive ideas present in our societies. He sees it as self-evident and uncontroversial, but it is not. Far from being a benign statement of fact, it is the result of a decision which already excludes from the dialogue those who believe that different values should be the organizing ones of the political order. Rawls, who considers that in our societies those values provide the criteria of moral reasonableness, rules out their objections. He is convinced that starting from those basic, reasonable premises, a process of neutral, rational reasoning leads to the formulation of a theory of justice that all reasonable and rational people should accept. In consequence, those who disagree with them are disqualified on the ground of being either unreasonable or irrational. This represents no problem for him since he believes that 'political institutions satisfying the principles of a liberal conception of justice realize political values and ideas that normally outweigh whatever values oppose them' (Rawls 1987, p. 24). Thanks to that wager, he whisks away not only the role of force in upholding the rules and institutions that produce the overlapping consensus, but also its 'outside'.

Pluralism and undecidability

As we can see, in order to create the conditions for successful argumentation, political liberals refuse to open rational dialogue to those who do not accept their 'rules of the game'. In a sense there is nothing objectionable about that, provided one is aware of the implications – but of course in this case the implications would defeat the very purpose of supposedly rational argumentation.

It is now generally acknowledged that argumentation is only possible when there is a shared framework. As Wittgenstein pointed out, to have agreement in opinions, there must first be agreement on the language used. But he also alerted us to the fact that those represented 'not agreement in opinions but in forms of life' (Wittgenstein 1958, 1: §241). In his view, to agree on the definition of a term is not enough and we need agreement in the way we use it. As he puts it: 'If language is to be a means of communication there must be agreement not only in definitions but also (queer as this may sound) in judgements' (ibid., 1: §242).

As John Gray indicates, Wittgenstein's analysis of rules and rule-following undermines the kind of liberal reasoning that envisages the common framework for argumentation on the model of a 'neutral' or 'rational' dialogue. According to a Wittgensteinian perspective:

> Whatever there is of definite content in contractarian deliberation and its deliverance, derives from particular judgments we are inclined to make as practitioners of specific forms of life. The forms of life in which we find ourselves are themselves held together by a network of precontractual agreements, without which there would be no possibility of mutual understanding or therefore, of disagreement.
>
> (Gray 1989, p. 252)

Such an approach offers a fruitful alternative to rationalist liberalism because it can be developed in a way that highlights the historical and contingent character of the discourses that construct our identities. This is exemplified by Richard Flathman when he notes that, notwithstanding the fact that a good deal of agreement has been achieved on many features of liberal democratic politics, certainty is not to be seen as necessary in any of the philosophical senses. In his view, 'Our agreement in these judgments constitutes the language of our politics. It is a language arrived at and continuously modified through no less than a history of discourse, a history in which we have thought about, as we became able to think in, that language' (Flathman 1989, p. 63).

This is, I believe, a very promising direction for political philosophy. Contrary to the current brand of liberalism, a reflection on liberal democracy on those lines would not present it as the rational, universal solution to the problem of political order. Neither would it attempt to deny its ultimately ungrounded status by making it appear as the outcome of a rational choice or a dialogical process of undistorted communication. Because of the central role it gives to practices, such a perspective could help us understand how our shared language of politics is entangled with power and needs to be apprehended in terms of hegemonic relations. It might also leave room for 'undecidability' and be better suited to account for conflict and antagonism.

Many rationalists will certainly accuse such a political philosophy of opening the way to 'relativism' and 'nihilism' and thus jeopardizing democracy. But the opposite is true because, instead of putting our liberal institutions at risk, the recognition that they do not have an ultimate foundation creates a more favourable terrain for their defence. When we realize that, far from being the necessary result of a moral evolution of mankind, liberal democracy is an ensemble of contingent practices, we can understand that it is a conquest that needs to be protected as well as deepened.

A political philosophy that makes room for contingency and undecidability is clearly at odds with liberal rationalism, whose typical move is to erase its very conditions of enunciation and deny its historical space of inscription. This was already constitutive of the 'hypocrisy' of the Enlightenment, as Reinhart Koselleck (1988) has shown. Many liberals follow suit by refusing to assume their political stand and pretending to be speaking from an impartial location. In that way they manage to present their views as the embodiment of 'rationality' and this enables them to exclude their opponents from 'rational dialogue'. However, the excluded do not disappear and, once their position has been declared 'unreasonable', the problem of neutrality remains unsolved. From their point of view, the 'neutral' principles of rational dialogue are certainly not so. For them, what is proclaimed as 'rationality' by the liberals is experienced as coercion.

It is not my intention to advocate a total pluralism and I do not believe it is possible to avoid excluding some points of view. No state or political order, even a liberal one, can exist without some forms of exclusion. My point is different: I want to argue that it is very important to recognize those forms of exclusion for what they are and the violence that they signify, instead of concealing them under the veil of rationality. To disguise the real nature of the necessary 'frontiers' and modes of exclusion required by a liberal democratic order by grounding them in the supposedly neutral character of 'rationality' creates effects of occultation which hinder the proper workings of democratic politics. William Connolly is right when he indicates that 'the pretense to neutrality functions to maintain established settlements below the threshold of public discourse' (Connolly 1991, p. 161).

The specificity of pluralist democracy does not reside in the absence of domination and violence but in the establishment of a set of institutions through which they can be limited and contested. It is for that reason that democracy 'maintains a split between law and justice: it accepts the fact that justice is "impossible", that it is an act which can never be wholly grounded in "sufficient (legal) reasons"' (Salecl 1991, p. 24). But this mechanism of 'self-binding' ceases to be effective if violence goes unrecognized and hidden behind appeals to rationality. Hence the importance of abandoning the mystifying illusion of a dialogue free from coercion. It might undermine democracy by closing the gap between justice and law which is a constitutive space of modern democracy.

In order to avoid the danger of such a closure, what must be relinquished is the very idea that there could be such a thing as a 'rational' political consensus, if that means a consensus that would not be based on any form of exclusion. To present the institutions of liberal democracy as the outcome of a pure deliberative rationality is to reify them and make them impossible to transform. The fact that, like any other regime, modern pluralist democracy constitutes a system of relations of power, is denied and the democratic challenging of those forms of power becomes illegitimate.

The political liberalism of Rawls and Larmore, far from being conducive to a pluralistic society, manifests a strong tendency toward homogeneity and leaves little space for dissent and contestation in the sphere of politics. By postulating that it is possible to reach a free moral consensus on political fundamentals through rational procedures and that such a consensus is provided by liberal institutions, it ends up endowing a historically specific set of arrangements with the character of universality and rationality. This is contrary to the indetermination that is constitutive of modern democracy. In the end, the rationalist defence of liberalism, by searching for an argument that is beyond argumentation and by wanting to define the meaning of the universal, makes the same mistake for which it criticizes totalitarianism: it rejects democratic indeterminacy and identifies the universal with a given particular.

Modern democratic politics, linked as it is to the declaration of human rights, does indeed imply a reference to universality. But this universality is conceived as a horizon that can never be reached. Every pretension to occupy the place of the universal, to fix its final meaning through rationality, must be rejected. The content of the universal must remain indeterminate since it is this indeterminacy that is the condition of existence of democratic politics.

The specificity of modern democratic pluralism is lost when it is envisaged merely as the empirical fact of a multiplicity of moral conceptions of the good. It needs to be understood as the expression of a symbolic mutation in the ordering of social relations: the democratic revolution envisaged in Claude Lefort's terms as 'the dissolution of the markers of certainty'. In a modern democratic society there can be no longer a substantive unity and division must be recognized as constitutive. It is 'a society in which Power, Law and Knowledge are exposed to a radical indeterminacy, a society that has become the theatre of an uncontrollable adventure' (Lefort 1986, p. 305).

Morality, unanimity and impartiality

What has been celebrated as a revival of political philosophy in the last decades is in fact a mere extension of moral philosophy; it is moral reasoning applied to the treatment of political institutions. This is manifest in the absence in current liberal theorizing of a proper distinction between moral discourse and political discourse. To recover the normative aspect of politics, moral concerns about impartiality and unanimity are introduced into political argumentation. The result is a public morality for liberal societies, a morality which is deemed to be 'political' because it is 'minimal' and avoids engaging with controversial conceptions of the good and because it provides the cement for social cohesion.[4]

There might well be a place for such an endeavour, but it cannot replace political philosophy and it does not provide us with the adequate understanding of the political that we urgently need. Moreover, its insistence on universalism and individualism can be harmful because it masks the real challenge that a reflection on pluralism faces today with the explosion of nationalisms and the multiplication of particularisms. Those phenomena need to be grasped in political terms, as forms of construction of a 'we/them' opposition, and consequently appeals to universality, impartiality and individual rights miss the mark.

The problems arising from the conflation of morality and politics are evident in the work of another liberal: Thomas Nagel. According to him, the difficulty for political theory is that

> political institutions and their theoretical justification try to externalize the demands of the impersonal standpoint. But they have to be staffed and supported and brought to life by individuals for whom the impersonal standpoint coexists with the personal, and this has to be reflected in their design.
>
> (Nagel 1991, p. 5)

Nagel believes that in order to be able to defend the acceptability of a political order, we need to reconcile an impartial concern for everyone with a view of how each individual can reasonably be expected to live. Nagel proposes that we should start with the conflict that each individual encounters in himself between the impersonal standpoint that produces a powerful demand for universal impartiality and equality and the personal standpoint that gives rise to individualistic motives which impede the realization of those ideals.

Central to political theory, in his view, is the question of political legitimacy, which requires the achievement of unanimity over the basic institutions of society. Like Rawls and Larmore, he rejects a Hobbesian solution because it does not integrate the impersonal standpoint and only considers personal motives and values, and he insists that some form of impartiality must be central to the pursuit of legitimacy. However, he considers that a legitimate system will have to reconcile the principle of impartiality with one of reasonable partiality so that no one could .object that the demands made on them are excessive.

With their insistence on 'partiality', Nagel's views represent, no doubt, progress with respect to the position of those liberals who equate the moral point of view with that of impartiality, and privilege it at the expense of all kinds of personal commitments. The problem is the emphasis he puts on unanimity and on his search for principles that no one could reasonably reject and that all could agree that everyone should follow. He sees the strength of such principles in the fact that they will have a moral character. As a consequence, he argues that when a system is legitimate,

> those living under it have no grounds for complaint against the way its basic structure accommodates their point of view, and no one is morally justified in withholding his cooperation from the functioning of the system, trying to subvert its results, or trying to overturn it if he has the power to do so.
>
> (Nagel 1991, p. 35)

We find again, stated openly in this case, the same attempt to foreclose the possibility of dissent in the public realm that we have already observed in Rawls and

Larmore. For those liberals, a fully realized liberal democratic order is one in which there is perfect unanimity concerning political arrangements and total coincidence between the individuals and their institutions. Their aim is to reach a type of consensus which, by its very nature, will disqualify every move to destabilize it. The pluralism they defend only resides in the private sphere and is restricted to philosophical, moral and religious issues. They do not seem to understand that there can also be unresolvable conflicts in the field of political values. It must be said that Nagel is not very sanguine about the possibility of realizing the type of consensus he promotes, but he entertains no doubt about its desirability. He declares:

> It would be morally preferable, and a condition of true political legitimacy, if the general principles governing agent-relative reasons limited the reach of those reasons in such a way that they left standing some solutions or distributions of advantages and disadvantages that no one could reasonably refuse, even if he were in a position to do so. Instead of morality being like politics in its sensitivity to the balance of power, we should want politics to be more like morality in its aim of unanimous acceptability.
>
> (Nagel 1991, p. 45)

This is, in my view, a dangerously misguided perspective, and people committed to democracy should be wary of all projects that aspire to create unanimity. Speaking about moral philosophy, Stuart Hampshire warns us that:

> Whether it is Aristotelian, Kantian, Humean, or utilitarian, moral philosophy can do harm when it implies that there ought to be, and that there can be, fundamental agreement on, or even a convergence in, moral ideals – the harm is that the reality of conflict, both within individuals and within societies, is disguised by the myth of humanity as a consistent moral unit across time and space. There is a false blandness in the myth, an aversion from reality.
>
> (Hampshire 1983, p. 155)

I think the same reasoning applies even more to political philosophy and that a democratic pluralist position cannot aim at establishing once and for all the definite principles and arrangements that the members of a well-ordered society should accept. Divisive issues cannot be confined to the sphere of the private, and it is an illusion to believe that it is possible to create a nonexclusive public sphere of rational argument where a noncoercive consensus could be attained. Instead of trying to erase the traces of power and exclusion, democratic politics requires that they be brought to the fore, making them visible so that they can enter the terrain of contestation.

Tackled from such a perspective, the question of pluralism is much more complex. It cannot be envisaged only in terms of already existing subjects and restricted to their conceptions of the good. What must be addressed is the very process of constitution of the subjects of pluralism. This is indeed where the more crucial issues lie today. And this is where the limitations of the current liberal approach – informed by essentialism and individualism – can have really damaging political consequences for democratic politics.[5]

What kind of consensus?

I agree with political liberals on the need to distinguish between liberalism as a comprehensive doctrine, a philosophy of man, and liberalism as a doctrine that is concerned with the institutions and values of the liberal society. And I am also committed – although in a way that differs from them – to elucidating the political dimension of liberalism. I want to scrutinize its contribution to the emergence of modern democracy as a new regime. But this requires recognition that the liberal democratic regime is not exhausted by its liberal component. For it consists in the articulation of two elements, the liberal one constituted by the institutions of the liberal state (rule of law, separation of powers, defence of individual rights) and the democratic one of popular sovereignty and majority rule. Moreover, liberty and equality, which constitute the political principles of the liberal democratic regime, can be interpreted in many different ways and ranked according to different priorities. This accounts for the multiple possible forms of liberal democracy. The 'liberals' privilege the values of liberty and individual rights, while the 'democrats' insist on equality and participation. But as long as neither side attempts to suppress the other, we are witnessing a struggle inside liberal democracy, over its priorities, and not one between alternative regimes.

To state, as Larmore does, that 'Liberalism and democracy are separate values whose relation ... consists largely in democratic self-government being the best means for protecting the principles of a liberal political order' (Larmore 1990, p. 359), is typically a liberal interpretation and is open to challenge. To be sure, the relation between liberalism and democracy has long been a controversial issue and will probably never be settled. A pluralist democracy is constantly pulled in opposite directions: towards exacerbation of differences and disintegration on one side; towards homogenization and strong forms of unity on the other. I consider, as I have argued elsewhere,[6] that the specificity of modern democracy as a new political form of society, as a new 'regime', lies precisely in the tension between the democratic logic of equality and the liberal logic of liberty. It is a tension that we should value and protect, rather than try to resolve, because it is constitutive of pluralist democracy. This does not mean that it does not create some specific problems; since the articulation between liberalism and democracy has been established, a recurrent concern of liberals has been how to put individual rights outside the reach of majoritarianism. To that effect they have wanted to put constraints on the democratic process of decision-making. Without being openly acknowledged, this is I believe one of the subtexts of the present discussion. Presenting liberal institutions as the outcome of a purely deliberative rationality might be seen as an attempt to provide them with a ground that forecloses the possibility of reasonable disagreement. This could be seen as a way to protect them against potential threats from democratic majorities.

There is, no doubt, a need to secure pluralism, individual rights and minorities against a possible majority tyranny. But the opposite danger also exists, of thereby naturalizing a given set of 'liberties' and existing rights, and at the same time buttressing many relations of inequality. The search for 'guarantees' can lead to the very destruction of pluralist democracy. Hence the importance of understanding that for democracy to exist no social agent should be able to claim any mastery of the foundation of society. The relation between social agents can only be termed 'democratic' in so far as they accept the particularity and the limitations of their claims – that is, only in so far as they recognize their mutual relations as ones from which power is ineradicable. This is why I have argued that the liberal evasion of the dimension of power is fraught with risks for democratic politics.

Like the exponents of 'political liberalism', I would like to see the creation of a wide consensus around the principles of pluralist democracy. But I do not believe that such a consensus should be grounded on rationality and unanimity or that it should manifest an impartial point of view. The real task, in my view, is to foster allegiance to our democratic institutions, and the best way to do this is not by demonstrating that they would be chosen by rational agents 'under the veil of ignorance' or in a 'neutral dialogue', but by creating strong forms of identification with them. This should be done by developing and multiplying in as many social relations as possible the discourses, the practices, the 'language games' that produce democratic 'subject positions'. The objective is to establish the hegemony of democratic values and practices.

This has to be envisaged as an 'ethico-political' enterprise, one that concerns the specific values that can be realized in the realm of politics through collective action, and which does not deny the constitutive role of conflict and antagonism and the fact that division is irreducible. This last point indicates why 'value pluralism' in its multiple dimensions has to be taken seriously by political philosophers. We need to make room for the pluralism of cultures, collective forms of life and regimes, as well as for the pluralism of subjects, individual choices and conceptions of the good. This has very important consequences for politics. For, in the realm of politics, once the plurality of values is granted along with their conflicting nature, undecidability cannot be the last word. Politics calls for decision and, despite the impossibility of finding a final grounding, any type of political regime consists in establishing a hierarchy among political values. A liberal democratic regime, while fostering pluralism, cannot equate all values, since its very existence as a political form of society requires a specific ordering of values which precludes a total pluralism. A political regime is always a case of 'undecidable decided' and this is why it cannot exist without a 'constitutive outside'.

Rawls indirectly points to this fact when he explains that 'a liberal view removes from the political agenda the most divisive issues' (Rawls 1993, p. 157). What is this, if not the drawing of a frontier between what is negotiable in a liberal society and what is not negotiable? What is this, if not a decision that establishes a distinction between the private and public spheres? No wonder that this process is experienced as coercion by those who do not accept such a separation. The advent of liberal pluralism as well as its continuance must be envisaged as a form of political intervention in a conflictual field, an intervention that implies the repression of other alternatives. Those other alternatives might be displaced and marginalized by the apparently irresistible march of liberal democracy, but they will never disappear completely and some of them can be reactivated. Our values, our institutions and way of life constitute one form of political order among a plurality of possible ones, and the consensus they command cannot exist without an 'outside' that will forever leave our liberal democratic values and our conception of justice open to challenge. For those who oppose these values – those who are disqualified as 'unreasonable' by our rationalist liberals and who do not participate in their overlapping consensus – the conditions imposed by the 'rational' dialogue are unacceptable because they deny some of the defining features of their identity. They might be forced to accept a *modus vivendi* but it is not one that will necessarily develop into a stable and enduring overlapping consensus as Rawls hopes. According to him, the liberal regime is a *modus vivendi* made necessary by the fact of pluralism. Yet it is a *modus vivendi* that he wants us to value and accept for moral not prudential reasons. But what about those who oppose the very idea of such a *modus vivendi*? There is obviously no place for their demands inside a liberal *modus vivendi*, even one whose scope would have been widened. Liberalism, for them, is a *modus vivendi* that they are forced to accept at the same time that it rejects their values.

I think there is no way to avoid such a situation and we have to face its implications. A project of radical and plural democracy has to come to terms with the dimension of conflict and antagonism within the political and has to accept the consequences of the irreducible plurality of values. This must be the starting point of our attempt to radicalize the liberal democratic regime and to extend the democratic revolution to an increasing number of social relations. Instead of shying away from the component of violence and hostility inherent in social relations, the task is to think how to create the conditions under which those aggressive forces can be defused and diverted and a pluralist democratic order made possible.

Notes

1 Some recent titles indicative of this trend are: Nancy L. Rosenblum, ed., *Liberalism and the Moral Life* (Cambridge, MA, 1989); R. B. Douglass, G. Mara and H. Richardson, eds., *Liberalism and the Good* (New York, 1990); Stephen Macedo, *Liberal Virtues. Citizenship, Virtue and Community in Liberal Constitutionalism* (Oxford, 1991); Galston (1991).

2 There are significant differences between Rawls and Larmore, but both defend a version of 'political liberalism' which has enough points in common to justify treating them under the same rubric.

3 This distinction was first formulated by Joshua Cohen in 'Moral Pluralism and Political Consensus', in D. Copp and J. Hampton (eds.), *The Idea of Democracy* (Cambridge, Cambridge University Press, 1993). Rawls (1993) has since then made extensive use of it.

4 I have developed this aspect of my critique in 'Rawls: Political Philosophy without Politics' in Mouffe (1993).
5 On this issue, see the stimulating article by Kirstie McClure, 'On the Subject of Rights: Pluralism, Plurality and Political Identity', in Mouffe (1993).
6 See my 'Pluralism and Modern Democracy: Around Carl Schmitt', in Mouffe (1993).

References

Ackerman, Bruce. 1989. *Social Justice and the Liberal State.* New Haven, CT: Yale University Press.
Butler, Judith. 1992. Contingent Foundations: Feminism and the Question of 'Post modernism'. In J. Butler and J. Scott, eds., *Feminists Theorize the Political.* New York and London.
Connolly, William E. 1991. *Identity/Difference: Democratic Negotiations of Political Paradox.* Ithaca, NY, and London: Cornell University Press.
Dworkin, Ronald. 1978. Liberalism. In Stuart Hampshire, ed., *Public and Private Morality.* Cambridge.
Flathman, Richard E. 1989. *Toward a Liberalism.* Ithaca, NY, and London: Cornell University Press.
Galston, William A. 1991. *Liberal Purposes: Goods, Virtues and Diversity in the Liberal State.* Cambridge.
Gray, John. 1989. *Liberalisms: Essays in Political Philosophy.* London and New York.
Hampshire, Stuart. 1983. *Morality and Conflict.* Cambridge, MA.
Koselleck, Reinhart. 1988. *Critique and Crisis: Enlightenment and the Pathogenesis of Modern Society.* Cambridge, MA.
Laclau, Ernesto. 1990. *New Reflections on the Revolution of Our Time.* London.
Larmore, Charles. 1987. *Patterns of Moral Complexity.* Cambridge.
——1990. Political Liberalism. *Political Theory* 18(3) August.
Lefort, Claude. 1986. *The Political Forms of Modern Society.* Cambridge: Polity Press.
Mouffe, Chantal. (Ed.) 1992. *Dimensions of Radical Democracy: Pluralism, Citizenship, Community.* London.
——1993. *The Return of the Political.* London.
Nagel, Thomas. 1991. *Equality and Partiality.* Oxford.
Rawls, John. 1987. The Idea of an Overlapping Consensus. *Oxford Journal of Legal Studies* 7(1).
——1993. *Political Liberalism.* New York.
Raz, Joseph. 1986. *The Morality of Freedom.* Oxford.
Salecl, Renata. 1991. Democracy and Violence. *New Formations* 14, Summer.
Schmitt, Carl. 1976. *The Concept of the Political.* New Brunswick, NJ.
Wittgenstein, Ludwig. 1958. *Philosophical Investigations.* Trans. G.E.M. Anscombe. Oxford.

7

FEMINISM, CITIZENSHIP AND RADICAL DEMOCRATIC POLITICS (1992)

Two topics have recently been the subject of much discussion among Anglo-American feminists: postmodernism and essentialism. Obviously they are related since the so-called "postmoderns" are also presented as the main critics of essentialism, but it is better to distinguish them since some feminists who are sympathetic to post-modernism have lately come to the defense of essentialism.[1] I consider that, in order to clarify the issues that are at stake in that debate, it is necessary to recognize that there is no such a thing as "postmodernism" understood as a coherent theo-retical approach and that the frequent assimilation between poststructuralism and postmodernism can only lead to confusion. Which is not to say that we have not been witnessing through the twentieth century a progressive questioning of the dominant form of rationality and of the premises of the modes of thought char-acteristic of the Enlightenment. But this critique of universalism, humanism, and rationalism has come from many different quarters and it is far from being limited to the authors called "poststructuralists" or "postmodernists." From that point of view, all the innovative currents of this century – Heidegger and the post-Heideggerian philosophical hermeneutics of Gadamer, the later Wittgenstein and the philosophy of language inspired by his work, psychoanalysis and the reading of Freud proposed by Lacan, American pragmatism – all have from diverse standpoints criticized the idea of a universal human nature, of a universal canon of rationality through which that human nature could be known as well as the traditional conception of truth. Therefore, if the term "postmodern" indicates such a critique of Enlightenment's universalism and rationalism, it must be acknowledged that it refers to the main currents of twentieth-century philosophy and there is no reason to single out poststructuralism as a special target. On the other side, if by "post-modernism" one wants to designate only the very specific form that such a critique takes in authors such as Lyotard and Baudrillard, there is absolutely no justification for putting in that category people like Derrida, Lacan, or Foucault, as has generally been the case. Too often a critique of a specific thesis of Lyotard or Baudrillard leads to sweeping conclusions about "the postmoderns" who by then include all the authors loosely connected with poststructuralism. This type of amalgamation is completely unhelpful when not clearly disingenuous.

Once the conflation between postmodernism and poststructuralism has been debunked, the question of essentialism appears in a very different light. Indeed, it is with regard to the critique of essentialism that a convergence can be established among many different currents of thought and similarities found in the work of authors as different as Derrida, Wittgenstein, Heidegger, Dewey, Gadamer, Lacan, Foucault, Freud, and others. This is very important because it means that such a critique takes many different forms and that if we want to scrutinize its relevance for feminist politics we must engage with all its modalities and implications and not quickly dismiss it on the basis of some of its versions.

My aim in this article will be to show the crucial insights that an anti-essentialist approach can bring to the elaboration of a feminist politics which is also informed by a radical democratic project. I certainly do not believe that essentialism necessarily entails conservative politics and I am ready to accept that it can be formulated in a progressive way. What I want to argue is that it presents some inescapable shortcomings for the construction of a democratic alternative whose objective is the articulation of the struggles linked to different forms of oppression. I consider that it leads to a view of identity that is at odds with a conception of radical and plural democracy and that it does not allow us to construe the new vision of citizenship that is required by such a politics.

The question of identity and feminism

One common tenet of critics of essentialism has been the abandoning of the category of the subject as a rational transparent entity that could convey a homogeneous meaning on the total field of her conduct by being the source of her action. For instance, psychoanalysis has shown that far from being organized around the transparency of an ego, personality is structured in a number of levels which lie outside of the consciousness and the rationality of the agents. It has therefore undermined the idea of the unified character of the subject. Freud's central claim is that the human mind is necessarily subject to division between two systems of which one is not and cannot be conscious. Expanding the Freudian vision, Lacan has shown the plurality of registers – the Symbolic, the Real, and the Imaginary – which penetrate any identity, and the place of the subject as the place of the lack which – though represented within the structure – is the empty place which at the same time subverts and is the condition of constitution of any identity. The history of the subject is the history of his/her identifications and there is no concealed identity to be rescued beyond the latter. There is thus a double movement. On the one hand, a movement of decentering which prevents the fixation of a set of positions around a preconstituted point. On the other hand, and as a result of this *essential* nonfixity, the opposite movement: the institution of nodal points, partial fixations which limit the flux of the signified under the signifier. But this dialectics at nonfixity/fixation is possible only because fixity is not given beforehand, because no center of subjectivity precedes the subject's identifications.

In the philosophy of language of the later Wittgenstein, we also find a critique of the rationalist conception of the subject that indicates that the latter cannot be the source of linguistic meanings since it is through participation in different language games that the world is disclosed to us. We encounter the same idea in Gadamer's philosophical hermeneutics in the thesis that there is a fundamental unity between thought, language, and the world and that it is within language that the horizon of our present is constituted. A similar critique of the centrality of the subject in modern metaphysics and of its unitary character can be found under several forms in the other authors mentioned earlier. However, my purpose here is not to examine those theories in detail but simply to indicate some basic convergences. I am not overlooking the fact that there are important differences among all those very diverse thinkers. But from the point of view of the argument that I want to make, it is important to grasp the consequences of their common critique of the traditional status of the subject and of its implications for feminism.

It is often said that the deconstruction of essential identities, which is the result of acknowledging the contingency and ambiguity of every identity, renders feminist political action impossible. Many feminists believe that, without seeing women as a coherent identity, we cannot ground the possiblity of a feminist political movement in which women could unite as women in order to formulate and pursue specific feminist aims. Contrary to that view, I will argue that, for those feminists who are committed to a radical democratic politics, the deconstruction of essential identities should be seen as the necessary condition for an adequate understanding of the variety of social relations where the principles of liberty and equality should apply. It is only when we discard the view of the subject as an agent both rational and transparent to itself, and discard as well the supposed unity and homogeneity of the ensemble of its positions, that we are in the position to theorize the multiplicity of relations of subordination. A single individual can be the bearer of this multiplicity and be dominant in one relation while subordinated in another. We can then conceive the social agent as constituted by an ensemble of "subject positions" that can never be totally fixed in a closed system of differences, constructed by a diversity of discourses among which there is no necessary relation, but a constant movement of overdetermination and displacement. The "identity" of such a multiple and contradictory subject is therefore always contingent and precarious, temporarily fixed at the intersection of those subject positions and dependent on specific forms of identification. It is therefore impossible to speak of the social agent as if we were dealing with a unified, homogeneous entity. We have rather to approach it as a plurality, dependent on the various subject positions through which it is constituted within various discursive formations. And to recognize that there is no *a priori*, necessary relation between the discourses that construct its different subject positions. But, for the reasons pointed out earlier, this plurality does not involve the *coexistence*, one by one, of a plurality of subject positions but rather the constant subversion and overdetermination of one by the others, which make possible the generation of "totalizing effects" within a field characterized by open and indeterminate frontiers.

Such an approach is extremely important to understand feminist as well as other contemporary struggles. Their central characteristic is that an ensemble of subject positions linked through inscription in social relations, hitherto considered as apolitical, have become loci of conflict and antagonism and have led to political mobilization. The proliferation of these new forms of struggle can only be theoretically tackled when one starts with the dialectics and decentering/recentering described earlier.

In *Hegemony and Socialist Strategy*,[2] Ernesto Laclau and I have attempted to draw the consequences of such a theoretical approach for a project of radical and plural democracy. We argued for the need to establish a chain of equivalence among the different democratic struggles so as to create an equivalent articulation between the demands of women, blacks, workers, gays, and others. On this point our perspective differs from other nonessentialist views where the aspect of detotalization and decentering prevails and where the dispersion of subject positions is transformed into an effective separation, as is the case with Lyotard and to some extent with Foucault. For us, the aspect of articulation is crucial. To deny the existence of an *a priori*, necessary link between subject positions does not mean that there are not constant efforts to establish between them historical, contingent, and variable links. This type of link, which establishes between various positions a contingent, unpredetermined relation is what we designated as "articulation." Even though there is no necessary link between different subject positions, in the field of politics there are always discourses that try to provide an articulation from different standpoints. For that reason every subject position is constituted within an essentially unstable discursive structure since it is submitted to a variety of articulatory practices that constantly subvert and transform it. This is why there is no subject position whose links with others is definitively assured and, therefore, no social identity that would be fully and permanently acquired. This does not mean, however, that we cannot retain notions like "working-class," "men," "women," "blacks," or other signifiers referring to collective subjects. However, once the existence of a common essence has been discarded, their status must be conceived in terms of what Wittgenstein designates as "family resemblances" and their unity must be seen as the result of the partial fixation of identities through the creation of nodal points.

For feminists to accept such an approach has very important consequences for the way we formulate our political struggles. If the category "woman" does not correspond to any unified and unifying essence, the question can no longer be to try to unearth it. The central issues become: how is "woman" constructed as a category within different discourses? how is sexual difference made a pertinent distinction in social relations? and how are relations of subordination constructed through such a distinction? The whole false dilemma of equality versus difference is exploded since we no longer have a homogeneous entity "woman" facing another homogeneous entity "man," but a multiplicity of social relations in which sexual difference is always constructed in very diverse ways and where the struggle against subordination has to be visualized in specific and differential forms. To ask if women should become identical to men in order to be recognized as equal, or if they should assert their difference at the cost of equality, appears meaningless once essential identities are put into question.[3]

Citizenship and feminist politics

In consequence, the very question of what a feminist politics should be, has to be posed in completely different terms. So far, most feminists concerned with the contribution that feminism could make to democratic politics have been looking either for the specific demands that could express women's interests or for the specific feminine values that should become the model for democratic politics. Liberal feminists have been fighting for a wide range of new rights for women to make them equal citizens, but without challenging the dominant liberal models of citizenship and politics. Their view has been criticized by other feminists who argue that the present conception of the political is a male one and that women's concerns cannot be accommodated within such a framework. Following Carol Gilligan, they oppose a feminist "ethics of care" to the male and liberal "ethics of justice." Against liberal individualist values, they defend a set of values based on the experience of women *as* women, that is, their experience of motherhood and care exercised in the private realm of the family. They denounce liberalism for having constructed modern citizenship as the realm of the public, identified with men, and for having excluded women by relegating them to the private realm. According to this view, feminists should strive for a type of politics that is guided by the specific values of love, care, the recognition of needs, and friendship. One of the clearest attempts to offer an alternative to liberal politics grounded in feminine values is to be found in "Maternal Thinking" and "Social Feminism" principally represented by Sara Ruddick and Jean Bethke Elshtain.[4] Feminist politics, they argue, should privilege the identity of "women as mothers" and the private realm of the family. The family is seen as having moral superiority over the public domain of politics because it constitutes our common humanity. For Elshtain, "the family remains the locus of the deepest and most resonant human ties, the most enduring hopes, the most intractable conflicts."[5] She considers that it is in the family that we should look for a new political morality to replace liberal individualism. In women's experience in the private realm as mothers, she says, a new model for the activity of citizenship is to be found. The maternalists want us to abandon the male liberal politics of the public informed by the abstract point of view of justice and the "generalized other" and adopt instead a feminist politics of the private, informed by the virtues of love, intimacy, and concern for the "concrete other" specific to the family.

An excellent critique of such an approach has been provided by Mary Dietz[6] who shows that Elshtain fails to provide a theoretical argument which links maternal thinking and the social practice of mothering to democratic values and democratic politics. Dietz argues that maternal virtues cannot be political because they are connected with and emerge from an activity that is special and distinctive. They are the expression of an unequal relation between mother and child which is also an intimate, exclusive, and particular activity. Democratic citizenship, on the contrary, should be collective, inclusive, and generalized. Since democracy is a condition in which individuals aim at being equals, the mother–child relationship cannot provide an adequate model of citizenship.

Yet a different feminist critique of liberal citizenship is provided by Carole Pateman.[7] It is more sophisticated, but shares some common features with "Maternal Thinking." Pateman's tone bears the traces of radical feminism, for the accent is put, not on the mother/child relation, but on the man/woman antagonism.

Citizenship is, according to Pateman, a patriarchal category: who a "citizen" is, what a citizen does and the arena within which he acts have been constructed in the masculine image. Although women in liberal democracies are now citizens, formal citizenship has been won within a structure of patriarchal power in which women's qualities and tasks are still devalued. Moreover, the call for women's distinctive capacities to be integrated fully into the public world of citizenship faces what she calls the "Wollstonecraft dilemma": to demand equality is to accept the patriarchal conception of citizenship which implies that women must become like men, while to insist that women's distinctive attributes, capacities, and activities be given expression and valued as contributing to citizenshp is to demand the impossible because such difference is precisely what patriarchal citizenship excludes.

Pateman sees the solution to this dilemma in the elaboration of a "sexually differentiated" conception of citizenship that would recognize women *as* women, with their bodies and all that they symbolize. For Pateman this entails giving political significance to the capacity that men lack: to create life, which is to say, *motherhood*. She declares that this capacity should be treated with equal political relevance for defining citizenship as what is usually considered the ultimate test of citizenship: a man's willingness to fight and to die for his country. She considers that the traditional patriarchal way of posing an alternative, where either the separation or the sameness of the sexes is valorized, needs to be overcome by a new way of posing the question of women. This can be done through a conception of citizenship that recognizes both the specificity of womanhood and the common humanity of men and women. Such a view "that gives due weight to sexual difference in a context of civil equality, requires the rejection of a unitary (i.e., masculine) conception of the individual, abstracted from our embodied existence and from the patriarchal division between the private and the public."[8] What feminists should aim for is the elaboration of a sexually differentiated conception of individuality and citizenship that would include "women *as* women in a context of civil equality and active citizenship."[9]

Pateman provides many very interesting insights into the patriarchal bias of the social contract theorists and the way in which the liberal individual has been constructed according to the male image. I consider that her own solution, however, is unsatisfactory. Despite all her provisos about the historically constructed aspects of sexual difference, her view still postulates the existence of some kind of essence corresponding to women *as* women. Indeed, her proposal for a differentiated citizenship that recognizes the specificity of womanhood rests on the identification of women *as* women with motherhood. There are for her two basic types of individuality that should be expressed in two different forms of citizenship: men *as* men and women *as* women. The problem according to her is that the category of the "individual," while based on the male model, is presented as the universal form of individuality. Feminists must uncover that false universality by asserting the existence of two sexually differentiated forms of universality; this is the only way to resolve the "Wollstonecraft dilemma," and to break free from the patriarchal alternatives of "othering" and "saming."

I agree with Pateman that the modern category of the individual has been constructed in a manner that postulates a universalist, homogeneous "public" that relegates all particularity and difference to the "private" and that this has very negative consequences for women. I do not believe, however, that the remedy is to replace it by a sexually differentiated, "bi-gendered" conception of the individual and to bring women's so-called specific tasks into the very definition of citizenship. It seems to me that such a solution remains trapped in the very problematic that Pateman wants to challenge. She affirms that the separation between public and private is the founding moment of modern patriarchalism because the separation of private and public is the separation of the world of natural subjection, i.e. women, from the world of conventional relations and individuals, i.e. men. The feminine, private world of nature, particularity, differentiation, inequality, emotion, love and ties of blood is set apart from the public, universal – and masculine – realm of convention, civil equality and freedom, reason, consent and contract.[10] It is for that reason that childbirth and motherhood have been presented as the antithesis of citizenship and that they have become the symbol of everything natural that cannot be part of the "public" but must remain in a separate sphere. By asserting the political value of motherhood, Pateman intends to overcome that distinction and contribute to the deconstruction of the patriarchal conception of citizenship and private and public life. As a result of her essentialism, however, she never deconstructs the very opposition of men/women. This is the reason that she ends up, like the maternalists, proposing an inadequate conception of what should be a democratic politics informed by feminism. This is why she can assert that "the most profound and complex problem for political theory and practice is how the two bodies of humankind and feminine and masculine individuality can be fully incorporated into political life."[11]

My own view is completely different. I want to argue that the limitations of the modern conception of citizenship should be remedied, not by making sexual difference politically relevant to its definition, but by constructing a new conception of citizenship where sexual difference should become effectively nonpertinent. This, of course, requires a conception of the social agent in the way that I have defended earlier, as the articulation of an ensemble of subject positions, corresponding to the multiplicity of social relations in which it is inscribed. This multiplicity is constructed within specific discourses which have no necessary relation but only contingent and precarious forms of articulation. There is no reason why sexual difference should be pertinent in all social relations. To be sure, today many different practices, discourses and institutions do construct men and women (differentially), and the masculine/feminine distinction exists as a pertinent one in many fields. But this does not imply that it should remain the case, and we can perfectly imagine sexual difference becoming irrelevant in many social relations where it is currently found. This is indeed the objective of many feminist struggles.

I am not arguing in favor of a total disappearance of sexual difference as a pertinent distinction; I am not saying either that equality between men and women requires gender-neutral social relations, and it is clear that, in many cases, to treat men and women equally implies treating them differentially. My thesis is that, in the domain of politics, and as far as citizenship is concerned, sexual difference should not be a pertinent distinction. I am at one with Pateman in criticizing the liberal, male conception of modern citizenship but I believe that what a project of radical and plural democracy needs is not a sexually differentiated model of citizenship in which the specific tasks of both men and women would be valued equally, but a truly different conception of what it is to be a citizen and to act as a member of a democratic political community.

A radical democratic conception of citizenship

The problems with the liberal conception of citizenship are not limited to those concerning women, and feminists committed to a project of radical and plural democracy should engage with all of them. Liberalism has contributed to the formulation of the notion of universal citizenship, based on the assertion that all individuals are born free and equal, but it has also reduced citizenship to a merely legal status, indicating the rights that the individual holds against the state. The way those rights are exercised is irrelevant as long as their holders do not break the law or interfere with the rights of others. Notions of public-spiritedness, civic activity and political participation in a community of equals are alien to most liberal thinkers. Besides, the public realm of modern citizenship was constructed in a universalistic and rationalistic manner that precluded the recognition of division and antagonism and that relegated to the private all particularity and difference. The distinction public/private, central as it was for the assertion of individual liberty, acted therefore as a powerful principle of exclusion. Through the identification between the private and the domestic, it played indeed an important role in the subordination of women. Recently, several feminists and other critics of liberalism have been looking to the civic republican tradition for a different, more active conception of citizenship that emphasizes the value of political participation and the notion of a common good, prior to and independent of individual desires and interests. Nevertheless, feminists should be aware of the limitations of such an approach and of the potential dangers that a communitarian type of politics presents for the struggle of many oppressed groups. The communitarian insistence on a substantive notion of the common good and shared moral values is incompatible with the pluralism that is constitutive of modern democracy and that I consider to be necessary to deepen the democratic revolution and accommodate the multiplicity of present democratic demands. The problems with the liberal construction of the public/private distinction would not be solved by discarding it, but only by reformulating it in a more adequate way. Moreover, the centrality of the notion of rights for a modern conception of the citizen should be acknowledged, even though these must be complemented by a more active sense of political participation and of belonging to a political community.[12]

The view of radical and plural democracy that I want to put forward sees citizenship as a form of political identity that consists in the identification with the political principles of modern pluralist democracy, namely, the assertion of liberty and equality for all. It would be a common political identity of persons who might be engaged in many different purposive enterprises and with differing conceptions of the good, but who are bound by their common identification with a given interpretation of a set of ethico-political values. Citizenship is not just one identity among others, as it is in liberalism, nor is it the dominant identity that overrides all others, as it is in Civic Republicanism. Instead, it is an articulating principle that affects the different subject positions of the social agent while allowing for a plurality of specific allegiances and for the respect of individual liberty. In this view, the public/private distinction is not abandoned, but constructed in a different way. The distinction does not correspond to discrete, separate spheres; every situation is an encounter between "private" and "public" because every enterprise is private while never immune from the public conditions prescribed by the principles of citizenship. Wants, choices and decisions are private because they are the responsibility of each individual, but performances are public because they have to subscribe to the conditions specified by a specific understanding of the ethico-political principles of the regime which provide the "grammar" of the citizen's conduct.[13]

It is important to stress here that if we affirm that the exercise of citizenship consists in identifying with the ethico-political principles of modern democracy, we must also recognize that there can be as many forms of citizenship as there are interpretations of those principles and that a radical democratic interpretation is one among others. A radical democratic interpretation will emphasize the numerous social relations in which situations of domination exist that must be challenged if the principles of liberty and equality are to apply. It indicates the common recognition by the different groups struggling for an extension and radicalization of democracy that they have a common concern. This should lead to the articulation of the democratic demands found in a variety of movements: women, workers, blacks, gays, ecological, as well as other "new social movements." The aim is to construct a "we" as radical democratic citizens, a collective political identity articulated through the principle of democratic *equivalence*. It must be stressed that such a relation of *equivalence* does not eliminate difference – that would be simple identity. It is only insofar as democratic differences are opposed to forces or discourses which negate all of them that these differences are substitutible for each other.

The view that I am proposing here is clearly different from the liberal as well as the civic republican one. It is not a gendered conception of citizenship, but neither is it a neutral one. It recognizes that every definition of a "we" implies the delimitation of a "frontier" and the designation of a "them." That definition of a "we" always takes place, then, in a context of diversity and conflict. Contrary to liberalism, which evacuates the idea of the common good, and Civic Republicanism, which reifies it, a radical democratic approach views the common good as a "vanishing point," something to which we must constantly refer when we are acting as citizens, but that can never be reached. The common good functions, on the one hand, as a "social imaginary": that is, as that for which the very impossibility of achieving full representation gives to it the role of an horizon which is the condition of possibility of any representation within the space that it delimits. On the other hand, it specifies what I have designated, following Wittgenstein, as a "grammar of conduct" that coincides with the allegiance to the constitutive ethico-political principles of modern democracy: liberty and equality for all. Yet, since those principles are open to many competing interpretations, one has to acknowledge that a fully inclusive political community can never be realized. There will always be a "constitutive outside," an exterior to the community that is the very condition of its existence. Once it is accepted that there cannot be a "we" without a "them" and that all forms of consensus are by necessity based on acts of exclusion, the question cannot be any more the creation of a fully inclusive community where antagonism, division, and conflict will have disappeared. Hence, we have to come to terms with the very impossibility of a full realization of democracy.

Such a radical democratic citizenship is obviously at odds with the "sexually differentiated" view of citizenship of Carole Pateman, but also with another feminist attempt to offer an alternative to the liberal view of the citizen: the "group differentiated" conception put forward by Iris Young.[14] Like Pateman, Young argues that modern citizenship has been constructed on a separation between "public" and "private" that presented the public as the realm of homogeneity and universality and relegated difference to the private. But she insists that this exclusion affects not only women but many other groups based on differences of ethnicity, race, age, disabilities, and so forth. For Young, the crucial problem is that the public realm of citizenship was presented as expressing a general will, a point of view that citizens held in common and that transcended their differences. Young argues in favor of a repoliticization of public life that would not require the creation of a public realm in which citizens leave behind their particular group affiliation and needs in order to discuss a presumed general interest or common good. In its place she proposes the creation of a "heterogeneous public" that provides mechanisms for the effective representation and recognition of the distinct voices and perspectives of those constituent groups that are oppressed or disadvantaged. In order to make such a project possible, she looks for a conception of normative reason that does not pretend to be impartial and universal and that does not oppose reason to affectivity and desire. She considers that, despite its limitations, Habermas's communicative ethics can contribute a good deal to its formulation.

Whereas I sympathize with Young's attempt to take account of other forms of oppression than the ones suffered by women, I nevertheless find her solution of "group differentiated citizenship" highly problematic. To begin with, the notion of a group that she identifies with comprehensive identities and ways of life might make sense for groups like Native Americans, but is completely inadequate as a description for many other groups whose demands she wants to take into account like women, the elderly, the differently abled, and others. She has an ultimately essentialist notion of "group," and this accounts for why, in spite of all her disclaimers, her view is not so different from the interest-group pluralism that she criticizes: there are groups with their interests and identities already given, and politics is not about the construction of new identities, but about finding ways to satisfy the demands of the various parts in a way acceptable to all. In fact, one could say that hers is a kind of "Habermasian version of interest group pluralism," according to which groups are not viewed as fighting for egoistic private interests but for justice, and where the emphasis is put on the need for argumentation and publicity. So politics in her work is still conceived as a process of dealing with already-constituted interests and identities while, in the approach that I am defending, the aim of a radical democratic citizenship should be the construction of a common political identity that would create the conditions for the establishment of a new hegemony articulated through new egalitarian social relations, practices and institutions. This cannot be achieved without the transformation of existing subject positions; this is the reason why the model of the rainbow coalition favored by Young can be seen only as a first stage toward the implementation of a radical democratic politics. It might indeed provide many opportunities for a dialogue among different oppressed groups, but for their demands to be construed around the principle of democratic equivalence, new identities need to be created: in their present state many of these demands are antithetical to each other, and their convergence can only result from a political process of hegemonic articulation, and not simply of free and undistorted communication.

Feminist politics and radical democracy

As I indicated at the outset, there has been a great deal of concern among feminists about the possibility of grounding a feminist politics once the existence of women *as* women is put into question. It has been argued that to abandon the idea of a feminine subject with a specific identity and definable interests was to pull the rug from under feminism as politics. According to Kate Soper,

> feminism, like any other politics, has always implied a banding together, a movement based on the solidarity and sisterhood of women, who are linked by perhaps very little else than their sameness and "common cause" as

women. If this sameness itself is challenged on the ground that there is no "presence" of womanhood, nothing that the term "woman" immediately expresses, and nothing instantiated concretely except particular women in particular situations, then the idea of a political community built around women – the central aspiration of the early feminist movement – collapses.[15]

I consider that Soper here construes an illegitimate opposition between two extreme alternatives: either there is an already given unity of "womanhood" on the basis of some *a priori* belonging or, if this is denied, no forms of unity and feminist politics can exist. The absence of a female essential identity and of a pregiven unity, however, does not preclude the construction of multiple forms of unity and common action. As the result of the construction of nodal points, partial fixations can take place and precarious forms of identification can be established around the category "women" that provide the basis for a feminist identity and a feminist struggle. We find in Soper a type of misunderstanding of the anti-essentialist position that is frequent in feminist writings and that consists in believing that the critique of an essential identity must necessarily lead to the rejection of any concept of identity whatsoever.[16]

In *Gender Trouble*, Judith Butler asks, "What new shape of politics emerges when identity as a common ground no longer constrains the discourse of feminist politics?"[17] My answer is that to visualize feminist politics in that way opens much greater opportunity for a democratic politics that aims at the articulation of the various different struggles against oppression. What emerges is the possibility of a project of radical and plural democracy.

To be adequately formulated, such a project requires discarding the essentialist idea of an identity of women *as* women as well as the attempt to ground a specific and strictly feminist politics. Feminist politics should be understood not as a separate form of politics designed to pursue the interests of women *as* women, but rather as the pursuit of feminist goals and aims within the context of a wider articulation of demands. Those goals and aims should consist in the transformation of all the discourses, practices and social relations where the category "woman" is constructed in a way that implies subordination. Feminism, for me, is the struggle for the equality of women. But this should not be understood as a struggle for realizing the equality of a definable empirical group with a common essence and identity, women, but rather as a struggle against the multiple forms in which the category "woman" is constructed in subordination. However, we must be aware of the fact that those feminist goals can be constructed in many different ways, according to the multiplicity of discourses in which they can be framed: Marxist, liberal, conservative, radical-separatist, radical-democratic, and so on. There are, therefore, by necessity many feminisms and any attempt to find the "true" form of feminist politics should be abandoned. I believe that feminists can contribute to politics a reflection on the conditions for creating an effective equality of women. Such a reflection is bound to be influenced by the existing political and theoretical discourses. Instead of trying to prove that a given form of feminist discourse is the one that corresponds to the "real" essence of womanhood, one should intend to show how it opens better possibilities for an understanding of women's multiple forms of subordination.

My main argument here has been that, for feminists who are committed to a political project whose aim is to struggle against the forms of subordination which exist in many social relations, and not only in those linked to gender, an approach that permits us to understand how the subject is constructed through different discourses and subject positions is certainly more adequate than one that reduces our identity to one single position – be it class, race, or gender. This type of democratic project is also better served by a perspective that allows us to grasp the diversity of ways in which relations of power are constructed and helps us to reveal the forms of exclusion present in all pretensions to universalism and in claims to have found the true essence of rationality. This is why the critique of essentialism and all its different forms – humanism, rationalism, universalism – far from being an obstacle to the formulation of a feminist democratic project, is indeed the very condition of its possibility.

Notes

1 See the issue of the journal *Differences*, 1 (September 1989), entitled "The Essential Difference: Another Look at Essentialism" as well as the recent book by Diana Fuss, *Essentially Speaking* (New York: Routledge, 1989).

2 Ernesto Laclau and Chantal Mouffe, *Hegemony and Socialist Strategy: Towards a Radical Democratic Politics* (London: Verso, 1985).

3 For an interesting critique of the dilemma of equality versus difference which is inspired by a similar *problematique* to the one I am defending here, see Joan W. Scott *Gender and the Politics of History* (New York: Columbia University Press, 1988), Part IV. Among feminists the critique of essentialism was first developed by the journal *m/f* which during its eight years of existence (1978–86) made an invaluable contribution to feminist theory. I consider that it has not yet been superseded and that the editorials as well as the articles by Parveen Adams still represent the most forceful exposition of the anti-essentialist stance. A selection of the best articles from the 12 issues of *m/f* are reprinted in *The Woman in Question*, edited by Parveen Adams and Elisabeth Cowie (Cambridge, Mass.: MIT Press, 1990 and London: Verso, 1990).

4 Sara Ruddick, *Maternal Thinking* (London: Verso, 1989); Jean Bethke Elshtain, *Public Man, Private Woman* (Princeton: Princeton University Press, 1981).

5 Jean Bethke Elshtain, "On 'The Family Crisis'," *Democracy*, 3, 1 (Winter 1983) p. 138.

6 Mary G. Dietz, "Citizenship with a Feminist Face. The Problem with Maternal Thinking," *Political Theory*, 13, 1 (February 1985).

7 Carole Pateman, *The Sexual Contract* (Stanford: Stanford University Press, 1988), and *The Disorder of Women* (Cambridge: Polity Press, 1989), as well as numerous unpublished papers on which I will also be drawing, especially the following: "Removing Obstacles to Democracy: The Case of Patriarchy"; "Feminism and Participatory Democracy: Some Reflections on Sexual Difference and Citizenship"; "Women's Citizenship: Equality, Difference, Subordination."

8 Carole Pateman, "Feminism and Participatory Democracy," unpublished paper presented to the Meeting of the American Philosophical Association, St. Louis, Missouri, May 1986, p. 24.

9 *Ibid.*, p. 26.

10 Carole Pateman, "Feminism and Participatory Democracy," pp. 7–8.

11 Carole Pateman, *The Disorder of Women*, p. 53.
12 I analyze in more detail the debate between liberals and communitarians in my article "American Liberalism and Its Critics: Rawls, Taylor, Sandel and Walzer," *Praxis International*, 8, 2 (July 1988).
13 The conception of citizenship that I am presenting here is developed more fully in my "Democratic Citizenship and The Political Community," in *Community at Loose Ends*, edited by the Miami Theory Collective (Minneapolis, MN: University of Minnesota Press, 1991).
14 Iris Marion Young, "Impartiality and the Civic Public," in *Feminism as Critique*, edited by Seyla Benhabib and Drucilla Cornell (Minneapolis: University of Minnesota Press, 1987) and "Polity and Group Difference: A Critique of the Ideal of Universal Citizenship," *Ethics*, 99 (January 1989).
15 Kate Soper, "Feminism, Humanism and Postmodernism," *Radical Philosophy*, 55 (Summer 1990), pp. 11–17.
16 We find a similar confusion in Diana Fuss who, as Anna Marie Smith indicates in her review of *Essentially Speaking, Feminist Review*, 38 (Summer 1991), does not realize that the repetition of a sign can take place without an essentialist grounding. It is for that reason that she can affirm that constructionism is essentialist as far as it entails the repetition of the same signifiers across different contexts.
17 Judith Butler, *Gender Trouble: Feminism and the Subversion of Identity* (New York: Routledge, 1990), p. xi.

8

FOR A POLITICS OF NOMADIC IDENTITY (1994)[1]

As we approach the end of the century, we are witnessing a vast process of redefinition of collective identities and the creation of new political frontiers. This is, of course, linked to the collapse of communism and the disappearance of the democracy/ totalitarianism opposition which had, at least since the end of the Second World War, served as the principal political boundary, enabling us to differentiate friend from foe. This, however, presents us with a double difficulty.

1 In Eastern Europe the unity that was forged in the fight against communism has evaporated and we are now seeing the multiplication of identities based on ethnic, regional and religious antagonisms. These represent a formidable challenge in the construction of a pluralist democracy in these countries.
2 In the West the meaning of democracy was founded on the differences established between its own system of governance and those of the 'other' that rejected it. Thus, the identity of democracy has now been destabilized by the loss of its erstwhile enemy; it has to be redefined by the creation of a new political frontier.

This situation tends to promote the growth of the extreme right, who can focus on a new enemy: the internal enemy represented by immigrants, particularly those who differentiate themselves by their ethnic origin or religion. These foreigners are portrayed as endangering national identity and sovereignty by various political movements which are doing their best to produce new collective identities and to re-create a political frontier by means of a nationalist and xenophobic discourse.

Today's democracies are thus confronted with a great challenge. In order to face up to this challenge, they must stop ignoring the political and must not delude themselves about the possibility of a consensus which would banish antagonism forever. This means questioning the liberal rationalism which is at the root of the current lack of vision afflicting political thought as it attempts to come to terms with the great upheavals taking place in the world today. It is as if the West were expecting to celebrate the ultimate victory for liberal democracy but can now only stand stunned by the conflicts over ethnic origin, religion and identity which, according to their theories, should be things of the past. In place of the generalization of post-conventional identities so dear to Habermas, and the disappearance of antagonisms proclaimed by liberals, today we can see only the multiplication of specificities and the emergence of new rivalries.

Some try to explain the situation as the perverse legacy of totalitarianism, others as a so-called 'return of the archaic', as if it were merely a temporary delay on the road leading to the universalization of liberal democracy. As 'the end of History' has already been declared, many seem to think that all this is no more than a slight hiccup, a bad spell to get through before rationality finds its feet again and imposes its order. In other words, one last desperate cry of the political before it is definitively destroyed by the forces of law and universal reason.

It is clearly the political itself and the question of its elimination which is at stake here. And it is the inability of liberal thought to understand the nature of the political and the fundamental part played by antagonism which makes it blind to the true nature of the present situation. This situation requires a clean break with the objectivism and essentialism which dominate political analysis. But liberal thought employs a logic of the social based on a conception of being as presence, and which conceives of objectivity as being inherent to things themselves. This is why it is impossible for liberal thought to recognize that there can only be an identity when it is constructed as a 'difference', and that any social objectivity is constituted by the enactment of power. What it refuses to admit is that any form of social objectivity is ultimately political and must bear the traces of the acts of exclusion which govern its constitution.

The political cannot be grasped by liberal rationalism as it shows the limits of any rational consensus, and reveals that any consensus is based on acts of exclusion. Liberalism affirms that general interest results from the free play of private interests, and its concept of politics is of the establishment of a compromise between the different competing forces in a society. Individuals are portrayed as rational beings driven by the maximization of their own interests and basically acting in the political world in an instrumental way. It is the idea of the market applied to the political; interests are already defined independently from the political; so what is important is the process of allocation which allows a consensus to be created between the different participants. Other liberals, those who rebel against this model and who want to create a link between politics and morality, believe that it is possible to create a rational and universal consensus by means of free discussion. They believe that by relegating disruptive issues to the private sphere, a rational agreement on principles should be enough to administer the pluralism present in modern society.

According to this rationalist theory, everything to do with passions and with antagonism which might lead to violence is thought of as archaic and irrational, the remains of a bygone age where 'soft commerce' had not yet established the superiority of interests over passions.

But this attempt to annihilate the political is doomed to failure because politics cannot be domesticated in this way. As was understood by Carl Schmitt – a man whose views it would be wrong to ignore because of his subsequent political activities – the political derives its energy from the most diverse sources and 'every religious, moral, economic, ethical, or other antithesis transforms into a political one if it is sufficiently strong to group human beings effectively according to friend and enemy' (Schmitt 1976, p. 37).

Confronted with the rise of particularisms and the resurgence of an ethnic and exclusive nationalism, the defence and extension of the democratic project require that we take multicultural issues into account. This means tackling the question of different types of identities in a new way, based on an understanding of the political: this is inevitably impossible for those who believe in the liberal rationalist and individualist conception. The latter does its utmost to get rid of the political as the domain of power struggles, violence and confrontations with the enemy. But the political cannot be made to disappear simply by denying it; such a rejection leads only to impotence – the impotence which characterizes liberal thought when it finds itself confronted with a multiplication of different forms of demands for identity. To solve this dilemma, we must understand that the condition governing the creation of any identity is the affirmation of a difference. Then we have to ask ourselves what type of relationship can be established between identity and otherness, to defuse the ever-present danger of exclusion which this identity–difference dynamic inevitably contains.

I shall use the concept of the 'constitutive outside' (*exterieur constitutif*) as a basis for tackling these different issues. This concept unites a number of the themes expounded by Jacques Derrida around his notions of 'supplement', 'trace' and '*différance*'. Its aim is to highlight the relationship between any identity and the fact that the creation of identity often implies the establishment of a hierarchy: for example, between form and matter; essence and contingency; black and white; man and woman. Once we have understood that every identity is relational and that the affirmation of a difference is a precondition for the existence of any identity (i.e. the perception of something 'other' than it which will constitute its 'exterior'), then we can begin to understand why such a relationship may always become a terrain for antagonism. Indeed, when it comes to the creation of a collective identity – basically the creation of an 'us' by the demarcation of a 'them' – then there will always be the possibility that this 'us/them' relationship will become one of 'friend and enemy', i.e. one of antagonism. This happens when the 'other', who up until now has been considered simply as different, starts to be perceived as someone who is rejecting 'my' identity and who is threatening 'my' existence. From that moment on, any form of us/them relationship – whether it be religious, ethnic, economic or other – becomes political.

Looking at the issue of identity in this way transforms the way we think of the political. The political can no longer be located as present only in a certain type of institution, as representative of a sphere or level of society. It should rather be understood as a dimension inherent in all human society which stems from our very ontological condition. To clarify this new approach, it is helpful to distinguish between 'the political' (which describes the dimension of antagonism and hostility between humans – an antagonism which can take many different forms and can emerge in any form of social relation) and 'politics' (which seeks to establish a certain order and to organize human co-existence in conditions that are permanently conflictual because they are affected by 'the political'). This view, which attempts to keep together the two meanings encompassed by the term 'politics' – that of 'polemos' and that of 'polis' – is totally foreign to liberal thought; that, incidentally, is the reason why liberal thought is powerless in the face of antagonism. But I believe that the future of democracy points towards the recognition of this dimension of the political, for to protect and consolidate democracy we have to see that politics consists of 'domesticating hostility' and of trying to defuse the potential antagonism inherent in human relations.

So politics concerns public activity and the formation of collective identities. Its aim is to create an 'us' in a context of diversity and conflict. But to construct an 'us', one has to be able to differentiate it from a 'them'. That is why the crucial question for democratic politics is not how to arrive at a consensus without exclusion, or how to create an 'us' which would not have a corresponding 'them', but rather it is how to establish this 'us' and 'them' discrimination in a way that is compatible with pluralist democracy. This presupposes that the 'other' is no longer seen as an enemy to be destroyed, but as a 'counterpart' who could be in our place in the future. The aim is to transform an antagonism into an agonism. Here we might take inspiration from the thoughts of Elias Canetti, who in *Crowds and Power* showed that the parliamentary system exploits the psychological structure of warring armies by presenting a combat where actual killing is rejected in favour of allowing the opinion of the majority to decide on the victor. According to Canetti:

> The actual vote is decisive, as the moment in which the one is really measured against the other. It is all that is left of the original lethal clash and is played out in many forms, with threats, abuse and physical provocation which may lead to blows or missiles. But the counting of the vote ends the battle.
>
> (Canetti 1973, p. 220)

Far from seeing democracy as something natural, arising independently and self-evidently as a necessary corollary to mankind's moral evolution, it is important that we realize its improbable and uncertain character.

Democracy is a fragile construction: never definitively acquired, it is a conquest which has to be forever defended against possible attacks. The prime task of democratic politics is not to eliminate passions, nor to relegate them to the private sphere in order to render rational consensus possible, but to mobilize these passions, and give them a democratic outlet. Instead of jeopardizing democracy, agonistic confrontation is its very condition of existence. Of course, democracy needs a certain degree of consensus – at least the rules of the democratic game have to be respected if it is to survive, but it also needs the constitution of collective identities around clearly differentiated positions. Voters must be given true choices and real alternatives amongst which they can choose. If Niklas Luhman is right and modern democracy does indeed essentially hinge on the 'splitting of the summit' which is created by the distinction between the government and the opposition, then we will also see the danger which the increasingly blurred boundaries between right- and left-wing opposition constitute. Unclear dividing lines block the creation of democratic political identities and fuel the disenchantment with traditional political parties. Thus they prepare the ground for various forms of populist and anti-liberal movements that target nationalist, religious and ethnic divides. When the agonistic dynamism of the pluralist system is unable to unfold because of a shortage of democratic identities with which one can identify, there is a risk that this will multiply confrontations over essentialist identities and non-negotiable moral values. It is only when we acknowledge that any identity is always relational and that it is defined in terms of difference that we are able to ask the crucial question: how can we fight the tendency towards exclusion? Again, Derrida's view might help us to find an answer. As the notion of a 'constitutive outside' itself implies, it is impossible to draw an absolute distinction between interior and exterior. Every identity is irremediably destabilized by its 'exterior'. This is an important point and I should therefore like to examine its political implications.

On a general philosophical level, it is obvious that if the constitutive outside is present inside every objectivity as its always real possibility, then the interior itself is something purely contingent, which reveals the structure of the mere possibility of every objective order. This questions every essentialist conception of identity and forecloses every attempt conclusively to define identity or objectivity. Inasmuch as objectivity always depends on an absent otherness, it is always necessarily echoed and contaminated by this otherness. Identity cannot, therefore, belong to one person alone, and no one belongs to a single identity. We might go further, and argue that not only are there no 'natural' and 'original' identities, since every identity is the result of a constituting process, but that this process itself must be seen as one of permanent hybridization and nomadization. Identity is, in effect, the result of a multitude of interactions that take place inside a space whose outlines are not clearly defined. Numerous feminist studies and investigations inspired by 'postcolonial' concerns have shown that this process is always one of 'over-determination' which establishes highly intricate links between the many forms of identity and a complex network of differences. For an appropriate definition of identity, we need to take into account both the multiplicity of discourses and the power structure that affects it, as well as the complex dynamic of complicity and resistance which underlies the practices in which this identity is implicated. Instead of seeing the different forms of identity as allegiances to a place or as a property, we ought to realise that they are the stake of a power struggle.

What we commonly call 'cultural identity' is both the scene and the object of political struggles. The social existence of a group is always constructed through conflict. It is one of the principal areas in which hegemony exists, because the definition of the cultural identity of a group, by reference to a specific system of contingent and particular social relations, plays a major role in the creation of 'hegemonic nodal points'.[2] These partially define the meaning of a 'signifying chain', allowing us to control the stream of signifiers, and temporarily to fix the discursive field. As for 'national' identities, the perspective based on concepts of hegemony and articulation allows us to come to grips with those identities, to transform them instead of rejecting them, whether in the name of anti-essentialism or universalism. In fact, it could be dangerous to ignore the libidinal cathexis which can be mobilized around the signifier 'nation', and it is a futile hope to expect the creation of a post 'conventional' identity. The struggle against the exclusive type of ethnic nationalism can be carried on only if some other form of nationalism is articulated, a kind of 'civic' nationalism, upholding pluralism and democratic values. Here we find questions that are of great import for democratic politics, and we should heed the warning offered us by the difficulties encountered in reunified Germany, namely that liberal and rationalist illusions of a 'post-nationalist' identity can have dangerous consequences.

Contrary to what is popularly believed, a 'European' identity, conceived as a homogeneous identity which could replace all other identifications and allegiances, will not be able to solve our problems. On the contrary, if we think of it in terms of 'aporia', of double genitive, as an 'experience of the impossible', to use Derrida's words from his *L'Autre cap*, then the notion of a 'European' identity could be a catalyst for a promising process, not unlike what Merleau-Ponty called 'lateral universalism', which implies that the universal lies at the very heart of specificities and differences, and that it is inscribed in respect for diversity. If we conceive of this European identity as a 'difference to oneself', as 'one's own culture' as 'someone else's culture' (Derrida 1991, p. 16), then we are in effect envisaging an identity that accommodates otherness, that demonstrates the porosity of frontiers, and opens up towards that 'exterior' which makes it possible. By accepting that only hybridity creates us as separate entities, it affirms and upholds the nomadic character of every identity.

By resisting the ever-present temptation to construct identity in terms of exclusion, and recognizing that identities comprise a multiplicity of elements, and that they are dependent and interdependent, we can 'convert an antagonism of identity into the agonism of difference', as William Connolly (1991, p. 178) put it, and thus stop the potential for violence that exists in every construction of an 'us and them'. Only if peoples' allegiances are multiplied and their loyalties pluralized will it be possible to create a truly 'agonistic pluralism'. Because where identities are multiplied, passions are divided.

If a discussion of identity is to be of real significance, it must be placed in the wider context of the paradoxes of pluralist democracy. Indeed, there is in such a democracy something enigmatic and paradoxical which several of its critics have emphasized and which stems from the articulation between liberalism and democracy which it has established. Undoubtedly there are two types of logic which come into conflict with each other because the final realization of the logic of democracy, which is a logic founded on identity and equivalence, is made impossible by the liberal logic of pluralism and difference, because the latter prevents the establishment of a complete system of identifications.

These two logics are incompatible, yet this does not mean that the system as such is not viable. On the contrary, it is precisely the existence of this *tension* between the logic of identity and the logic of difference which makes pluralist democracy a regime particularly suited to the indeterminacy of modern politics. There is no doubt that due to this articulation between liberalism and democracy, liberal logic – which tends to construct every identity as positivity and as a difference – necessarily subverts the totalization which is the aim of the democratic logic of equivalence. Far from complaining about this, we should rejoice, because it is this tension between the logic of equivalence and the logic of difference, between equality and liberty, and between our identity as individuals and our identity as citizens, which provides the best protection against every attempt to effect either a complete fusion or a total separation. We should therefore avoid suppressing this tension because if we try to eliminate the political we risk destroying democracy. The experience of modern democracy is based on the realization that these conflicting logics exist – one aiming to achieve complete equivalence, the other to preserve all differences – and that their articulation is necessary. This articulation must be constantly recreated and renegotiated: there is no point of equilibrium where final harmony could be attained. It is only in this precarious 'in-between' that we can experience pluralism, that is to say, that this democracy will always be 'to come', to use Derrida's expression, which emphasizes not only the unrealized possibilities but also the radical impossibility of final completion. Far from creating the necessary background for pluralism, any belief in a final resolution of all conflict, even if it is conceived as an asymptotic approach to the regulative idea of non-distorted communication as expounded by Habermas, will put it in danger because paradoxically the very moment that it was completed would also be the moment of its destruction. True pluralist democracy is therefore to be seen as an 'impossible good', that is to say, as something that exists only as long as it cannot be perfectly achieved. The existence of pluralism implies the permanence of conflict and antagonism and these should not be seen as empirical obstacles which would make impossible the perfect realization of an ideal existing in a harmony which we cannot reach because we will never be capable of perfectly coinciding with our rational selves.

It is therefore important for democracy and for the construction of democratic identities to have a framework that allows us to think of difference as being the condition of both possibility and impossibility to create unity and totality. This framework invites us to abandon the dangerous illusion of a possible resumption of otherness in a unified and harmonious whole, and to admit that the other and its otherness are irreducible. This is an otherness which cannot be domesticated, and as Rodolphe Gasché has said:

This alterity forever undermines, but also makes possible, the dream of autonomy achieved through a reflexive coiling upon self, since it names a structural precondition of such a desired state, a precondition that represents the limit of such a possibility.

(Gasché 1986, p. 105)

Notes

1 This paper was originally published in a different translation in *REPRESENTATIVES: Andrea Fraser, Christian Philipp Muller, Gerwald Rockenschaub*, the catalogue of the Austrian Pavilion at the 45th Venice Biennale, 1993 (Bundesministerium für Unterricht und Kunst, Vienna, 1993).
2 For a discussion of this concept, see Laclau and Mouffe (1985), ch. 3.

References

Canetti, Elias. 1973. *Crowds and Power.* Harmondsworth: Penguin Books.
Connolly, William E. 1991. *Identity/Difference.* Ithaca, NY: Cornell University Press.
Derrida, Jacques. 1991. *L'Autre cap.* Paris: Editions de Minuit.
Gasché, Rodolphe. 1986. *The Taint of the Mirror: Derrida and the Philosophy of Reflection.* Cambridge, MA: Harvard University Press.
Laclau, Ernesto, and Mouffe, Chantal. 1985. *Hegemony and Socialist Strategy: Towards a Radical Democratic Politics.* London: Verso.
Schmitt, Carl. 1976. *The Concept of the Political.* New Brunswick, NJ: Rutgers University Press.

PART III
The Political

A politics beyond consensus

9

THE RADICAL CENTRE

A politics without adversary (1998)[1]

Tales of the end of the right/left distinction have been with us for some time. Since the late 1980s this was accelerated by the collapse of communism – we have witnessed a clear move towards the centre in most socialist parties. But with New Labour in power a new twist has been added to this tale. We are told that a third way is now available: the 'radical centre'. After promoting the label of 'centre-left', Blair and his advisers now seem to prefer avoiding altogether any reference to the left. Since its victory, New Labour has begun to market itself as a radical movement, albeit of a new type. The novelty of this third way of 'radical centrism' supposedly consists in occupying a position which, by being located above left and right, manages to overcome the old antagonisms. Unlike the traditional centre, which lies in the middle of the spectrum between right and left, this is a centre that transcends the traditional left/right division by articulating themes and values from both sides in a new synthesis.

This radical centre, presented as the new model for progressive politics and as the most promising alternative to old-fashioned social democracy, draws on ideas developed by Anthony Giddens in his book *Beyond Left and Right* (1994). Socialism, argues Giddens, was based on a 'cybernetic model' of social life which worked reasonably well in a world of 'simple modernisation', but which cannot work any more in a globalised, post-traditional social order characterised by the expansion of social reflexivity. In this brave new world of 'reflexive modernisation' we need a new type of radical politics, a 'generative' politics that allows people to make things happen and provides a framework for the life-political decisions of the individuals. Democracy should become 'dialogic' and, far from being limited to the political sphere, it should reach the various areas of personal life, aiming at a 'democracy of the emotions'. This new 'life' politics overcomes, in his view, the traditional left/right divide since it draws from philosophical conservatism while preserving some of the core values usually associated with socialism.

Alas, when examined more closely, stripped of its theoretical jargon and New Age rhetorical flourish, this radical centrism is oddly reminiscent of the strategy of 'triangulation' designed by Dick Morris for Bill Clinton's second term campaign. In the case of Clinton there is no doubt that as an instrument of electoral propaganda it worked. By drawing on Republican ideas that resonated with voters – taxes, crime, welfare and the federal budget – and articulating them with leftist policies on abortion, education and the environment, Clinton managed to neutralise his adversaries and adroitly turn the tables in his favour. But who would want to call this radical politics?

Let me make clear at the outset that the problem I see in this notion of the radical centre is not its rejection of traditional left solutions. The critique of statism and productivism is far from new, and many people who still identify with the left have long been aware of the shortcomings of traditional social democracy. The problem is not in the radical centre's embracing some conservative themes either. The postmodern critique of Enlightenment epistemology has for some time stressed the possibility of, and the need to, dissociate the left project from its rationalistic premises. Several attempts to reformulate the aims of the left in terms of 'radical and plural democracy' have pointed out how, by helping us to problematise the idea of progress inherited from the Enlightenment, traditional conservative philosophers could contribute to the elaboration of a radical politics.

What is really the problem with the advocates of the 'radical centre' is, I believe, their claim that the left/right divide, an inheritance of 'simple modernisation', is no longer relevant in our era of 'reflexive modernisation'. By asserting that a radical politics today should transcend this divide and conceive democratic life as a dialogue, they imply that we live in a society which is no longer structured by social division. Relations of power and their constitutive role in society are disregarded; the conflicts that they entail are reduced to a simple competition between interests which can be harmonised through dialogue. This is the typical liberal perspective that envisages democracy as a struggle among elites, taking place in a neutral terrain, thereby making adversary forces invisible and reducing politics to an exchange of arguments and the negotiation of compromises. I want to argue that to present such a view of politics as 'radical' is disingenuous, and that instead of being conducive to a greater democracy the radical centrism advocated by New Labour is in fact a renunciation of the basic tenet of radical politics: the definition of the adversary.

Conflict and modern democracy

One of the main problems nowadays is that the left's coming to terms with the importance of pluralism, and of liberal democratic institutions, has been accompanied by the mistaken belief that this means abandoning any attempt to offer an alternative to the present hegemonic order. Hence the sacralisation of consensus, the blurring of the left/right distinction and the present urge of many left parties to locate themselves at the centre. But this is to miss a crucial point, not only about the primary reality of strife in social life, but also about the integrative role which conflict plays in modern democracy. The specificity of modern democracy lies in the recognition and the legitimation of conflict and the refusal to suppress it through the imposition of an authoritarian order. Breaking with the symbolic representation of society as an organic body – which is characteristic of the holist mode of social organisation – a democratic society asserts pluralism and makes room for the expression of conflicting interests and values. A well-functioning democracy calls for a vibrant clash of democratic political positions. If this is missing there is always the danger that this democratic confrontation will be replaced by a confrontation between non-negotiable moral values or essentialist forms of identifications as is the case with identity politics. Too much emphasis on consensus, together with aversion towards confrontations, leads to apathy and to disaffection with political participation. Worse still, it may backfire with the result being an explosion of antagonisms unmanageable by the democratic process. This is why a vibrant democratic life requires real debate about possible alternatives. In other words while consensus is indeed necessary, it must be accompanied by dissent. There is no contradiction in saying that, as some would pretend. Consensus is needed on the institutions which are constitutive of democracy, but there will always be disagreement concerning the way social justice should be implemented in and through these institutions. In a pluralist democracy such disagreement should be considered legitimate and indeed welcome. We can agree on the importance of 'liberty and equality for all', while disagreeing sharply about their meaning and the way they should be implemented.

It is precisely this kind of disagreement which provides the stuff of democratic politics, and it is what the struggle between left and right should be about. This is why, instead of giving up 'left' and 'right' as outdated terms, we should redefine them. When political frontiers become blurred, the dynamics of politics are obstructed and the constitution of distinctive political identities is hindered. Disaffection towards political parties sets in and in turn discourages participation in the political process. Alas, as we have begun to witness in many countries, the result is not a more mature, reconciled society, but the growth of other types of collective identities around religious, nationalist or ethnic forms of identifications. Antagonisms can take many forms, and it is illusory to believe that they could ever be eliminated. This is why it is preferable to give them a political outlet within a pluralistic democratic system. The deplorable spectacle of the United States with the trivialisation of political stakes, reduced to the unmasking of sex scandals, provides a good example of the degeneration of the democratic public sphere. The focus on Clinton's sexual history is a direct consequence of this new kind of bland, homogenised political world resulting from the effects of triangulation. The development of a moralistic discourse and the obsessive unveiling of scandals, as well as the growth of various types of religious integrisms, are too often the consequence of the void created in political life by the absence of democratic forms of identifications informed by competing political values.

However, the problem is not specific to the US. A look at other countries where, because of different traditions, the sexual card cannot be played in the same way as in the Anglo-American world shows that the crusade against corruption and shabby deals can play a similar role in replacing the missing political line of demarcation between adversaries. In other circumstances yet, the political frontier might be drawn around religious identities or around non-negotiable moral values, as in the case of abortion. But in all cases what this reveals is a democratic deficit created by the blurring of the left/right divide and the trivialisation of political discourse.

Another, perhaps more worrying, consequence of the same phenomenon is the increasing role played by extreme right-wing parties in many European countries. Indeed I submit that the rise of the far-right in France and Austria, for instance, should be understood in the context of the 'consensus at the centre' type of politics that has resulted in these particular countries from the growing ideological convergence between the main governing parties. This has allowed the National Front in France and the Freedom Party in Austria – the only parties to challenge the dominant consensus – to appear as anti-Establishment forces representing the will of the people. Thanks to a skilful populist rhetoric, they have been able to articulate many demands of the ordinary people, scorned as retrograde by the modernising elites, and they are trying to present themselves as the only guarantors of the sovereignty of the people. Such a situation, I believe, would not have been possible had more real political choices been available within the traditional democratic spectrum.

Politics and the political

Unfortunately, political theory, dominated as it is by a rationalistic and individualistic perspective, is completely unable to help us understand what is happening. Hence the urgency to develop an alternative approach. Against the views that envisage democracy as a 'dialogue', it is important to grasp the role of power relations in society and the ever present possibility of antagonism. In order to begin delineating a different conception of politics, one which acknowledges the centrality of antagonism, it may be useful to make a distinction between 'the political' and 'politics'. By 'the political', I mean the potential antagonism inherent in social relations, antagonism which can manifest itself in many different forms. 'Politics' refers to the ensemble of discourses, institutions and practices whose objective is to establish an order, to organise human coexistence in a context that is always conflictual because of the presence of 'the political'. Politics is concerned with the formation of an 'us' as opposed to a 'them'. It aims at the creation of unity in a context which is always one of conflict and diversity.

Envisaged from that angle, the novelty of democratic politics is not the overcoming of this us/them opposition, but the different way in which it is established. A pluralist democratic order supposes that the opponent is not considered as an enemy to be destroyed but as an adversary whose existence is legitimate and must be tolerated. We will fight against her ideas but we will not put into question her right to defend them. This category of the adversary does not eliminate antagonism, though, and it should be distinguished from the liberal notion of the competitor with which it is sometimes identified. An adversary, we could say, is an enemy with whom we have in common a shared adhesion to the ethico-political principles of democracy while disagreeing about their interpretation and implementation. However, this disagreement is not one that could be resolved through rational argument because it involves power relations. Hence the antagonistic element in the relation.

To come to accept the position of the adversary is to undergo a radical change in political identity and it implies a shift in power relations. Certainly, compromises are possible and they are part of the process of politics, but these are only temporary respites in an ongoing confrontation in which it is impossible to satisfy everybody. There is a distinction which I take to be crucial for grasping the specificity of modern democratic politics: the distinction between antagonism and agonism. A relation of antagonism is one that takes place between enemies, while a relation of agonism takes place between adversaries. Against the two dominant models of democratic politics (the 'aggregative' one that reduces politics to the negotiation of interests, and the 'deliberative' or 'dialogic' one which believes that decisions on matters of common concern should result from the free and unconstrained public deliberation of all) I envisage democratic politics as a form of 'agonistic pluralism'. This is a way to envisage democracy which, starting with the recognition of power relations and the conflicts that they entail, stresses that in modern democratic politics the crucial problem is how to transform antagonism into agonism. In other words, the aim of democratic institutions from this perspective is not to establish a rational consensus in the public sphere; it is to provide democratic channels of expression for the forms of conflicts considered as legitimate.

Envisaging modern democracy as a form of agonistic pluralism has very important consequences for politics. Once it is acknowledged that this type of agonistic confrontation is what is specific to a pluralist democracy, we can understand why such a democracy requires the creation of collective identities around clearly differentiated positions, as well as the possibility to choose between real alternatives. This is precisely the function of the left/right distinction. The left/right opposition is the means through which legitimate conflict is given form and institutionalised. If this framework does not exist or is weakened, the process of transformation of antagonism into agonism is hindered, and this can have dire consequences for democracy. This is why discourses about the 'end of politics' and the irrelevance of the left/right distinction should not be cause for celebration, but for concern. The traditional framework of left and right is in serious need of overhauling, and it is not a question of merely reasserting the old slogans and the dogmatic certainties. However, it would be a mistake to believe that such a distinction could be transcended and that a radical politics could exist without defining an adversary.

Which globalisation?

Those who argue for the need to go beyond right and left affirm that in the type of globalised, reflexive society in which we live, neither conservatism nor socialism can provide adequate solutions. But to infer from that empirical fact a thesis concerning the necessary irrelevance of such a distinction, or to make a value judgement about the desirability of its disappearance, is another matter. This might make sense from the perspective of a liberal approach unable to recognise the constitutive role of relations of power and the ineradicability of antagonism; but for those who aim at formulating a progressive politics it is necessary to acknowledge the dimension of what I have called 'the political' and the impossibility of a reconciled society. Our task should be to redefine the left in order to re-activate the democratic struggle, not to proclaim its obsolescence. There is in advanced democratic societies an urgent need to re-establish the centrality of politics, and this requires drawing new political frontiers capable of giving a real impulse to democracy. One of the crucial stakes for left democratic politics is to begin providing an alternative to neo-liberalism. It is the current unchallenged hegemony of the neo-liberal discourse which explains why the left is without any credible project. Paradoxically, while increasingly victorious politically – since it is in power in many European countries – the left is still thoroughly out-manoeuvred ideologically. This is why it is unable to take the intellectual initiative. Instead of trying to build a new hegemony, it has capitulated to the neo-liberal one. Witness the desperate strategy of 'triangulation' whose outcome is the 'Thatcherism with a human face' trademark of New Labour.

Globalisation is the usual justification given for the 'there is no alternative' dogma. Indeed, the argument most often rehearsed against redistributive type social-democratic policies is that the tight fiscal restraints faced by the government are the only realistic possibility in a world where voters refuse to pay more taxes and where global markets would not allow any deviation from neo-liberal orthodoxy. This kind of argument takes for granted the ideological terrain which has been established as a result of years of neo-liberal hegemony and transforms what is a conjunctural state of affairs into an historical necessity. Here, as in many other cases, the mantra of globalisation is invoked to justify the status quo and reinforce the power of big transnational corporations.[2]

When it is presented as driven exclusively by the information revolution, globalisation becomes detached from its political dimension and appears as a fate to which we all have to submit. This is precisely where our critique should begin. Scrutinising this conception, André Gorz (1997) has recently argued that, instead of being seen as the necessary consequence of a technological revolution, the process of globalisation must be understood as a move by capital to provide what was a fundamentally political answer to the 'crisis of governability' of the 1970s. In his view, the crisis of the Fordist model of development led to a divorce between the interests of capital and those of the nation state. The space of politics became dissociated from the space of the economy. This phenomenon of globalisation was made possible by new forms of technology. But this technological revolution required for its implementation a profound transformation in the relations of power among social groups and between capitalist corporations and the state. The political move was the crucial one. The result is that today corporations have gained a sort of extra-territoriality. They have managed to emancipate themselves from political power and to appear the real locus of sovereignty. No wonder the resources needed to finance the welfare state are diminishing since the states are unable to tax the transnational corporations.

By unveiling the strategies of power which have informed the process of globalisation, Gorz's approach allows us to see the possibility for a counter strategy. Of course it is vain to simply attempt to resist globalisation from the context of the nation state. It is only by opposing the power of transnational capital – another globalisation, informed by a different political project – that we could have a chance to resist successfully neo-liberalism and to install a new hegemony. However, such a counter-hegemonic strategy is precisely what is precluded by the very idea of a radical centrism which denies the existence of antagonisms and the need for political frontiers. To believe that one can accommodate the aims of the big corporations with those of the weaker sectors of society is already to have capitulated to their power. It is to have accepted their globalisation as the only possible one and to act within the constraints that capital is imposing on national governments. The adherents of such a view see politics as a game where potentially the demands of all could be met without anybody having to lose. For New Labour there is of course neither enemy nor adversary. For them everybody or organisation are part of 'the people'. The interests of Murdoch, Formula One, or the rich transnational corporations, can be happily reconciled with those of the unemployed, single mothers and the disabled. Social cohesion is to be secured not through equality and solidarity but through strong families and shared moral values.

A new left-wing project

Radical politics cannot be located at the centre because to be radical – as Margaret Thatcher, contrary to Tony Blair, very well knew – is to aim at a profound transformation of power relations. This cannot be done without drawing political frontiers and defining an adversary or even an enemy. Of course, a radical project cannot be successful without winning over many of those who are located at the centre. All significant victories of the left have been the result of an alliance of important sectors of the middle classes, whose interests have been articulated, and those of the popular sectors. Today more than ever such an alliance is vital for the formulation of a radical project. But this does not mean that such an alliance requires taking the middle ground and trying to establish a compromise between neo-liberalism and the groups that it oppresses. There are many issues concerning the provision of decent public services and the creation of good conditions of life on which a broad alliance could be established. However, this cannot take place without the elaboration of new hegemonic project that would put again on the agenda the struggle for equality which has been discarded by the advocates of neo-liberalism.

Perhaps the clearest sign of New Labour's renunciation of its left identity is that it has abandoned such a struggle for equality. Under the pretence of formulating a modern, post-social democratic conception of equality, Blairites have eschewed the language of redistribution in order to speak exclusively in terms of inclusion and exclusion. As if the very condition for inclusion of the excluded were not a drastic redistribution and a correction of the profound inequalities which the neo-liberal long decade has brought about.

The current avoidance by New Labour of the theme of equality, and its increasing acceptance of inequalities, is very symptomatic indeed. As Norberto Bobbio (1996) recently reminded us, it is the idea of equality which provides the backbone of the left vision while the right has always defended diverse forms of inequality. The fact that a certain type of egalitarian ideology has been used to justify totalitarian forms of politics in no way forces us to relinquish the struggle for equality. What a left-wing project today requires is to envisage this struggle for equality in a way that takes account of the multiplicity of social relations in which inequality needs to be challenged. This will of course require a critique of the shortcomings of traditional social democracy. If Thatcherism was successful it is in part because it was able to re-articulate in its favour the popular resentment against those shortcomings. I have no problem therefore with the idea of a 'post-social democratic politics', on condition that this does not mean regressing behind social democracy to some pre-social democratic liberal view. Yet this type of regression appears to be precisely the kind of move that is behind the logic of the welfare-to-work policies advocated by Blairites.

John Gray, another of Blair's advisers, celebrates New Labour for having abandoned a redistributive, social democratic idea of justice but worries that they have not put anything in its place. He urges them to re-invent liberal Britain by embracing the New Liberalism advocated in the early decades of this century by L.T. Hobhouse and T.H. Green. According to such a liberalism, says Gray (1997), economic inequalities were not unfair and the important issue was to reconcile the demands of individual choice with the needs for social cohesion.

While agreeing with Gray in his critique of 'egalitarianism', I believe that he establishes a false dichotomy between equality and individual freedom. To be sure there will always be a tension between those values, and it is unrealistic to believe that they could be perfectly reconciled, but it does not mean that they are incompatible and that we have to discard one in pursuit of the other. For those who still identify with the left there are ways to envisage a social justice which is committed to both pluralism and equality. Several theorists have been concerned with developing such a perspective. For instance, in *Spheres of Justice*, Michael Walzer (1983) elaborates a conception which he calls 'complex equality'. He argues that if one wants to make equality a central objective of a politics that also respects liberty it is necessary to abandon the idea of 'simple equality' which tends to render people as equal as possible in all areas. Equality in his view is a complex relationship between persons mediated by a series of social goods; it does not consist in an identity of possession. According to the complex view of equality that he advocates, social goods should be distributed, not in a uniform manner but in terms of a diversity of criteria which reflect the diversity of those social goods and the meaning attached to them. The important thing, he argues, is not to violate the principles of distribution proper to each sphere. One needs to preclude success in one sphere implying the possibility of exercising preponderance in others, as is now the case with wealth. It is essential that no social good be used as the means of domination and that concentration of political power, wealth, honour and offices in the same hands should be avoided. Thinking along those lines would allow us to envisage the struggle against inequality in a way that would respect and deepen pluralism instead of stifling individual freedom.

The main problem that a post-social democratic vision informed by a view of complex equality will have to tackle, a problem of which the welfare-to-work policies of New Labour seem to be unaware, is the crucial transformation with which our societies are confronted: the crisis of work and the exhaustion of the wage society. In this area, more than any other perhaps, it is evident that we have entered a quite different world in which neither *laissez-faire* liberalism nor Keynesianism will be able to provide a solution. The problem of unemployment calls for new radical thinking. Without a realisation that there will be no return to full employment (if that ever existed) and that a new model of economic development is urgently needed, no alternative to neo-liberalism will ever take off. The Americanisation of Europe will proceed under the liberal motto of 'flexibilisation'.

A truly radical project needs to start by acknowledging that, as a consequence of the information revolution, there is a growing dissociation between the production of wealth and the quantity of work needed to produce it. Without a drastic redistribution in the average effective duration of work, society will become increasingly polarised between those who work in stable, regular jobs and the rest who are either unemployed or have part-time, precarious and unprotected jobs. Jointly with such a redistribution, a plural economy should be developed where the associative sector would play an important role alongside the market and the state sector. Many activities, of crucial social utility but discarded by the logic of the market, could, through public financing, be carried out in this solidaristic economy. There is, however, a third element to take into account. Indeed the condition for the success of such initiatives is the implementation of some form of citizen's income that would guarantee a decent minimum for everybody. This is an idea that has recently been gaining an increasing number of supporters who argue that the reform of the welfare state would be better approached by envisaging the different modalities of such an income than by replacing it by workfare.

Implemented together, these measures could create the basis for a post-social democratic answer to neo-liberalism. Of course such an answer could only be carried out successfully in a European context, and this is why a left-wing project today could only be a European one. In this time of globalisation the taming of capitalism cannot be realised at the level of the nation state. Only within the context of an integrated Europe, in which the different states would unite their forces, could the attempt to make finance capital more accountable succeed. If, instead of competing among themselves in order to establish the more attractive deals for transnational corporations, the different European states would agree on common policies, another type of globalisation could be possible. That the traditional conceptions of both the left and the right are inadequate for the problems that we are facing at the eve of the new millennium is something that I readily accept, but to believe that the antagonisms that those categories evoke have disappeared in our globalised world is to fall prey to the hegemonic neo-liberal discourse of the end of politics. Far from having lost their relevance, the stakes to which the left and the right allude are more pertinent than ever.

A last word on New Labour. Given its mistaken conception of the democratic process, we should not be surprised at the fact that it is unable to accept the expression of dissent in its midst. Its authoritarianism chimes with its conception of a consensual politics of dialogue from which strife has been eliminated. Such a conception cannot make room for the conflict inherent in social life. As I have tried to show, the radical centre is unable to acknowledge the importance of an agonistic confrontation. Every expression of dissent is therefore seen as the manifestation of an antagonism that will threaten Labour's existence. However, this politics without an adversary is a flawed conception. By wanting to include everybody in 'the people', and have the powerful cohabit with the oppressed, New Labour perpetuates the continued subordination of the very people that it was meant to defend and represent. In the end it cannot do without adversaries, except that since it cannot see them in Murdoch and his like, it must resort to the part of 'the people' that resists being 'dialogically' domesticated: 'Old Labour', which is depicted as the enemy. Alas politics always calls for decision. When the stakes are on the table, one needs to choose one's camp, there is no 'third way'. The centre – radical or not – has to take sides. We can only hope that New Labour will not learn that lesson too late.

Notes

1 This article is dedicated to the memory of Ralph Miliband, who, on this issue, I hope would have agreed.
2 For a similar argument, see the editorial of *Soundings* No 7, 'States of Africa', by Doreen Massey.

References

Bobbio, Norberto. 1996. *Left and Right*. Cambridge: Polity.
Giddens, Anthony. 1994. *Beyond Left and Right*. Cambridge: Polity.
Gorz, André. 1997. *Misères du present, Richesse du possible*. Paris: Galilee.
Gray, John. 1997. Goodbye to Rawls. *Prospect* (November).
Walzer, Michael. 1983. *Spheres of Justice*. New York: Basic.

10

CARL SCHMITT AND THE PARADOX OF LIBERAL DEMOCRACY (1997, REV. 2000)

In his introduction to the paperback edition of *Political Liberalism*, John Rawls, referring to Carl Schmitt's critique of parliamentary democracy, suggests that the fall of Weimar's constitutional regime was in part due to the fact that German elites no longer believed in the possibility of a decent liberal parliamentary regime. In his view, this should make us realize the importance of providing convincing arguments in favour of a just and well ordered constitutional democracy. 'Debates about general philosophical questions', he says, 'cannot be the daily stuff of politics, but that does not make these questions without significance, since what we think their answers are will shape the underlying attitudes of the public culture and the conduct of politics' (Rawls 1996, lxi).

I agree with Rawls on the practical role that political philosophy can play in shaping the public culture and contributing to the creation of democratic political identities. But I consider that political theorists, in order to put forward a conception of a liberal-democratic society able to win the active support of its citizens, must be willing to engage with the arguments of those who have challenged the fundamental tenets of liberalism. This means confronting some disturbing questions, usually avoided by liberals and democrats alike.

My intention in this chapter is to contribute to such a project by scrutinizing Carl Schmitt's critique of liberal democracy. Indeed, I am convinced that a confrontation with his thought will allow us to acknowledge – and, therefore, be in a better position to try to negotiate – an important paradox inscribed in the very nature of liberal democracy. To bring to the fore the pertinence and actuality of Schmitt's questioning, I will organize my argument around two topics which are currently central in political theory: the boundaries of citizenship and the nature of a liberal-democratic consensus.[1]

Democracy, homogeneity and the boundaries of citizenship

The boundaries of citizenship have recently provoked much discussion. Several authors have argued that in an age of globalization, citizenship cannot be confined within the boundaries of nation-states; it must become transnational. David Held (1995), for instance, advocates the advent of a 'cosmopolitan citizenship', and asserts the need for a cosmopolitan democratic law to which citizens whose rights have been violated by their own states could appeal. Richard Falk (1995), for his part, envisages the development of 'citizen pilgrims' whose loyalties would belong to an invisible political community of their hopes and dreams.

Other theorists, however, particularly those who are committed to a civic republican conception of citizenship, are deeply suspicious of such prospects, which they view as endangering democratic forms of government. They assert that the nation state is the necessary locus for citizenship, and that there is something inherently contradictory in the very idea of cosmopolitan citizenship. I see this debate as a typical example of the problems arising from the conflict between democratic and liberal requirements. Schmitt, I submit, can help us to clarify what is at stake in this issue by making us aware of the tension between democracy and liberalism.

As a starting point, let us take his thesis that 'homogeneity' is a condition of possibility of democracy. In the preface to the second edition of *The Crisis of Parliamentary Democracy* (1926), he declares: 'Every actual democracy rests on the principle that not only are equals equal but unequals will not be treated equally. Democracy requires, therefore, first homogeneity and second – if the need arises – elimination or eradication of heterogeneity' (Schmitt 1985, p. 9). I do not want to deny that, given its author's later political evolution, this assertion has a chilling effect. I consider, however, that it would be short-sighted to dismiss Schmitt's claim on the necessity of homogeneity in a democracy for that reason. It is my contention that this provocative thesis – interpreted in a certain way – may force us to come to terms with an aspect of democratic politics that liberalism tends to eliminate.

The first thing to do is to grasp what Schmitt means by 'homogeneity'. He affirms that homogeneity is inscribed at the very core of the democratic conception of equality, insofar as it must be a *substantive* equality. His argument is that democracy requires a conception of equality as substance, and cannot satisfy itself with abstract conceptions like the liberal one, since 'equality is only interesting and invaluable politically so long as it has substance, and for that reason at least the possibility and the risk of inequality' (ibid., p. 9). In order to be treated as equals, citizens must, he says, partake of a common substance.

As a consequence, he rejects the idea that the general equality of mankind could serve as a basis for a state or any form of government. Such an idea of human equality – which comes from liberal individualism – is, says Schmitt, a non-political form of equality, because it lacks the correlate of a possible inequality from which every equality receives its specific meaning. It does not provide any criteria for establishing political institutions: 'The equality of all persons as persons is not democracy but a certain kind of liberalism, not a state form but an individualistic-humanitarian ethic and *Weltanschauung*. Modern mass democracy rests on the confused combination of both' (ibid., p. 13).

Schmitt asserts that there is an insuperable opposition between liberal individualism, with its moral discourse centred around the individual, and the democratic ideal, which is essentially political, and aims at creating an identity based on homogeneity. He claims that liberalism negates democracy and democracy negates liberalism, and that parliamentary democracy, since it consists in the articulation between democracy and liberalism, is therefore a non-viable regime.

In his view, when we speak of equality, we need to distinguish between two very different ideas: the liberal one and the democratic one. The liberal conception of equality postulates that every person is, as a person, automatically equal to every other person. The democratic conception, however, requires the possibility of distinguishing who belongs to the demos and who is exterior to it; for that reason, it cannot exist without the necessary correlate of inequality. Despite liberal claims, a democracy of mankind, if it was ever likely, would be a pure abstraction, because equality can exist only through its specific meanings in particular spheres – as political equality, economic equality, and so forth. But those specific equalities always entail, as their very condition of possibility, some form of inequality. This is why he concludes that an absolute human equality would be a practically meaningless, indifferent equality.

Schmitt makes an important point when he stresses that the democratic concept of equality is a *political* one which therefore entails the possibility of a *distinction*. He is right to say that a political democracy cannot be based on the generality of all mankind, and that it must belong to a specific people. It is worth indicating in this context that – contrary to several tendentious interpretations – he never postulated that this belonging to a people could be envisaged only in racial terms. On the contrary, he insisted on the multiplicity of ways in which the homogeneity constitutive of a demos could be manifested. He says, for instance, that the substance of equality 'can be found in certain physical and moral qualities, for example, in civic virtue, in *arete*, the classical democracy of vertus [vertu]' (ibid., p. 9). Examining this question from a historical angle, he also points out that 'In the democracy of English sects during the seventeenth century equality was based on a consensus of religious convictions. However, since the nineteenth century it has existed above all in membership in a particular nation, in national homogeneity' (ibid., p. 9).

It is clear that what is important for Schmitt is not the nature of the similarity on which homogeneity is based. What matters is the possibility of tracing a line of demarcation between those who belong to the demos – and therefore have equal rights – and those who, in the political domain, cannot have the same rights because they are not part of the demos. Such a democratic equality – expressed today through citizenship – is, for him, the ground of all the other forms of equality. It is through their belonging to the demos that democratic citizens are granted equal rights, not because they participate in an abstract idea of humanity. This is why he declares that the central concept of democracy is not 'humanity' but the concept of the 'people', and that there can never be a democracy of mankind. Democracy can exist only for a people. As he puts it:

> In the domain of the political, people do not face each other as abstractions but as politically interested and politically determined persons, as citizens,

governors or governed, politically allied or opponents – in any case, therefore, in political categories. In the sphere of the political, one cannot abstract out what is political, leaving only universal human equality.

(ibid., p. 11)

In order to illustrate his point, Schmitt indicates that even in modern democratic states, where a universal human equality has been established, there is a category of people who are excluded as foreigners or aliens, and that there is therefore no absolute equality of persons. He also shows how the correlate of the equality among the citizenry found in those states is a much stronger emphasis on national homogeneity, and on the line of demarcation between those who belong to the state and those who remain outside it. This, he notes, is to be expected, and if it were not the case, and if a state attempted to realize the universal equality of individuals in the political realm without concern for national or any other form of homogeneity, the consequence would be a complete devaluation of political equality, and of politics itself. To be sure, this would in no way mean the disappearance of substantive inequalities, but, says Schmitt:

> they would shift into another sphere, perhaps separated from the political and concentrated in the economic, leaving this area to take on a new, disproportionately decisive importance. Under the conditions of superficial political equality, another sphere in which substantial inequalities prevail (today for example the economic sphere) will dominate politics.

(ibid., p. 12)

It seems to me that, unpleasant as they are to liberal ears, these arguments need to be considered carefully. They carry an important warning for those who believe that the process of globalization is laying the basis for worldwide democratization and the establishment of a cosmopolitan citizenship. They also provide important insights into the current dominance of economics over politics. We should indeed be aware that without a demos to which they belong, those cosmopolitan citizen pilgrims would in fact have lost the possibility of exercising their democratic rights of law-making. They would be left, at best, with their liberal rights of appealing to transnational courts to defend their individual rights when these have been violated. In all probability, such a cosmopolitan democracy, if it were ever to be realized, would be no more than an empty name disguising the actual disappearance of democratic forms of government and indicating the triumph of the liberal form of governmental rationality.

The democratic logic of inclusion-exclusion

It is true that by reading him in this way, I am doing violence to Schmitt's questioning, since his main concern is not democratic participation but *political unity*. He considers that such a unity is crucial, because without it the state cannot exist. But his reflections are relevant to the issue of democracy, since he considers that in a democratic state, it is through their participation in this unity that citizens can be treated as equals and exercise their democratic rights. Democracy, according to Schmitt, consists fundamentally in the identity between rulers and ruled. It is linked to the fundamental principle of the unity of the demos and the sovereignty of its will. But if the people are to rule, it is necessary to determine who belongs to the people. Without any criterion to determine who are the bearers of democratic rights, the will of the people could never take shape.

It could, of course, be objected that this is a view of democracy which is at odds with the liberal-democratic one, and some would certainly claim that this should be called not democracy but populism. To be sure, Schmitt is no democrat in the liberal understanding of the term, and he had nothing but contempt for the constraints imposed by liberal institutions on the democratic will of the people. But the issue he raises is a crucial one, even for those who advocate liberal-democratic forms. The logic of democracy does indeed imply a moment of closure which is required by the very process of constituting the 'people'. This cannot be avoided, even in a liberal-democratic model; it can only be negotiated differently. But this in turn can be done only if this closure, and the paradox it implies, are acknowledged.

By stressing that the identity of a democratic political community hinges on the possibility of drawing a frontier between 'us' and 'them', Schmitt highlights the fact that democracy always entails relations of inclusion-exclusion. This is a vital insight that democrats would be ill-advised to dismiss because they dislike its author. One of the main problems with liberalism – and one that can endanger democracy – is precisely its incapacity to conceptualize such a frontier. As Schmitt indicates, the central concept of liberal discourse is 'humanity', which – as he rightly points out – is not a political concept, and does not correspond to any political entity. The central question of the political constitution of 'the people' is something that liberal theory is unable to tackle adequately, because the necessity of drawing such a 'frontier' contradicts its universalistic rhetoric. Against the liberal emphasis on 'humanity', it is important to stress that the key concepts of democracy are the 'demos' and the 'people'.

Contrary to those who believe in a necessary harmony between liberalism and democracy, Schmitt makes us see how they conflict, and the dangers the dominance of liberal logic can bring to the exercise of democracy. No doubt there is an opposition between the liberal 'grammar' of equality, which postulates universality and reference to 'humanity', and the practice of democratic equality, which requires the political moment of discrimination between 'us' and 'them'. However, I think that Schmitt is wrong to present this conflict as a contradiction that is bound to lead liberal democracy to self-destruction. We can accept his insight perfectly well without agreeing with the conclusions he draws. I propose to acknowledge the crucial difference between the liberal and the democratic conceptions of equality, while envisaging their articulation and its consequences in another way. Indeed, such an articulation can be seen as the locus of a *tension* that installs a very important dynamic, which is constitutive of the specificity of liberal democracy as a new political form of society. The democratic logic of constituting the people, and inscribing rights and equality into practices, is necessary to subvert the tendency towards abstract universalism inherent in liberal discourse. But the articulation with the liberal logic allows us constantly to challenge – through reference to 'humanity' and the polemical use of 'human rights' – the forms of exclusion that are necessarily inscribed in the political practice of installing those rights and defining 'the people' which is going to rule.[2] Notwithstanding the ultimate contradictory nature of the two logics, their articulation therefore has very positive consequences, and there is no reason to share Schmitt's pessimistic verdict concerning liberal democracy. However, we should not be too sanguine about its prospect either. No final resolution or equilibrium between those two conflicting logics is ever possible, and there can be only temporary, pragmatic, unstable and precarious negotiations of the tension between them. Liberal-democratic politics consists, in fact, in the constant process of negotiation and renegotiation – through different hegemonic articulations – of this constitutive paradox.

Deliberative democracy and its shortcomings

Schmitt's reflections on the necessary moment of closure entailed by the democratic logic have important consequences for another debate, the one about the nature of the consensus that can obtain in a liberal-democratic society. Several issues are at stake in that debate, and I will examine them in turn.

One of the implications of the argument presented above is the impossibility of establishing a rational consensus without exclusion. This raises several problems for the model of democratic politics, which has been receiving quite a lot of attention recently under the name 'deliberative democracy'. No doubt, the aim of the theorists who advocate the different versions of such a model is commendable. Against the interest-based conception of democracy, inspired by economics and sceptical about the virtues of political participation, they want to introduce questions of morality and justice into politics, and envisage democratic citizenship in a different way. However, by proposing to view reason and rational argumentation, rather than interest and aggregation of preferences, as the central issue of politics, they simply replace the economic model with a moral one which – albeit in a different way – also misses the specificity of the political. In their attempt to overcome the limitations of interest-group pluralism, deliberative democrats provide a telling illustration of Schmitt's point that 'In a very systematic fashion liberal thought evades or ignores state and politics and moves instead in a typical, always recurring polarity of two heterogeneous spheres, namely ethics and economics, intellect and trade, education and property' (Schmitt 1976, p. 70).

Since I cannot examine all the different versions of deliberative democracy here, I will concentrate on the model developed by Habermas and his followers. To be sure, there are several differences among the advocates of this new paradigm. But there is enough convergence among them to affirm that none of them can deal adequately with the paradox of democratic politics.[3]

According to Seyla Benhabib, the main challenge confronting democracy is how to reconcile rationality with legitimacy – or, to put it differently, the crucial question that democracy needs to address is how the expression of the common good can be made compatible with the sovereignty of the people. She presents the answer offered by the deliberative model:

> legitimacy and rationality can be attained with regard to collective decision-making processes in a polity if and only if the institutions of this polity and their interlocking relationship are so arranged that what is considered in the common interest of all results from processes of collective deliberation conducted rationally and fairly among free and equal individuals.
>
> (Benhabib 1994, p. 30)

In this view, the basis of legitimacy in democratic institutions derives from the fact that those who claim obligatory power do so on the presumption that their decisions represent an *impartial standpoint* which is *equally in the interests of all*. If this presumption is to be fulfilled, those decisions must be the result of appropriate public processes of deliberation which follow the procedures of the Habermasian discourse model. The basic idea behind this model is that:

> only those norms, i.e. general rules of action and institutional arrangements, can be said to be valid which would be agreed to by all those affected by their consequences, if such agreement were reached as a consequence of a process of deliberation which has the following features:
>
> (a) participation in such deliberation is governed by the norms of equality and symmetry; all have the same chance to initiate speech acts, to question, interrogate, and to open debate;
> (b) all have the right to question the assigned topics of conversation;
> (c) all have the right to initiate reflexive arguments about the very rules of the discourse procedure and the way in which they are applied or carried out. There is no *prima facie* rule limiting the agenda or the conversation, nor the identity of the participants, as long as each excluded person or group can justifiably show that they are relevantly affected by the proposed norm under question.
>
> (Benhabib 1994, p. 31)

Let us examine this model of deliberative democracy closely. In their attempt to ground legitimacy on *rationality*, these theorists have to distinguish between mere agreement and rational consensus. That is why they assert that the process of public discussion must realize the conditions of ideal discourse. This sets the values of the procedure, which are impartiality and equality, openness and lack of coercion, and unanimity. The combination of those values in the discussion guarantees that its outcome will be legitimate, since it will produce generalizable interests on which all participants can agree.

Habermasians do not deny that there will, of course, be obstacles to the realization of the ideal discourse, but these obstacles are conceived of as *empirical*. They are due to the fact that it is unlikely, given the practical and empirical limitations of social life, that we will ever be completely able to leave all our particular interests aside in order to coincide with our universal rational self. This is why the ideal speech situation is presented as a regulative idea.

However, if we accept Schmitt's insight about the relations of inclusion-exclusion which are necessarily inscribed in the political constitution of 'the people' – which is required by the exercise of democracy – we have to acknowledge that the obstacles to the realization of the ideal speech situation – and to the consensus without exclusion that it would bring about – are inscribed in the democratic logic itself. Indeed, the free and unconstrained public deliberation of all on matters of common concern goes against the democratic requisite of drawing a frontier between 'us' and 'them'. We could say – this time using Derridean terminology – that the very conditions of possibility of the exercise of democracy constitute simultaneously the conditions of impossibility of democratic legitimacy as envisaged by deliberative democracy. Consensus in a liberal-democratic society is – and will always be – the expression of a hegemony and the crystallization of power relations. The frontier that it establishes between what is and what is not legitimate is a political one, and for that reason it should remain contestable. To deny the existence of such a moment of closure, or to present the frontier as dictated by rationality or morality, is to naturalize what should be perceived as a contingent and temporary hegemonic articulation of 'the people' through a particular regime of inclusion-exclusion. The result of such an operation is to reify the identity of the people by reducing it to one of its many possible forms of identification.

Pluralism and its limits

Because it postulates the availability of a consensus without exclusion, the model of deliberative democracy is unable to envisage liberal-democratic pluralism in an adequate way. Indeed, one could indicate how, in both Rawls and Habermas – to take the best-known representatives of that trend – the very condition for the creation of consensus is the elimination of pluralism from the public sphere.[4] Hence the incapacity of deliberative democracy to provide a convincing refutation of Schmitt's critique of liberal pluralism. It is this critique that I will now examine, to see how it could be answered.

Schmitt's best-known thesis is certainly that the criterion of the political is the friend-enemy distinction. Indeed, for him, the political 'can be understood only in the context of the ever present possibility of the friend-and-enemy grouping' (Schmitt 1976, p. 35). Because of the way this thesis is generally interpreted, he is often taken to task for neglecting the 'friend' side of his friend-enemy opposition.

In his remarks on homogeneity, however, we can find many indications of how this grouping should be envisaged, and this has important implications for his critique of pluralism.

Let us return to the idea that democracy requires political equality, which stems from partaking in a common substance – this, as we have seen, is what Schmitt means by the need for homogeneity. So far, I have stressed the necessity of drawing a frontier between the 'us' and the 'them'. But we can also examine this question by focusing on the 'us' and the nature of the bond that unites its components. Clearly, to assert that the condition of possibility of an 'us' is the existence of a 'them' does not exhaust the subject. Different forms of unity can be established among the components of the 'us'. To be sure, this is not what Schmitt believes, since in his view unity can exist only on the mode of identity. But this is precisely where the problem with his conception lies. It is useful, therefore, to examine both the strengths and the weaknesses of his argument.

By asserting the need for homogeneity in a democracy, Schmitt is telling us something about the kind of bond that is needed if a democratic political community is to exist. In other words, he is analysing the nature of the 'friendship' which defines the 'us' in a democracy. This, for him, is, of course, a way of taking issue with liberalism for not recognizing the need for such a form of commonality, and for advocating pluralism. If we take his target to be the liberal model of interest-group pluralism which postulates that agreement on mere procedures can assure the cohesion of a liberal society, he is no doubt right. Such a vision of a pluralist society is certainly inadequate. Liberalism simply transposes into the public realm the diversity of interests already existing in society and reduces the political moment to the process of negotiation among interests independently of their political expression. There is no place in such a model for a common identity of democratic citizens; citizenship is reduced to a legal status, and the moment of the political constitution of the people is foreclosed. Schmitt's critique of that type of liberalism is convincing, and it is interesting to note that it chimes with what Rawls says when he rejects the 'modus vivendi' model of constitutional democracy because it is very unstable, always liable to dissolution, and declares that the unity it creates is insufficient.

Having discarded the view that grounds it in a mere convergence of interests and a neutral set of procedures, how, then, should we envisage the unity of a pluralist society? Isn't any other type of unity incompatible with the pluralism advocated by liberal societies? On this issue, Schmitt's answer is, of course, unequivocal: there is no place for pluralism inside a democratic political community. Democracy requires the existence of a homogeneous demos, and this precludes any possibility of pluralism. This is why, in his view, there is an insurmountable contradiction between liberal pluralism and democracy. For him, the only possible and legitimate pluralism is a pluralism of states. Rejecting the liberal idea of a world state, he affirms that the political world is a 'pluriverse', not a 'universe'. In his view: 'The political entity cannot by its very nature be universal in the sense of embracing all of humanity and the entire world' (Schmitt 1976, p. 53).

In *The Concept of the Political* – taking as his target the kind of pluralism advocated by the pluralist school of Harold Laski and G.D.H. Cole – Schmitt argues that the state cannot be considered as one more association among others, which would be on the same level as a church or a trade union. Against liberal theory, whose aim is to transform the state into a voluntary association through the theory of the social contract, he urges us to acknowledge that the political entity is something different and more decisive. For him, to deny this is to deny the political:

> Only as long as the essence of the political is not comprehended or not taken into consideration is it possible to place a political association pluralistically on the same level with religious, cultural, economic, or other associations and permit it to compete with these.
>
> (ibid., p. 45)

A few years later, in his important article 'Ethic of State and Pluralistic State', again discussing Laski and Cole, he notes that the actuality of their pluralist theory comes from the fact that it corresponds to the empirical conditions existing in most industrial societies. The current situation is one in which

> the state, in fact, does appear to be largely dependent on social groups, sometimes as sacrifice to, sometimes as result of, their negotiations – an object of compromise among the powerful social and economic groups, an agglomeration of heterogeneous factors, political parties, combines, unions, churches, and so on ...
>
> (Schmitt 1999)

The state is therefore weakened, and becomes some kind of clearing house, a referee between competing factions. Reduced to a purely instrumental function, it cannot be the object of loyalty; it loses its ethical role and its capacity to represent the political unity of a people. While he deplores such a situation, Schmitt nonetheless admits that as far as their empirical diagnostic is concerned, the pluralists have a point. In his opinion, the interest of their theory lies in the 'appreciation of the concrete empirical power of social groups, and of the empirical situation as it is determined by the ways in which individuals belong to several of such social groups' (ibid.).

Schmitt, it must be said, does not always see the existence of parties as being absolutely incompatible with the existence of an ethical state. In the same article, he even seems willing to admit at least the possibility of some form of pluralism that does not negate the unity of the state. But he quickly rejects it, declaring that it will inevitably lead to the type of pluralism that will dissolve political unity:

> If the state then becomes a pluralistic party state, the unity of the state can be maintained only as long as two or more parties agree to recognize common premises. That unity then rests in particular on the constitution recognized

by all parties, which must be respected without qualification as the common foundation. The ethic of state then amounts to a constitutional ethic. Depending on the substantivity, unequivocality and authority of the constitution, a very effective unity can be found there. But it can also be the case that the constitution dwindles into mere rules of the game, its ethic of state into a mere ethic of fair play; and that it finally, in a pluralistic dissolution of the unity of the political whole, gets to the point where the unity is only an agglomeration of changing alliances between heterogeneous groups. The constitutional ethic then dwindles even further, to the point of the ethic of state being reduced in the proposition *pacta sunt servanda*.

(ibid.)

Schmitt's false dilemma

I think Schmitt is right to stress the deficiencies of the kind of pluralism that negates the specificity of the political association, and I concur with his assertion that it is necessary to constitute the people *politically*. But I do not believe that this must commit us to denying the possibility of any form of pluralism within the political association. To be sure, liberal theory has so far been unable to provide a convincing solution to this problem. This does not mean, however, that it is insoluble. In fact, Schmitt presents us with a false dilemma: either there is unity of the people, and this requires expelling every division and antagonism outside the demos – the exterior it needs if it is to establish its unity; or some forms of division inside the demos are considered legitimate, and this will lead inexorably to the kind of pluralism which negates political unity and the very existence of the people. As Jean-François Kervégan points out:

> For Schmitt, either the State imposes its order and its rationality to a civil society characterized by pluralism, competition and disorder, or, as is the case in liberal democracy, social pluralism will empty the political entity of its meaning and bring it back to its *other*, the state of nature.
>
> (Kervégan 1992, p. 259)

What leads Schmitt to formulate such a dilemma is the way he envisages political unity. The unity of the state must, for him, be a concrete unity, already given and therefore stable. This is also true of the way he envisages the identity of the people: it also must exist as a given. Because of that, his distinction between 'us' and 'them' is not really politically constructed; it is merely a recognition of already-existing borders. While he rejects the pluralist conception, Schmitt is nevertheless unable to situate himself on a completely different terrain because he retains a view of political and social identities as empirically given. His position is, in fact, ultimately contradictory. On the one hand, he seems seriously to consider the possibility that pluralism could bring about the dissolution of the unity of the state. If that dissolution is, however, a distinctive *political* possibility, it also entails that the existence of such a unity is itself a contingent fact which requires a political construction. On the other hand, however, the unity is presented as a *factum* whose obviousness could ignore the political conditions of its production. Only as a result of this sleight of hand can the alternative be as inexorable as Schmitt wants it to be.

What Schmitt fears most is the loss of common premisses and consequent destruction of the political unity which he sees as inherent in the pluralism that accompanies mass democracy. There is certainly a danger of this happening, and his warning should be taken seriously. But this is not a reason to reject all forms of pluralism. I propose to refuse Schmitt's dilemma, while acknowledging his argument for the need of some form of 'homogeneity' in a democracy. The problem we have to face becomes, then, how to imagine in a different way what Schmitt refers to as 'homogeneity' but that – in order to stress the differences with his conception – I propose to call, rather, 'commonality'; how to envisage a form of commonality strong enough to institute a 'demos' but nevertheless compatible with certain forms of pluralism: religious, moral and cultural pluralism, as well as a pluralism of political parties. This is the challenge that engaging with Schmitt's critique forces us to confront. It is indeed a crucial one, since what is at stake is the very formulation of a pluralistic view of democratic citizenship.

I obviously do not pretend to provide a solution within the confines of this chapter, but I would like to suggest some lines of reflection. To offer a different – resolutely non-Schmittian – answer to the compatibility of pluralism and liberal democracy requires, in my view, putting into question any idea of 'the people' as already given, with a substantive identity. What we need to do is precisely what Schmitt does not do: once we have recognized that the unity of the people is the result of a political construction, we need to explore all the logical possibilities that a *political* articulation entails. Once the identity of the people – or rather, its multiple possible identities – is envisaged on the mode of a political articulation, it is important to stress that if it is to be a real political articulation, not merely the acknowledgement of empirical differences, such an identity of the people must be seen as the *result* of the political process of hegemonic articulation. Democratic politics does not consist in the moment when a fully constituted people exercises its rule. The moment of rule is indissociable from the very struggle about the definition of the people, about the constitution of its identity. Such an identity, however, can never be fully constituted, and it can exist only through multiple and competing forms of *identifications*. Liberal democracy is precisely the recognition of this constitutive gap between the people and its various identifications. Hence the importance of leaving this space of contestation forever open, instead of trying to fill it through the establishment of a supposedly 'rational' consensus.

To conceive liberal-democratic politics in such a way is to acknowledge Schmitt's insight into the distinction between 'us' and 'them', because this struggle over the constitution of the people always takes place within a conflictual field, and implies the existence of competing forces. Indeed, there is no hegemonic articulation without the determination of a frontier, the definition of a 'them'. But in the case of liberal-democratic politics this frontier is an internal one, and the 'them' is not a permanent outsider. We can begin to realize, therefore, why such a regime requires pluralism. Without a plurality of competing forces which attempt to define the common good, and aim at fixing the identity of the community, the political articulation of the demos could not take place. We would be in the field either of the aggregation of interests, or of a process of deliberation which eliminates the moment of decision. That is – as Schmitt pointed out – in the field of economics or of ethics, but not in the field of politics.

Nevertheless, by envisaging unity only under the mode of substantive unity, and denying the possibility of pluralism within the political association, Schmitt was unable to grasp that there was another alternative open to liberals, one that could render the articulation between liberalism and democracy viable. What he could not conceive of, owing to the limits of his problematic, he deemed impossible. Since his objective was to attack liberalism, such a move is not surprising but it certainly indicates the limits of his theoretical reflection.

Despite these shortcomings, Schmitt's questioning of liberalism is a very powerful one. It reveals several weaknesses of liberal democracy, and brings its blind spot to the fore. Those deficiencies cannot be ignored. If we are to elaborate a view of democratic society which is convincing and worthy of allegiance, they have to be addressed. Schmitt is an adversary from whom we can learn, because we can draw on his insights. Turning them against him, we should use them to formulate a better understanding of liberal democracy, one that acknowledges its paradoxical nature. Only by coming to terms with the double movement of inclusion-exclusion that democratic politics entails can we deal with the challenge with which the process of globalization confronts us today.

Notes

1 I would have thought everybody should be able to understand that it is possible to use Schmitt against Schmitt – to use the insights of his critique of liberalism in order to consolidate liberalism – while recognizing that this was not, of course, his aim. However, it does not seem to be the case, since W.E. Scheuermann, in *Between the Norm and the Exception* (Cambridge, MA: MIT Press, 1994, p. 8), criticizes me for presenting Schmitt as a theorist of radical pluralist democracy!

2 I have put forward a similar argument about the tension that exists between the articulation of the liberal logic of difference and the democratic logic of equivalence in my discussion of Schmitt in *The Return of the Political* (London: Verso, 1993), chapters 7 and 8.

3 For a critique of the Rawlsian model and its incapacity to acknowledge the political nature of the discrimination it establishes between 'simple' and 'reasonable' pluralism, see chapter 1 of Mouffe, *The Democratic Paradox* (London: Verso, 2000).

4 This, of course, takes place in a different way in both authors. Rawls relegates pluralism to the private sphere, while Habermas screens it out, so to speak, from the public sphere through the procedures of argumentation. In both cases, however, the result is the elimination of pluralism from the public sphere.

References

Benhabib, Seyla. 1994. Deliberative Rationality and Models of Democratic Legitimacy. *Constellations* 1:1 (April).
Falk, Richard. 1995. *On Human Governance*. Cambridge: Polity.
Held, David. 1995. *Democracy and the Global Order*. Cambridge: Polity.
Kervégan, Jean-François. 1992. *Carl Schmitt et Hegel: Le politique entre métaphysique et positivité*. Paris: PUF.
Rawls, John. 1996. *Political Liberalism*. New York: Columbia University Press.
Schmitt, Carl. 1976. *The Concept of the Political*. Trans. George Schwab. New Brunswick, NJ: Rutgers University Press.
——1985. *The Crisis of Parliamentary Democracy*. Trans. Ellen Kennedy. Cambridge, MA: MIT Press.
——1999. Staatsethik und pluralistischer Staat. *Kantstudien* 35:1 (1930). Trans. in *The Challenge of Carl Schmitt*. Ed. Chantal Mouffe. London: Verso, pp. 195–208.

11

POLITICS AND PASSIONS

The stakes of democracy (2002)[1]

For some time I have been concerned with what I see as our growing inability to envisage in political terms the problems facing our societies: that is, to see them as problems the solutions to which entail not just technical but political decisions. These decisions would be made between real alternatives, the existence of which implied the presence of conflicting but legitimate projects of how to organize our common life. We appear to be witnessing not the end of history but the end of politics. Is this not the message of recent trends in political theory and sociology as well as of the practices of mainstream political parties? They all claim that the adversarial model of politics has become obsolete and that we have entered a new phase of reflexive modernity, one in which an inclusive consensus can be built around a 'radical centre'. All those who disagree with this consensus are dismissed as archaic or condemned as evil. Morality has been promoted to the position of a master narrative; as such, it replaces discredited political and social discourses as a framework for collective action. Morality is rapidly becoming the only legitimate vocabulary: we are now urged to think not in terms of right and left, but of right and wrong.

This displacement of politics by morality means that there is now no properly 'agonistic' debate in the democratic political public sphere about possible alternatives to the existing hegemonic order; as a consequence, this sphere has been seriously weakened. Hence the growing disaffection with liberal democratic institutions, a disaffection which manifests itself in declining electoral participation and in the attraction exerted by right-wing populist parties that challenge the political establishment.

There are many reasons for the disappearance of a properly political perspective: they include the predominance of a neo-liberal regime of globalization, and the influence of the individualistic consumer culture which now pervades most advanced industrial societies. From a more strictly political perspective, it is clear that the collapse of communism and the disappearance of the political frontiers that structured the political imaginary for most of the last century have caused the political markers of society to crumble. The steady blurring of the distinction between right and left which so many celebrate as progress is, in my view, one of main reasons for the growing irrelevance of the democratic, political public sphere. It has negative consequences for democratic politics. Before returning to this point I would like to examine the responsibility of political theory for our current inability to think in political terms – a phenomenon with which I, as a political theorist, am particularly concerned.

The shortcomings of liberal democratic theory

In recent years the traditional understanding of democracy as an aggregation of interests – the 'aggregative' model – has been increasingly displaced by a new paradigm: 'deliberative democracy'. One of the main tenets of this new model is that political questions are, by nature, moral and can, therefore, be addressed rationally. The objective of a democratic society, in this view is the creation of a rational consensus. This consensus would be reached by using deliberative procedures with the aim of producing outcomes that were impartial and met everyone's interests equally. All those who question the possibility of achieving such a rational consensus, and who claim, instead, that the political is a domain in which one should always rationally expect to find discord, are accused of undermining the very possibility of democracy. As Jürgen Habermas has put it:

> If questions of justice cannot transcend the ethical self-understanding of competing forms of life, and existentially relevant value conflicts and oppositions must penetrate all controversial questions, then in the final analysis we will end up with something resembling Carl Schmitt's understanding of politics.
>
> (Habermas 1996, p. 1493)

This trend in political theory of conflating politics with morality – understood in rationalistic and universalistic terms – tries to eradicate an aspect of politics that cannot, in fact, be eradicated: antagonism. This approach has contributed to the current displacement of the political by the juridical and the moral, each of which is perceived to be a terrain on which impartial decisions can be reached. There is, therefore, a strong link between this kind of political theory and the retreat of the political. That is why I am concerned by the fact the deliberative model of democracy is often presented as being well suited to the present stage of democracy. No doubt this type of theory chimes with 'third way' politics and its pretensions to be located 'beyond left and right'; but, as I argue below, it is precisely this post-political perspective which makes us incapable of thinking politically, of asking political questions, and of offering political answers.

This displacement of the political by the juridical is very clear in the work of John Rawls. Rawls offers the US Supreme Court as the best example of what he calls the 'free exercise of public reason', in his view the very model of democratic deliberation. Another example is Ronald Dworkin, who, in many of his essays, gives primacy to the independent judiciary, which he sees as the interpreter of the political morality of a community. According to Dworkin all the fundamental questions that a political community faces – to do with employment, education, censorship, freedom of association, and so on – are better resolved by judges, providing they interpret the constitution with reference to the principle of political equality. There is, in Dworkin's worldview, very little left over for discussion in the political arena to resolve.

Even a pragmatist such as Richard Rorty, despite his important and far-reaching critique of the rationalist approach, fails to provide an adequate alternative to it. Rorty, too, privileges consensus and neglects the dimension of the political. Of course, the consensus he advocates is reached through persuasion and 'sentimental education', not rational argumentation; nevertheless, he believes in the possibility of an all-encompassing consensus and, thus, in the elimination of antagonism.

The current situation can be seen as the fulfilment of a tendency which, as Carl Schmitt argued, is inscribed in liberalism, with its constitutive inability to think in truly political terms and its consequent resorting to other discourses: economic, moral, or juridical. It might seem paradoxical, even perverse, to refer to Schmitt, a declared adversary of liberal democracy, in an attempt to remedy the deficiencies of liberal democratic theorists. However, I am convinced that we can often learn more from intransigent critics than from bland apologists.

The strength of Schmitt's critique is that it highlights the main shortcoming of liberal thought: its inability to apprehend the specificity of the political. In *The Concept of the Political* Schmitt writes:

> In a very systematic fashion liberal thought evades or ignores state and politics and moves instead in a typical recurring polarity of two heterogeneous spheres, namely ethics and economics, intellect and trade, education and property. The critical distrust of state and politics is easily explained by the principles of a system whereby the individual must remain *terminus a quo* and *terminus ad quem*.
>
> (Schmitt, 1976, p. 70)

In other words liberal thought is necessarily blind to the political: liberalism's individualism means it cannot understand the formation of collective identities. Yet the political is from the outset concerned with collective forms of identification; the political always has to do with the formation of an 'Us' as opposed to a 'Them', with conflict and antagonism; its *differentia specifica*, as Schmitt puts it, is the friend-enemy distinction. Rationalism, however, entails the negation of the ineradicability of antagonism. It is no wonder, then, that liberal rationalism cannot grasp the nature of the political. Liberalism has to negate antagonism, since antagonism, by highlighting the inescapable moment of decision – in the strong sense of having to make a decision on an undecidable terrain – reveals the limits of any rational consensus.

In my view this denial of antagonism is what prevents liberal theory from understanding democratic politics. The political in its antagonistic dimension cannot be made to disappear simply by denying it, by wishing it away (the typical liberal gesture): such a negation only leads to impotence; and liberal thought *is* impotent when confronted by antagonisms which it believes belong to a bygone age when reason did not control archaic passions. This impotence, as I show below, is at the root of the current inability to grasp the nature and causes of the new phenomenon of right-wing populism spreading throughout Europe. That is why it is extremely important to listen to Schmitt when he states that the political can be understood 'only in the context of the ever present possibility of the friend-and-enemy groupings, regardless of the aspects which this possibility implies for morality, aesthetics, and economics' (ibid., p. 35). With this crucial insight, Schmitt is drawing our attention to the fact that the political is linked to the existence of hostility in human societies, a hostility which can take many forms and manifests itself in many kinds of social relations. In my view, recognizing this is the starting point for thinking properly about the aims of democratic politics.

Schmitt never developed these insights theoretically. That is why, in my work, I have tried to formulate them more rigorously on the basis of a critique of essentialism developed in several currents of contemporary thought. This critique shows that one of the main weaknesses of liberalism is that it deploys a logic of the social based on a conception of being as presence, conceiving of objectivity as being inherent in things themselves. As a result it cannot apprehend the process by which political identities are constructed. It is unable to recognize that identity is always constructed as 'difference' and that social objectivity is constituted through acts of power. What liberalism refuses to admit is that any form of social objectivity is ultimately political and that it bears the traces of the acts of exclusion which govern its constitution.

The notion of the 'constitutive outside' clarifies this point. Henry Staten uses this term to refer to a number of themes developed by Jacques Derrida with notions such as *supplement, trace* and *difference* (Staten, 1985). The term 'constitutive outside' is meant to highlight the fact that the creation of an identity implies the establishment of a difference, one which is often constructed on the basis of a hierarchy: for example between form and matter, black and white, man and woman. Once we have understood that every identity is relational and that the affirmation of a difference – that is, the perception of something 'Other' that constitutes an 'exterior' – is a precondition for the existence of any identity, we can formulate better Schmitt's point about the ever present possibility of the friend-enemy relationship. Put another way, we can begin to envisage how social relations can become the breeding ground of antagonism.

Indeed – as already indicated – political identities, which are always collective identities, entail the creation of an 'Us' that only exists by distinguishing itself from a 'Them'. Such a relation is not necessarily antagonistic. But there is always the possibility that an 'Us'–'Them' relationship can become a friend-enemy relationship. This happens when the 'Other', until now merely considered to be different, begins to be perceived as questioning our identity and threatening our existence. From that moment, any form of 'Us'–'Them' relationship – religious, ethnic or economic – becomes the locus of an antagonism.

It is important to acknowledge that the very condition of possibility of the formation of political identities is at the same time the condition of impossibility of a society from which antagonism has been eliminated. Antagonism – as Schmitt repeatedly stressed – is an ever present possibility. This antagonistic dimension is what I call the 'the political'; I distinguish it from 'politics', which refers to the set of practices and institutions the aim of which is to create order, to organize human coexistence in conditions which are always conflictual because they are traversed by 'the political'. To use Heideggerian terminology, one could say that 'the political' is situated at the level of the ontological, while politics belongs to the ontic.

Agonistic pluralism

These considerations on the shortcomings of liberal democratic theory should make clear the basis of my conviction that, in order to understand the nature of democratic politics and the challenges with which it is confronted, we need an alternative to the two main approaches in democratic political theory. One of those approaches, the aggregative model, sees political actors as being moved by the pursuit of their interests; the other, the deliberative model, stresses the role of reason and moral considerations. *Both* of these models leave aside the central role of 'passions' in the creation of collective political identities. In my view one cannot understand democratic politics without acknowledging passions as the moving force in the field of politics. That is why I am working on a new model: 'agonistic pluralism'. This attempts to tackle all the issues which the two other models, with their rationalist, individualistic frameworks, cannot properly address.

My argument is this. Once we acknowledge the dimension of 'the political' we begin to realize that one of the main challenges facing democratic politics is how to domesticate hostility and to defuse the potential antagonism in all human relations. The fundamental question for democratic politics is not how to arrive at a rational consensus, that is, a consensus not based on exclusion: this would require the construction of an 'Us' that did not have a corresponding 'Them'; an impossible feat because – as we have seen – the condition of the constitution of an 'Us' is the demarcation of a 'Them'. The crucial issue for democratic politics, instead, is how to establish this 'Us'–'Them' distinction in a way that is compatible with pluralism. The specificity of modern democracy is precisely its recognition and legitimation of conflict; in democratic societies, therefore, conflict cannot and should not be eradicated. Democratic politics requires that the others be seen not as enemies to be destroyed but as adversaries whose ideas should be fought, even fiercely, but whose right to defend those ideas will never be questioned. Put differently, what is important is that conflict does not take the form of 'antagonism' (struggle between enemies) but of 'agonism' (struggle between adversaries). The aim of democratic politics is to transform potential antagonism into agonism.

This is why the central category of democratic politics is the category of the 'adversary', the opponent with whom we share a common allegiance to the democratic principle of 'liberty and equality for all' while disagreeing about its interpretation. Adversaries fight each other because they want their interpretation to become hegemonic; but they do not question their opponents' right to fight for the victory of their position. The 'agonistic struggle' – the very condition of a vibrant democracy – consists of this confrontation between adversaries.[2] In the agonistic model the prime task of democratic politics is neither to eliminate passions nor to relegate them to the private sphere in order to establish a rational consensus in the public sphere; it is, rather, to 'tame' these passions by mobilizing them for democratic ends and by creating collective forms of identification around democratic objectives.

This understanding of the term 'adversary' needs to be distinguished sharply from its use in liberal discourse. In this understanding the presence of antagonism is not eliminated, but 'sublimated'. By contrast, what liberals mean by 'adversary' is simply 'competitor'. They envisage the field of politics as a neutral terrain on which different groups compete for positions of power. These groups do not question the dominant hegemony nor wish to transform the relations of power; their aim is to dislodge others so that they can occupy their place. This is merely competition among elites. In the agonistic model, however, the antagonistic dimension is always present; there is a constant struggle between opposing hegemonic projects which can never be reconciled rationally; one of them needs to be defeated. This is a real confrontation but one that is played out under conditions regulated by a set of democratic procedures accepted by the adversaries.

Liberal theorists are unable to acknowledge not only the presence of strife in social life and the impossibility of finding rational, impartial solutions to political issues, but also the integrative role that conflict plays in modern democracy. A well-functioning democracy requires confrontation between democratic political positions. Without this there is always a danger that democratic confrontation will be replaced by confrontation between non-negotiable moral values or essentialist forms of identification. Too much emphasis on consensus, together with an aversion towards confrontation, produces both apathy as well as a lack of interest in political participation. This is why a democratic society requires a debate about possible alternatives. It must provide political forms of identification around clearly differentiated democratic positions; or, in Niklas Luhman's words, there must be a clear 'splitting of the summit', a real choice between the policies put forward by the government and those of the opposition (Luhman 1990, p. 51). Consensus is necessary, but it must be accompanied by dissent. Consensus is needed both about the institutions which constitute democracy and about the ethico-political values that should inform the political association. There will always be disagreements, however, about the meaning of these values and how they should be implemented.

In a pluralist democracy such disagreements, which allow people to identify themselves as citizens in different ways, are not just legitimate but necessary; they are the stuff of democratic politics. When the agonistic dynamics of pluralism are obstructed because of a lack of democratic forms of identification, passions have no democratic outlet. This lays the ground for forms of politics that articulate essentialist identities – nationalist, religious or ethnic – and for increased confrontations over non-negotiable moral values.

Beyond left and right

This is why we should be suspicious of the current tendency to celebrate the blurring of the frontiers between left and right and to advocate a politics 'beyond left and right'. A well-functioning democracy needs vibrant clashes of democratic political positions. Antagonism can take many forms; it is illusory to believe that it can be eradicated. In order to allow for the possibility of transforming antagonistic into agonistic relations there must be political outlets for the expression of conflict within a pluralistic democratic system that offers opportunities of identification around democratic political alternatives.

In this context I would like to emphasize the pernicious consequences of the fashionable thesis – put forward by Ulrich Beck and Anthony Giddens – that the adversarial model of politics has become obsolete. In their view the friend-enemy model of politics is characteristic of classical industrial modernity, the 'first modernity'. Now, they claim, we live in a different, 'second', 'reflexive', modernity, in which the emphasis should be put on 'sub-politics', on the issues of 'life and death'.

At the core of this conception of reflexive modernity – as in the case of deliberative democracy, though in a different form – is the view that the antagonistic dimension of the political can be eliminated and the belief that friend-enemy relations have been eradicated. In post-traditional societies, it is claimed, collective identities are no longer constructed in terms of 'Us' and 'Them'. This means that political frontiers have evaporated and that politics must therefore, in Beck's expression, be 'reinvented'. Indeed, Beck pretends that the generalized scepticism and the doubt prevalent today preclude the emergence of antagonistic relations. We have entered an era of ambivalence in which nobody believes any more that they possess the truth. As it was precisely this belief from which antagonisms stemmed there is, without it, no longer any reason for antagonism to exist. Any attempt to organize collective identities in terms of left and right and to define an adversary is thereby discredited as being 'archaic' or (to talk like Tony Blair) 'Old Labour'.

Conflictual politics is deemed to belong to the past; the favoured type of democracy is consensual and depoliticized. Nowadays the key terms of political discourse are 'good governance' and 'partisan-free democracy'. In my view it is the inability of traditional parties to provide distinctive forms of identification around possible alternatives which has created a terrain on which right-wing populism can flourish. Indeed, right-wing populist parties are often the only ones which attempt to mobilize passions and to create collective forms of identifications. By contrast with all those who believe that politics can be reduced to individual motivation, they are well aware that politics consists in the creation of an 'Us' counterposed to a 'Them' and that it requires the creation of collective identities. Hence the powerful appeal of their discourse: it provides collective forms of identification around the notion of 'the people'.

In addition, social-democratic parties in many countries, under the banner of 'modernization', identify more or less exclusively with the middle classes and have stopped addressing the concerns of those groups whose demands are considered to be 'archaic' or 'retrograde'. In view of all this, it is no surprise if those groups who feel excluded from an effective exercise of citizenship by what they perceive as the 'establishment elites' are becoming increasingly alienated. In a context in which the dominant discourse proclaims that there is no alternative to the current neo-liberal form of globalization – and that we have to accept its dictates – it is small wonder that more and more people are keen to listen to those who claim that alternatives do exist and that they will give back to the people the power to make decisions. When democratic politics can no longer shape the discussion about how we should organize our common life, when it is limited to securing the necessary conditions for the smooth functioning of the market: in these circumstances the conditions are ripe for talented demagogues to articulate popular frustration. We should realize that to a great extent the success of right wing populist parties is due to the fact that they provide people with some form of hope, with the belief that things can be different. Of course this is an illusory hope, founded on false premises and on unacceptable mechanisms of exclusion in which xenophobia usually plays a central role. But when these parties are the only ones offering an outlet for political passions their claim to offer an alternative can be seductive. As a result, their appeal is likely to grow. In order to formulate an adequate response to them, it is necessary to understand the economic, social and political conditions in which they have emerged. The ability to do this presupposes a theoretical approach that does not deny the antagonistic dimension of the political.

Politics in the moral register

It is crucial to understand that the rise of right-wing populism cannot be stopped by moral condemnation: this, the dominant response to this phenomenon – and a predictable one, for it chimes with the dominant post-political perspective – has so far been completely inadequate. It is, however, a reaction worth examining closely as doing so will provide some insight into the form in which political antagonisms take today.

As already indicated, the dominant discourse asserts that the adversarial model of politics is at an end and that a consensual society, beyond left and right, has arrived. However, politics, as I have argued, always entails an 'Us'-'Them' distinction. This is why the consensus advocated by the defenders of partisan-free democracy cannot exist without a political frontier being created and an exterior being defined, a 'Them' which assures the identity of the consensus and the coherence of the 'Us'.

This 'Them' is today conveniently designated as the 'extreme right', a term which refers to an amalgam of groups and parties covering a wide spectrum, from fringe groups of extremists and neo-Nazis through to the authoritarian right and up to the various new, right-wing populist parties. Of course, such a heterogeneous construct cannot help one grasp the nature and the causes of the new right-wing populism. It is, however, very useful as a way of securing the identity of the 'good democrats'. Indeed, since politics has supposedly become non-adversarial, the 'Them' necessary to secure the 'Us' of the good democrats cannot be envisaged as a political adversary. So the extreme right comes in very handy because it allows one to draw a frontier at the moral level, between 'the good democrats' and the 'evil extreme right'; the latter can then be condemned morally instead of being fought politically. This is why moral condemnation and the establishment of a 'cordon sanitaire' around the 'extreme right' have become the dominant answer to the rise of right-wing populist movements.

However, what is in fact happening is very different from what the advocates of the post-political approach would have us believe. Politics, with its supposedly old-fashioned antagonisms, has not been superseded by moral concerns about 'life issues' and 'human rights'. Antagonistic politics is very much alive, except that now it is being played out in the register of morality. Indeed, far from having disappeared, frontiers between 'Us' and 'Them' are constantly being created; but, since the 'Them' can no longer be defined in political terms, these frontiers are drawn in moral terms, between 'us, the good' and 'them, the evil ones'.

My concern is that this type of politics – one played out in the moral register – is not conducive to the creation of the 'agonistic public sphere', which, as I have argued, is necessary for a robust democratic life. When the opponent is defined not in political but in moral terms, he can be envisaged only as an enemy, not an adversary: no agonistic debate is possible with the 'evil them'; they must be eradicated.

It should therefore be clear that the approach which claims that the friend-enemy model of politics has been superseded in fact ends up reinforcing the antagonistic model of politics that it has declared obsolete; it does so by constructing the 'Them' as a moral, that is, as an 'absolute' enemy, which, by its nature, cannot be transformed into an 'adversary'. Instead of helping to create a vibrant, agonistic public sphere with which democracy can be kept alive and indeed deepened, all those who proclaim the end of antagonism and the arrival of a consensual society are – by creating the conditions for the emergence of antagonisms that democratic institutions will be unable to manage – actually jeopardizing democracy.

Unless there is both a profound transformation in the way democratic politics is envisaged and a serious attempt to address the absence of forms of identification which would allow for a democratic mobilization of passions, the challenge posed by right-wing populist parties is unlikely to diminish. As the recent success of Le Pen in France, the Pim Fortuyn List in Holland, the People's Party in Denmark, and the Progress Party in Norway – not to mention the important advances already made by similar parties in Italy, Austria, Belgium and Switzerland – new political frontiers are being drawn in European politics. There is a danger that the old left–right distinction could soon be replaced by another distinction, one much less conducive to pluralistic democratic debate. Hence the urgent need to relinquish the illusions of the consensual model of politics and to create the foundations of an agonistic public sphere.

By limiting themselves to calls for reason, moderation and consensus, democratic parties display their lack of understanding of the workings of political logic. They do not understand the need to counter right-wing populism by mobilizing affects and passions towards democratic ends. They do not grasp that democratic politics needs to have a real purchase on people's desires and fantasies and that, instead of opposing interests to sentiments and reason to passions, it should offer forms of identifications which challenge those promoted by the right. This is not to say that reason and rational argument should disappear from politics; rather, that their place in it needs to be rethought. I am convinced that what is at stake in this enterprise is no less than the very future of democracy.

Notes

1 This article was first presented as an inaugural professorial lecture at the University of Westminster in May 2002.
2 For a development of this argument, see Chantal Mouffe, *The Democratic Paradox* (London: Verso, 2000).

References

Habermas, Jürgen. 1996. Reply to Symposium Participants. *Cardozo Law Review* 17: 4–5 (March).
Luhman, Niklas. 1990. The future of democracy. *Thesis 11*, no. 26.
Schmitt, Carl. 1976. *The Concept of the Political*. New Brunswick, NJ: Rutgers University Press.
Staten, Henry. 1985. *Wittgenstein and Derrida*. Oxford: Blackwell.

12

FOR AN AGONISTIC MODEL OF DEMOCRACY (2000)

As this turbulent century draws to a close, liberal democracy seems to be recognized as the only legitimate form of government. But does that indicate its final victory over its adversaries, as some would have it? There are serious reasons to be sceptical about such a claim. For once, it is not clear how strong is the present consensus and how long it will last. While very few dare to openly challenge the liberal-democratic model, the signs of disaffection with present institutions are becoming widespread. An increasing number of people feel that traditional parties have ceased to take their interests into account, and extreme right wing parties are making important inroads in many European countries. Moreover, even among those who are resisting the call of the demagogues, there is a marked cynicism about politics and politicians, and this has a very corrosive effect on popular adhesion to democratic values. There is clearly a negative force at work in most liberal-democratic societies, which contradicts the triumphalism that we have witnessed since the collapse of Soviet communism.

It is with those considerations in mind that I will be examining the present debate in democratic theory. I want to evaluate the proposals that democratic theorists are offering in order to consolidate democratic institutions. I will concentrate my attention on the new paradigm of democracy, the model of 'deliberative democracy', which is currently becoming the fastest-growing trend in the field. To be sure, the main idea – that in a democratic polity political decisions should be reached through a process of deliberation among free and equal citizens – has accompanied democracy since its birth in fifth-century BCE Athens. The ways of envisaging deliberation and the constituency of those entitled to deliberate have varied greatly, but deliberation has long played a central role in democratic thought. What we see today is therefore the revival of an old theme, not the sudden emergence of a new one.

What needs scrutinizing, though, is the reason for this renewed interest in deliberation, as well as its current modalities. One explanation has certainly to do with the problems facing democratic societies today. Indeed, one proclaimed aim of deliberative democrats is to offer an alternative to the understanding of democracy which has become dominant in the second half of the twentieth century, the 'aggregative model'. Such a model was initiated by Joseph Schumpeter's (1947) seminal work, *Capitalism, Socialism and Democracy*, which argued that, with the development of mass democracy, popular sovereignty as understood by the classical model of democracy had become inadequate. A new understanding of democracy was needed, putting the emphasis on aggregation of preferences, taking place through political parties for which people would have the capacity to vote at regular intervals. Hence Schumpeter's proposal to define democracy as the system in which people have the opportunity of accepting or rejecting their leaders thanks to a competitive electoral process.

Further developed by theorists like Anthony Downs (1957) in *An Economic Theory of Democracy*, the aggregative model became the standard one in the field which called itself 'empirical political theory'. The aim of this current was to elaborate a descriptive approach to democracy, in opposition to the classical normative one. The authors who adhered to this school considered that under modern conditions, notions like 'common good' and 'general will' had to be relinquished and that the pluralism of interests and values had to be acknowledged as coextensive with the very idea of 'the people'. Moreover, given that in their view, self-interest was what moved individuals to act, not the moral belief that they should do what was in the interests of the community, they declared that it was interests and preferences that should constitute the lines over which political parties should be organized and provide the matter over which bargaining and voting would take place. Popular participation in the taking of decisions should rather be discouraged, since it could only have dysfunctional consequences for the working of the system. Stability and order were more likely to result from compromise among interests than from mobilizing people towards an illusory consensus on the common good. As a consequence, democratic politics was separated from its normative dimension and began to be envisaged from a purely instrumentalist standpoint.

The dominance of the aggregative view, with its reduction of democracy to procedures for the treatment of interest-group pluralism, is what the new wave of normative political theory, inaugurated by John Rawls (1971) with the publication of his book *A Theory of Justice*, began to put into question and that the deliberative model is today challenging. They declare it to be at the origin of the current disaffection with democratic institutions and of the rampant crisis of legitimacy affecting western democracies. The future of liberal democracy, in their view, depends on recovering its moral dimension. While not denying 'the fact of pluralism' (Rawls) and the necessity to make room for many different conceptions of the good, deliberative democrats affirm that it is nevertheless possible to reach a consensus that would be deeper than a 'mere agreement on procedures', a consensus that could qualify as 'moral'.

Deliberative democracy: its aims

In wanting to offer an alternative to the dominant aggregative perspective, with its impoverished view of the democratic process, deliberative democrats are, of course, not alone. The specificity of their approach resides in promoting a form of *normative* rationality. Distinctive is also their attempt to provide a solid basis of allegiance to liberal democracy by reconciling the idea of democratic sovereignty with the defence of liberal institutions. Indeed, it is worth stressing that, while critical of a certain type of modus-vivendi liberalism, most of the advocates of deliberative democracy are not anti-liberals. Unlike previous Marxist critics, they stress the central role of liberal values in the modern conception of democracy. Their aim is not to relinquish liberalism but to recover its moral dimension and establish a close link between liberal values and democracy.

Their central claim is that it is possible, thanks to adequate procedures of deliberation, to reach forms of agreement that would satisfy both rationality (understood as defence of liberal rights) and democratic legitimacy (as represented by popular sovereignty). Their move consists in reformulating the democratic principle of popular sovereignty in such a way as to eliminate the dangers that it could pose to liberal values. It is the consciousness of those dangers that has often made liberals wary of popular participation and keen to find ways to discourage or limit it. Deliberative democrats believe that those perils can be avoided, thereby allowing liberals to embrace the democratic ideals with much more enthusiasm than they have done so far. One proposed solution is to reinterpret popular sovereignty in intersubjective terms and to redefine it as 'communicatively generated power'.[1]

There are many different versions of deliberative democracy but they can roughly be classified under two main schools, the first broadly influenced by John Rawls, and the second by Jürgen Habermas. I will therefore concentrate on these two authors, jointly with two of their followers, Joshua Cohen, for the Rawlsian side, Seyla Benhabib, for the Habermasian one. I am of course not denying that there are differences between the two approaches – which I will indicate during my discussion – but there are also important convergences which, from the point of view of my enquiry, are more significant than the disagreements.

As I have already indicated, one of the aims of the deliberative approach – an aim shared by both Rawls and Habermas – consists in securing a strong link between democracy and liberalism, refuting all those critics who – from the right as well as from the left – have proclaimed the contradictory nature of liberal democracy. Rawls, for instance, declares that his ambition is to elaborate a democratic liberalism which would answer to the claim of both liberty and equality. He wants to find a solution to the disagreement which has existed in democratic thought over the past centuries,

> between the tradition associated with Locke, which gives greater weight to what Constant called 'the liberties of the moderns', freedom of thought and conscience, certain basic rights of the person and of property and the rule of law, and the tradition associated with Rousseau, which gives greater weight

to what Constant called the 'liberties of the ancients', the equal political liberties and the values of public life.

(Rawls 1993, p. 5)

As far as Habermas is concerned, his recent book *Between Facts and Norms* makes it clear that one of the objectives of his procedural theory of democracy is to bring to the fore the 'co-originality' of fundamental individual rights and of popular sovereignty. On one side self-government serves to protect individual rights; on the other side, those rights provide the necessary conditions for the exercise of popular sovereignty. Once they are envisaged in such a way, he says, 'then one can understand how popular sovereignty and human rights go hand in hand, and hence grasp the co-originality of civic and private autonomy' (Habermas 1996, p. 127).

Their followers Cohen and Benhabib also stress the reconciliatory move present in the deliberative project. While Cohen states that it is mistaken to envisage the 'liberties of the moderns' as being exterior to the democratic process and that egalitarian and liberal values are to be seen as elements of democracy rather than as constraints upon it (Cohen 1988, p. 187), Benhabib declares that the deliberative model can transcend the dichotomy between the liberal emphasis on individual rights and liberties and the democratic emphasis on collective formation and will-formation (Benhabib 1996, p. 77).

Another point of convergence between the two versions of deliberative democracy is their common insistence on the possibility of grounding authority and legitimacy on some forms of public reasoning and their shared belief in a form of rationality which is not merely instrumental but has a normative dimension: the 'reasonable' for Rawls, 'communicative rationality' for Habermas. In both cases a strong separation is established between 'mere agreement' and 'rational consensus', and the proper field of politics is identified with the exchange of arguments among reasonable persons guided by the principle of impartiality.

Both Habermas and Rawls believe that we can find in the institutions of liberal democracy the idealized content of practical rationality. Where they diverge is in their elucidation of the form of practical reason embodied in democratic institutions. Rawls emphasizes the role of principles of justice reached through the device of the 'original position' that forces the participants to leave aside all their particularities and interests. His conception of 'justice as fairness' – which states the priority of basic liberal principles jointly with the 'constitutional essentials' – provides the framework for the exercise of 'free public reason'. As far as Habermas is concerned, he defends what he claims to be a strictly proceduralist approach in which no limits are put on the scope and content of the deliberation. It is the procedural constraints of the ideal speech situation that will eliminate the positions which cannot be agreed to by the participants in the moral 'discourse'. As recalled by Benhabib, the features of such a discourse are the following:

(1) participation in such deliberation is governed by the norms of equality and symmetry; all have the same chances to initiate speech acts, to question,

to interrogate, and to open debate; (2) all have the right to question the assigned topics of the conversation; and (3) all have the right to initiate reflexive arguments about the very rules of the discourse procedure and the way in which they are applied and carried out. There are no *prima facie* rules limiting the agenda of the conversation, or the identity of the participants, as long as any excluded person or group can justifiably show that they are relevantly affected by the proposed norm under question.

(Benhabib 1996, p. 70)

For this perspective the basis of legitimacy of democratic institutions derives from the fact that the instances which claim obligatory power do so on the presumption that their decisions represent an impartial standpoint which is equally in the interests of all. Cohen, after stating that democratic legitimacy arises from collective decisions among equal members, declares: 'According to a *deliberative* conception, a decision is collective just in case it emerges from arrangements of binding collective choices that establish conditions of *free public reasoning among equals who are governed by the decisions*' (Cohen 1988, p. 186).

In such a view it is not enough for a democratic procedure to take account of the interests of all and to reach a compromise that will establish a modus vivendi. The aim is to generate 'communicative power' and this requires establishing the conditions for a freely given assent of all concerned, hence the importance of finding procedures that would guarantee moral impartiality. Only then can one be sure that the consensus that is obtained is a rational one and not a mere agreement. This is why the accent is put on the nature of the deliberative procedure and on the types of reasons that are deemed acceptable for competent participants. Benhabib puts it in the following way:

According to the deliberative model of democracy, it is a necessary condition for attaining legitimacy and rationality with regard to collective decision making processes in a polity, that the institutions of this polity are so arranged that what is considered in the common interest of all results from processes of collective deliberation conducted rationally and fairly among free and equal individuals.

(Benhabib 1996, p. 69)

For the Habermasians, the process of deliberation is guaranteed to have reasonable outcomes to the extent that it realizes the condition of the 'ideal discourse': the more equal and impartial, the more open the process is, and the less the participants are coerced and ready to be guided by the force of the better argument, the more likely truly generalizable interests will be accepted by all those relevantly affected. Habermas and his followers do not deny that there will be obstacles to the realization of the ideal discourse, but those obstacles are conceived as empirical ones. They are due to the fact that it is unlikely, given the practical and empirical limitations of social life, that we will ever be able to completely leave aside all our particular interests in order to coincide with our universal rational self. This is why the ideal speech situation is presented as a 'regulative idea'.

Moreover, Habermas now accepts that there are issues that have to remain outside the practices of rational public debate, like existential issues which concern not questions of 'justice' but the 'good life' – this is for him the domain of ethics – or conflicts between interest groups about distributive problems that can only be resolved by means of compromises. But he considers that 'this differentiation within the field of issues that requires political decisions negates neither the prime importance of moral considerations nor the practicability of rational debate as the very form of political communication' (Habermas 1991, p. 448). In his view fundamental political questions belong to the same category as moral questions, and they can be decided rationally. Contrary to ethical questions, they do not depend on their context. The validity of their answers comes from an independent source and has a universal reach. He remains adamant that the exchange of arguments and counter-arguments as envisaged by his approach is the most suitable procedure for reaching the rational formation of the will from which the general interest will emerge.

Deliberative democracy, in both versions considered here, does concede to the aggregative model that under modern conditions a plurality of values and interests must be acknowledged and that consensus on what Rawls calls 'comprehensive' views of a religious, moral or philosophical nature has to be relinquished. But its advocates do not accept that this entails the impossibility of a rational consensus on political decisions, understanding by that not a simple modus vivendi but a moral type of agreement resulting from free reasoning among equals. Provided that the procedures of the deliberation secure impartiality, equality, openness and lack of coercion, they will guide the deliberation towards generalizable interests which can be agreed by all participants, thereby producing legitimate outcomes. The issue of legitimacy is more heavily stressed by the Habermasians, but there is no fundamental difference between Habermas and Rawls on this question. Indeed, Rawls defines the liberal principle of legitimacy in a way which is congruent with Habermas's view: 'Our exercise of political power is proper and hence justifiable only when it is exercised in accordance with a constitution the essentials of which all citizens may reasonably be expected to endorse in the light of principles and ideals acceptable to them as reasonable and rational' (Rawls 1993, p. 217). This normative force given to the principle of general justification chimes with Habermas's discourse ethics, and this is why one can certainly argue for the possibility of reformulating Rawlsian political constructivism in the language of discourse ethics.[2] In fact this is to some extent what Cohen does, and this is why he provides a good example of the compatibility between the two approaches. He particularly stresses the deliberative processes and affirms that, when envisaged as a system of social and political arrangements linking the exercise of power to free reasoning among equals, democracy requires the participants not only to be free and equal but also to be 'reasonable'. By this he means that 'they aim to defend and criticize institutions and programs in terms of considerations that others, as free and equal, have *reason to accept*, given the fact of reasonable pluralism' (Cohen 1988, p. 194).

The flight from pluralism

After having delineated the main ideas of deliberative democracy, I will now examine in more detail some points of the debate between Rawls and Habermas in view of bringing to the fore what I see as the crucial shortcoming of the deliberative approach. There are two issues which I take as particularly relevant.

The first is that one of the central claims of the 'political liberalism' advocated by Rawls is that it is a liberalism which is political, not metaphysical, and which is independent of comprehensive views. A clear-cut separation is established between the realm of the *private* – where a plurality of different and irreconcilable comprehensive views coexist – and the realm of the *public*, where an overlapping consensus can be established over a shared conception of justice.

Habermas contends that Rawls cannot succeed in his strategy of avoiding philosophically disputed issues, because it is impossible to develop his theory in the freestanding way that he announces. Indeed, his notion of the 'reasonable' as well as his conception of the 'person' necessarily involve him with questions concerning concepts of rationality and truth that he pretends to bypass (Habermas 1995, p. 126). Moreover, Habermas declares that his own approach is superior to the Rawlsian one because of its strictly procedural character which allows him to 'leave more questions open because it entrusts more to the *process* of rational opinion and will formation' (ibid., p. 131). By not positing a strong separation between public and private, it is better adapted to accommodate the wide-ranging deliberation that democracy entails. To that, Rawls retorts that Habermas's approach cannot be as strictly procedural as he pretends. It must include a substantive dimension, given that issues concerning the result of the procedures cannot be excluded from their design (Rawls 1995, pp. 170–74).

I think that they are both right in their respective criticisms. Indeed, Rawls's conception is not as independent of comprehensive views as he believes, and Habermas cannot be as purely proceduralist as he claims. That both are unable to separate the public from the private or the procedural from the substantial as clearly as they declare is very telling. What this reveals is the impossibility of achieving what each of them, albeit in different ways, is really aiming at, that is, circumscribing a domain that would not be subject to the pluralism of values and where a consensus without exclusion could be established. Indeed, Rawls's avoidance of comprehensive doctrines is motivated by his belief that no rational agreement is possible in this field. This is why, in order for liberal institutions to be acceptable to people with differing moral, philosophical and religious views, they must be neutral with respect to comprehensive views. Hence the strong separation that he tries to install between the realm of the private – with its pluralism of irreconcilable values – and the realm of the public, where a political agreement on a liberal conception of justice would be secured through the creation of an overlapping consensus on justice.

In the case of Habermas, a similar attempt of escaping the implications of value pluralism is made through the distinction between *ethics* – a domain which allows for competing conceptions of the good life – and *morality* – a domain where a strict proceduralism can be implemented and impartiality reached leading to the formulation of universal principles. Rawls and Habermas want to ground adhesion to liberal democracy on a type of rational agreement that would preclude the possibility of contestation. This is why they need to relegate pluralism to a non-public domain in order to insulate politics from its consequences. That they are unable to maintain the tight separation they advocate has very important implications for democratic politics. It highlights the fact that the domain of politics – even when fundamental issues like justice or basic principles are concerned – is not a neutral terrain that could be insulated from the pluralism of values and where rational, universal solutions could be formulated.

The second issue is another question that concerns the relation between private autonomy and political autonomy. As we have seen, both authors aim at reconciling the 'liberties of the ancients' with the 'liberties of the moderns' and they argue that the two types of autonomy necessarily go together. However, Habermas considers that only his approach manages to establish the co-originality of individual rights and democratic participation. He affirms that Rawls subordinates democratic sovereignty to liberal rights because he envisages public autonomy as a means to authorize private autonomy. But as Charles Larmore has pointed out, Habermas, for his part, privileges the democratic aspect, since he asserts that the importance of individual rights lies in their making democratic self-government possible (Larmore 1996, p. 217). So we have to conclude that, in this case again, neither of them is able to deliver what they announce. What they want to deny is the paradoxical nature of modern democracy and the fundamental tension between the logic of democracy and the logic of liberalism. They are unable to acknowledge that, while it is indeed the case that individual rights and democratic self-government are constitutive of liberal democracy – whose novelty resides precisely in the articulation of those two traditions – there exists between their respective 'grammars' a tension that can never be eliminated. To be sure, contrary to what adversaries like Carl Schmitt have argued, this does not mean that liberal democracy is a doomed regime. Such a tension, though ineradicable, can be negotiated in different ways. Indeed, a great part of democratic politics is precisely about the negotiation of that paradox and the articulation of precarious solutions.[3] What is misguided is the search for a final rational resolution. Not only can it not succeed, but moreover it leads to putting undue constraints on the political debate. Such a search should be recognized for what it really is, another attempt at insulating politics from the effects of the pluralism of value, this time by trying to fix once and for all the meaning and hierarchy of the central liberal-democratic values. Democratic theory should renounce those forms of escapism and face the challenge that the recognition of the pluralism of values entails. This does not mean accepting a total pluralism, and some limits need to be put to the kind of confrontation which is going to be seen as legitimate in the public sphere. But the political nature of the limits should be acknowledged instead of being presented as requirements of morality or rationality.

Which allegiance for democracy?

If both Rawls and Habermas, albeit in different ways, aim at reaching a form of rational consensus instead of a 'simple modus vivendi' or a 'mere agreement', it is because they believe that, by procuring stable grounds for liberal democracy, such a consensus will contribute to securing the future of liberal-democratic institutions. As we have seen, while Rawls considers that the key issue is justice, for Habermas it has to do with legitimacy. According to Rawls, a well-ordered society is one which functions according to the principles laid down by a shared conception of justice. This is what produces stability and citizens' acceptance of their institutions. For Habermas a stable and well-functioning democracy requires the creation of a polity integrated through rational insight into legitimacy. This is why for Habermasians the central issue lies in finding a way to guarantee that decisions taken by democratic institutions represent an impartial standpoint expressing equally the interests of all, which requires establishing procedures able to deliver rational results through democratic participation. As put by Seyla Benhabib, 'legitimacy in complex democratic societies must be thought to result from the free and unconstrained public deliberation of all on matters of common concern' (Benhabib 1996, p. 68).

In their desire to show the limitations of the democratic consensus as envisaged by the aggregative model – only concerned with instrumental rationality and the promotion of self-interest – deliberative democrats insist on the importance of another type of rationality, the rationality at work in communicative action and free public reason. They want to make it the central moving force of democratic citizens and the basis of their allegiance to their common institutions.

Their concern with the current state of democratic institutions is one that I share, but I consider their answer as being profoundly inadequate. The solution to our current predicament does not reside in replacing the dominant 'means-ends rationality' by another form of rationality, a 'deliberative' and 'communicative' one. True, there is space for different understandings of reason and it is important to complexify the picture offered by the holders of the instrumentalist view. However, simply replacing one type of rationality by another is not going to help us address the real problem that the issue of allegiance poses. As Michael Oakeshott has reminded us, the authority of political institutions is not a question of *consent* but of the continuous acknowledgement of *cives* who recognize their obligation to obey the conditions prescribed in *respublica* (Oakeshott 1975, pp. 149–58). Following that line of thought we can realize that what is really at stake in the allegiance to democratic institutions is the constitution of an ensemble of practices that make possible the creation of democratic citizens. This is not a matter of *rational justification* but of *availability* of democratic forms of individuality and sub-jectivity. By privileging rationality, both the deliberative and the aggregative per-spectives leave aside a central element which is the crucial role played by passions and affects in securing allegiance to democratic values. This cannot be ignored, and it entails envisaging the question of democratic citizenship in a very different way.

The failure of current democratic theory to tackle the question of citizenship is the consequence of their operating with a conception of the subject which sees individuals as prior to society, bearers of natural rights, and either utility maximizing agents or rational subjects. In all cases, they are abstracted from social and power relations, language, culture and the whole set of practices that make agency possible. What is precluded in these rationalistic approaches is the very question of what are the conditions of existence of the democratic subject.

The view that I want to put forward is that it is not by providing arguments about the rationality embodied in liberal democratic institutions that one can contribute to the creation of democratic citizens. Democratic individuals can only be made possible by multiplying the institutions, the discourses, the forms of life that foster identification with democratic values. This is why, although agreeing with deliberative democrats about the need for a different understanding of democracy, I see their proposals as counterproductive. To be sure, we need to formulate an alternative to the aggregative model and to the instrumentalist conception of politics that it fosters. It has become clear that by discouraging the active involvement of citizens in the running of the polity and by encouraging the privatization of life, they have not secured the stability that they were announcing. Extreme forms of individualism have become widespread which threaten the very social fabric. On the other side, deprived of the possibility of identifying with valuable conceptions of citizenship, many people are increasingly searching for other forms of collective identification, which can very often put into jeopardy the civic bond that should unite a democratic political association. The growth of various religious, moral and ethnic fundamentalisms is, in my view, the direct consequence of the democratic deficit which characterizes most liberal-democratic societies.

To seriously tackle those problems, the only way is to envisage democratic citizenship from a different perspective, one that puts the emphasis on the types of *practices* and not the forms of *argumentation*. In *The Return of the Political*, I have argued that the reflections on civil association developed by Michael Oakeshott in *On Human Conduct* are very pertinent for envisaging the modern form of political community and the type of bond uniting democratic citizens, the specific language of civil intercourse that he calls the *respublica* (Mouffe 1993, ch. 4). But we can also take inspiration from Wittgenstein, who, as I have shown,[4] provides very important insights for a critique of rationalism. Indeed, in his later work he has highlighted the fact that, in order to have agreement in opinions, there must first be agreement in forms of life. In his view, to agree on the definition of a term is not enough and we need agreement in the way we use it. This means that procedures should be envisaged as a complex ensemble of practices. It is because they are inscribed in shared forms of life and agreements in judgments that procedures can be accepted and followed. They cannot be seen as rules that are created on the basis of principles and then applied to specific cases. Rules for Wittgenstein are always abridgements of practices, they are inseparable from specific forms of life. This indicates that a strict separation between 'procedural' and 'substantial' or between 'moral' and 'ethical', separations which are central to the Habermasian approach, cannot be maintained. Procedures always involve substantial ethical commitments, and there can never be such a thing as purely neutral procedures.

Viewed from such a standpoint, allegiance to democracy and belief in the value of its institutions do not depend on giving them an intellectual foundation. It is more in the nature of what Wittgenstein likens to 'a passionate commitment to a system of reference. Hence, although it's *belief*, it is really a way of living, or of assessing one's life' (Wittgenstein 1980, p. 85e). Contrary to deliberative democracy, such a perspective also implies, to acknowledge the limits of consensus: 'Where two principles really do meet which cannot be reconciled with one another, then each man declares the other a fool and an heretic. I said I would "combat" the other man, – but wouldn't I give him reasons? Certainly; but how far do they go? At the end of reasons comes persuasion' (Wittgenstein 1969, p. 81e).

Seeing things in that way should make us realize that taking pluralism seriously requires that we give up the dream of a rational consensus which entails the fantasy that we could escape from our human form of life. In our desire for a total grasp, says Wittgenstein, 'We have got on to the slippery ice where there is no friction and so in a certain sense the conditions are ideal, but also, just because of that, we are unable to walk: so we need *friction*. Back to the rough ground' (ibid., p. 46e).

Back to the rough ground here means coming to terms with the fact that, far from being merely empirical or epistemological, the obstacles to rationalist devices like the 'original condition' or 'the ideal discourse' are ontological. Indeed, the free and unconstrained public deliberation of all on matters of common concern is a conceptual impossibility, since the particular forms of life which are presented as its 'impediments' are its very condition of possibility. Without them no communication, no deliberation, would ever take place. There is absolutely no justification for attributing a special privilege to a so-called 'moral point of view' governed by rationality and impartiality and where a rational universal consensus could be reached.

An 'agonistic' model of democracy

Besides putting the emphasis on practices and language-games, an alternative to the rationalist framework also requires coming to terms with the fact that power is constitutive of social relations. One of the shortcomings of the deliberative approach is that, by postulating the availability of a public sphere where power would have been eliminated and where a rational consensus could be realized, this model of democratic politics is unable to acknowledge the dimension of antagonism that the pluralism of values entails and its ineradicable character. This is why it is bound to miss the specificity of the political which it can only envisage as a specific domain of morality. Deliberative democracy provides a very good illustration of what Carl Schmitt had said about liberal thought: 'In a very systematic fashion liberal thought evades or ignores state and politics and moves instead in a typical always recurring polarity of two heterogeneous spheres, namely ethics and economics' (Schmitt 1976, p. 70). Indeed, to the aggregative model, inspired by economics, the only alternative deliberative democrats can oppose is one that collapses politics into ethics.

In order to remedy this serious deficiency, we need a democratic model able to grasp the nature of the political. This requires developing an approach which places the question of power and antagonism at its very centre. It is such an approach that I want to advocate and whose theoretical bases have been delineated in *Hegemony and Socialist Strategy* (Laclau and Mouffe, 1985). The central thesis of the book is that social objectivity is constituted through acts of power. This implies that any social objectivity is ultimately political and that it has to show the traces of exclusion which governs its constitution. This point of convergence – or rather mutual collapse – between objectivity and power is what we meant by 'hegemony'. This way of posing the problem indicates that power should not be conceived as an external relation taking place between two preconstituted identities, but rather as constituting the identities themselves. Since any political order is the expression of a hegemony, of a specific pattern of power relations, political practice cannot be envisaged as simply representing the interests of preconstituted identities, but as constituting those identities themselves in a precarious and always vulnerable terrain.

To assert the hegemonic nature of any kind of social order is to operate a displacement of the traditional relation between democracy and power. According to the deliberative approach, the more democratic a society is, the less power would be constitutive of social relations. But if we accept that relations of power are constitutive of the social, then the main question for democratic politics is not how to eliminate power but how to constitute forms of power more compatible with democratic values.

Coming to terms with the constitutive nature of power implies relinquishing the ideal of a democratic society as the realization of a perfect harmony or transparency. The democratic character of a society can only be given by the fact that no limited social actor can attribute to herself or himself the representation of the totality and claim to have the 'mastery' of the foundation.

Democracy requires, therefore, that the purely constructed nature of social relations finds its complement in the purely pragmatic grounds of the claims to power legitimacy. This implies that there is no unbridgeable gap between power and legitimacy – not obviously in the sense that all power is automatically legitimate, but in the sense that: (a) if any power has been able to impose itself, it is because it has been recognized as legitimate in some quarters; and (b) if legitimacy is not based in an aprioristic ground, it is because it is based in some form of successful power. This link between legitimacy and power and the hegemonic ordering that this entails is precisely what the deliberative approach forecloses by positing the possibility of a type of rational argumentation where power has been eliminated and where legitimacy is grounded on pure rationality.

Once the theoretical terrain has been delineated in such a way, we can begin formulating an alternative to both the aggregative and the deliberative model, one that I propose to call 'agonistic pluralism'.[5] A first distinction is needed in order to clarify the new perspective that I am putting forward, the distinction between 'politics' and 'the political'. By 'the political', I refer to the dimension of antagonism that is inherent in human relations, antagonism that can take many forms and emerge in different types of social relations. 'Politics', on the other side, indicates the ensemble of practices, discourses and institutions which seek to establish a certain order and organize human coexistence in conditions that are always potentially conflictual because they are affected by the dimension of 'the political'. I consider that it is only when we acknowledge the dimension of 'the political' and understand that 'politics' consists in domesticating hostility and in trying to defuse the potential antagonism that exists in human relations, that we can pose what I take to be the central question for democratic politics. This question, *pace* the rationalists, is not how to arrive at a consensus without exclusion, since this would imply the eradication of the political. Politics aims at the creation of unity in a context of conflict and diversity; it is always concerned with the creation of an 'us' by the determination of a 'them'. The novelty of democratic politics is not the overcoming of this us/them opposition – which is an impossibility – but the different way in which it is established. The crucial issue is to establish this us/them discrimination in a way that is compatible with pluralist democracy.

Envisaged from the point of view of 'agonistic pluralism', the aim of democratic politics is to construct the 'them' in such a way that it is no longer perceived as an enemy to be destroyed, but as an 'adversary', that is, somebody whose ideas we combat but whose right to defend those ideas we do not put into question. This is the real meaning of liberal-democratic tolerance, which does not entail condoning ideas that we oppose or being indifferent to standpoints that we disagree with, but treating those who defend them as legitimate opponents. This category of the 'adversary' does not eliminate antagonism, though, and it should be distinguished from the liberal notion of the competitor with which it is sometimes identified. An adversary is an enemy, but a legitimate enemy, one with whom we have some common ground because we have a shared adhesion to the ethico-political principles of liberal democracy: liberty and equality. But we disagree concerning the meaning and implementation of those principles, and such a disagreement is not one that could be resolved through deliberation and rational discussion. Indeed, given the ineradicable pluralism of value, there is no rational resolution of the conflict, hence its antagonistic dimension.[6] This does not mean, of course, that adversaries can never cease to disagree, but that does not prove that antagonism has been eradicated. To accept the view of the adversary is to undergo a radical change in political identity. It is more a sort of *conversion* than a process of rational persuasion (in the same way as Thomas Kuhn has argued that adherence to a new scientific paradigm is a conversion). Compromises are, of course, also possible; they are part and parcel of politics; but they should be seen as temporary respites in an ongoing confrontation.

Introducing the category of the 'adversary' requires complexifying the notion of antagonism and distinguishing two different forms in which it can emerge, *antagonism* properly speaking and *agonism*. *Antagonism* is struggle between enemies, while *agonism* is struggle between adversaries. We can therefore reformulate our problem by saying that envisaged from the perspective of 'agonistic pluralism' the aim of democratic politics is to transform *antagonism* into *agonism*. This requires providing channels through which collective passions will be given ways to express themselves over issues which, while allowing enough possibility for identification, will not construct the opponent as an enemy but as an adversary. An important difference with the model of 'deliberative democracy' is that for 'agonistic pluralism', the prime task of democratic politics is not to eliminate passions from the sphere of the public, in order to render a rational consensus possible, but to mobilize those passions towards democratic designs.

One of the keys to the thesis of agonistic pluralism is that, far from jeopardizing democracy, agonistic confrontation is in fact its very condition of existence. Modern democracy's specificity lies in the recognition and legitimation of conflict and the refusal to suppress it by imposing an authoritarian order. Breaking with the symbolic representation of society as an organic body – which was characteristic of the holist mode of social organization – a democratic society acknowledges the pluralism of values, the 'disenchantment of the world' diagnosed by Max Weber and the unavoidable conflicts that it entails.

I agree with those who affirm that a pluralist democracy demands a certain amount of consensus and that it requires allegiance to the values which constitute its 'ethico-political principles'. But since those ethico-political principles can only exist through many different and conflicting interpretations, such a consensus is bound to be a 'conflictual consensus'. This is indeed the privileged terrain of agonistic confrontation among adversaries. Ideally such a confrontation should be staged around the diverse conceptions of citizenship which correspond to the different interpretations of the ethico-political principles: liberal-conservative, social-democratic, neo-liberal, radical-democratic, and so on. Each of them proposes its own interpretation of the 'common good', and tries to implement a different form of hegemony. To foster allegiance to its institutions, a democratic system requires the availability of those contending forms of citizenship identification. They provide the terrain in which passions can be mobilized around democratic objectives and antagonism transformed into agonism.

A well-functioning democracy calls for a vibrant clash of democratic political positions. If this is missing there is the danger that this democratic confrontation will be replaced by a confrontation among other forms of collective identification, as is the case with identity politics. Too much emphasis on consensus and the refusal of confrontation lead to apathy and disaffection with political participation. Worse still, the result can be the crystallization of collective passions around issues which cannot be managed by the democratic process and an explosion of antagonisms that can tear up the very basis of civility.

It is for that reason that the ideal of a pluralist democracy cannot be to reach a rational consensus in the public sphere. Such a consensus cannot exist. We have to accept that every consensus exists as a temporary result of a provisional hegemony, as a stabilization of power, and that it always entails some form of exclusion. The ideas that power could be dissolved through a rational debate and that legitimacy could be based on pure rationality are illusions which can endanger democratic institutions.

What the deliberative-democracy model is denying is the dimension of undecidability and the ineradicability of antagonism which are constitutive of the political. By postulating the availability of a non-exclusive public sphere of deliberation where a rational consensus could obtain, they negate the inherently conflictual nature of modern pluralism. They are unable to recognize that bringing a deliberation to a close always results from a *decision* which excludes other possibilities and for which one should never refuse to bear responsibility by invoking the commands of general rules or principles. This is why a perspective like 'agonistic pluralism', which reveals the impossibility of establishing a consensus without exclusion, is of fundamental importance for democratic politics. By warning us against the illusion that a fully achieved democracy could ever be instantiated, it forces us to keep the democratic contestation alive. To make room for dissent and to foster the institutions in which it can be manifested is vital for a pluralist democracy, and one should abandon the very idea that there could ever be a time in which it would cease to be necessary because the society is now 'well-ordered'. An 'agonistic' approach acknowledges the real nature of its frontiers and the forms of exclusion that they entail, instead of trying to disguise them under the veil of rationality or morality. Coming to terms with the hegemonic nature of social relations and identities, it can contribute to subverting the ever present temptation existing in democratic societies to naturalize its frontiers and essentialize its identities. For this reason it is much more receptive than the deliberative model to the multiplicity of voices that contemporary pluralist societies encompass and to the complexity of their power structure.

Notes

1 See, for instance, Jürgen Habermas, 'Three Normative Models of Democracy', in Seyla Benhabib (ed.), *Democracy and Difference* (Princeton, NJ: Princeton University Press, 1996).

2 Such an argument is made by Rainer Forst in his review of 'Political Liberalism' in *Constellations* 1:1, p. 169.

3 I have developed this argument in my article 'Carl Schmitt and the Paradox of Liberal Democracy', in Chantal Mouffe (ed.), *The Challenge of Carl Schmitt* (London, 1999); also Mouffe (2000), ch. 2.

4 Mouffe (2000), ch. 3.

5 'Agonistic pluralism' as defined here is an attempt to operate what Richard Rorty would call a 'redescription' of the basic self-understanding of the liberal-democratic regime, one which stresses the importance of acknowledging its conflictual dimension. It therefore needs to be distinguished from the way the same term is used by John Gray to refer to the larger rivalry between whole forms of life which he sees as 'the deeper truth of which agonistic liberalism is only one exemplar'. In John Gray, *Enlightenment's Wake: Politics and Culture at the Close of the Modern Age* (London: 1995), p. 84.

6 This antagonistic dimension, which can never be completely eliminated but only 'tamed' or 'sublimated' by being, so to speak, 'played out' in an agonistic way, is what, in my

view, distinguishes my understanding of agonism from the one put forward by other 'agonistic theorists', those who are influenced by Nietzsche or Hannah Arendt, like William Connolly or Bonnie Honig. It seems to me that their conception leaves open the possibility that the political could under certain conditions be made absolutely congruent with the ethical, optimism which I do not share.

References

Benhabib, Seyla. 1996. Toward a Deliberative Model of Democratic Legitimacy. In *Democracy and Difference*, ed. Seyla Benhabib. Princeton, NJ: Princeton University Press.
Cohen, Joshua. 1988. Democracy and Liberty. In *Deliberative Democracy*, ed. J. Elster. Cambridge: Cambridge University Press.
Downs, Anthony. 1957. *An Economic Theory of Democracy*. New York: Harper & Row.
Habermas, Jürgen. 1991. Further Reflections on the Public Sphere. In *Habermas and the Public Sphere*, ed. C. Calhoun. Cambridge, MA: MIT Press.
——1995. 'Reconciliation Through the Public Use of Reason: Remarks on John Rawls's 'Political Liberalism'. *Journal of Philosophy* XCII.
——1996. *Between Facts and Norms: Contributions to a Discourse Theory of Law and Democracy*. Cambridge: Polity.
Laclau, Ernesto and Mouffe, Chantal. 1985. *Hegemony and Socialist Strategy*. London: Verso.
Larmore, Charles. 1996. *The Morals of Modernity*. Cambridge: Cambridge University Press.
Mouffe, Chantal. 1993. *The Return of the Political*. London: Verso.
——2000. *The Democratic Paradox*. London: Verso.
Oakeshott, Michael. 1975. *On Human Conduct*. Oxford: Clarendon Press.
Rawls, John. 1971. *A Theory of Justice*. Cambridge, MA: Harvard University Press.
——1993. *Political Liberalism*. New York: Columbia University Press.
——1995. 'Reply to Habermas'. *Journal of Philosophy* XCII: 3.
Schmitt, Carl. 1976. *The Concept of the Political*. New Brunswick, NJ: Rutgers University Press.
Schumpeter, Joseph. 1947. *Capitalism, Socialism and Democracy*. New York: Harper.
Wittgenstein, Ludwig. 1958. *Philosophical Investigations*. Oxford: Blackwell.
——1969. *On Certainty*. New York: Harper.
——1980. *Culture and Value*. Chicago: University of Chicago Press.

13

CULTURAL WORKERS AS ORGANIC INTELLECTUALS (2008)

Can artistic and cultural practices still play a critical role in societies in which every critical gesture is quickly recuperated and neutralized by the dominant powers? Such a question is increasingly raised, and there is no agreement about the answer. Many people argue that in our consumer societies aesthetics has triumphed in all realms and that the effect of this triumph has been the creation of a hedonistic culture in which there is no longer any place for art to provide a truly subversive experience. The blurring of the lines between art and advertising is such that the possibility of critical public spaces has lost its meaning. We are now living in societies where even the public has become privatized.

Indeed, reflecting on the growth of the global culture industry some theorists claim that Adorno's and Horkheimer's worst nightmares have become true. The production of symbols is today a central goal of capitalism, and, through the development of the creative industries, individuals are now totally subjugated to the control of capital. Not just consumers but also cultural producers are prisoners of the culture industry dominated by media and entertainment corporations. They have been transformed into passive effects of the capitalist system.

Fortunately, this pessimistic diagnosis is not shared by everybody. For instance there are theorists who claim that the analysis of Adorno and Horkheimer, based as it is on the Fordist model, no longer provides a useful guide to examine the new forms of production that have become dominant in the current post-Fordist mode of capitalist regulation. They see those new forms of production as creating new modes of resistance pointing towards a revitalization of an emancipatory project to which artistic practices could make a decisive contribution. Such a view is supported by insights from André Gorz, who has said:

> When self-exploitation acquires a central role in the process of valorization, the production of subjectivity becomes a terrain of the central conflict …

social relations that elude the grasp of value, competitive individualism and market exchange make the latter appear by contrast in their political dimension, as extensions of the power of capital. A front of total resistance to this power is made possible which necessarily overflows the terrain of production of knowledge towards new practices of living, consuming and collective appropriation of common spaces and everyday culture.

(Gorz 2004, p. 209)

Those who defend this approach affirm that the field of artistic intervention should be widened by intervening directly in a multiplicity of social spaces in order to oppose the program of the total social mobilization of capitalism. The objective, they say, should be to undermine the imaginary environment necessary for its reproduction.

I agree that artistic practices could still play a critical role and that they could make a decisive contribution to the struggle against capitalist domination. However I will argue that this requires not only an adequate grasp of the nature of the transition undergone by advanced industrial societies during the last decades of the 20th century, but also a proper understanding of the dynamic of democratic politics; an understanding which, I contend, can only be obtained by acknowledging its hegemonic nature. I will examine those two points in turn.

From Fordism to post-Fordism

As far as the changes that have affected capitalist societies are concerned, different theories conceptualize them either as a transition from industrial to post-industrial society, a move from Fordism to post-Fordism, or a progression from a disciplinary society to a society of control. I will concentrate my attention on the first perspective: from Fordism to post-Fordism and discuss it by examining the differences between the approaches influenced by the critical theory of Adorno and Horkheimer and those that are influenced by the Italian autonomist tradition. Their main disagreement lies in the role that the culture industry has played in the transformations of capitalism. It is well known that Adorno and Horkheimer saw the development of the culture industry as the moment when the Fordist mode of production finally managed to enter into the field of culture. They present this evolution as a further stage in the process of commodification and of subjugation of society to the requisites of capitalist production. For Paolo Virno and some other post-Operaists, on the contrary, it is the culture industry that played an important role in the transition between Fordism and post-Fordism. According to them it is in that field that new production practices emerged which led to the overcoming of Fordism. In his book *A Grammar of the Multitude* Virno (2004) asserts that the spaces granted to the informal, the unexpected and the unplanned, which for Horkheimer and Adorno were uninfluential remnants of the past, should be seen as anticipatory omens. With the development of immaterial labor, they began to play an increasingly important role and opened the way for new forms of social relations. In advanced capitalism, according to Virno, the labor process has become performative, and it mobilizes the most universal requisites of the species: perception, language, memory and feelings. Contemporary production is 'virtuosic' and productive labor in its totality appropriates the special characteristics of the performing artist. This is why he argues that the culture industry should be seen as the matrix of post-Fordism.

Theorists influenced by the autonomist tradition share the conviction that the transition from Fordism to post-Fordism has to be understood, not as dictated by the logic of the development of capitalist forces of production, but as a reaction to new practices of resistance on the part of workers. Disagreements exist among them, however, about the political consequences of this transition. Although many of them use the notion of 'multitude' to refer to a new type of political agent characteristic of the current period, they do not envisage its role in the same way. Some, like Michael Hardt and Antonio Negri, celebrate in the 'multitude' the emergence of a new revolutionary subject that will necessarily bring down the new forms of domination embodied in empire (Hardt and Negri 2000; 2004). Incorporating – although not always in a faithful way – the analyses of Foucault and Deleuze, Hardt and Negri claim that the end of the disciplinary regime that was exercised over bodies in enclosed spaces like schools, factories and asylums and its replacement by procedures of control linked to the growth of networks, is leading to a new type of governance which permits more autonomous and independent forms of subjectivity. With the expansion of new forms of cooperative communication and the invention of new communicative forms of life, those subjectivities, they write, can express themselves freely and contribute to the formation of a new set of social relations that will finally replace the capitalist system.

While acknowledging the potential opened in the post-Fordist stage for new forms of life, other post-Operaist theorists are not so sanguine about the future. For instance, Virno sees the growth of the multitude as an ambivalent phenomenon and he acknowledges the new forms of subjection and precarisation that are typical of the post-Fordist stage. It is true that people are not as passive as before, but it is because they have now become active actors of their own precarisation. So instead of seeing in the generalization of immaterial labor a type of 'spontaneous communism', as Hardt and Negri do, Virno tends to see post-Fordism as a manifestation of the 'communism of capital'. This does not mean that he abandons every hope for emancipation, but it is in the refusal to work and the different forms of exodus and disobedience that he locates such hope.

I would certainly not deny the crucial transformations in the mode of regulation of capitalism represented by the transition to post-Fordism, but I consider that the dynamics of this transition are better apprehended within the framework of the theory of hegemony. I agree with those who insist on the importance of not seeing those transformations as the mere consequence of technological progress, and of bringing to the fore their political dimension. These transformations should indeed be understood as a move by capital to provide what was a fundamentally political answer to the crisis of governability of the 1970s. What I want to stress however is that many factors have contributed to this transition and that it is necessary to recognize its complex nature.

My problem with Operaist and some post-Operaist views is that, by putting an exclusive emphasis on workers' struggles, they tend to see this transition as if it was exclusively driven by one single logic: workers' resistances to the process of exploitation forcing the capitalists to reorganize the process of production and to move to the post-Fordist era with its centrality of immaterial labor. This logic is accompanied by the assumption by some theorists like Hardt and Negri that those resistances will necessarily lead to the final collapse of the system. In their view, capitalism can only be reactive, and, differing with Deleuze and Guattari, they refuse to accept the creative roles played by both capital and the working class. What they deny is, in fact, the role played in this transition by the hegemonic struggle, and this is why their conception of politics is a flawed one.

A hegemonic approach

According to the approach that I am advocating and whose theoretical bases have been established in *Hegemony and Socialist Strategy: Towards a Radical Democratic Politics* (Laclau and Mouffe, 1985) the two key concepts needed to address the question of the political are 'antagonism' and 'hegemony'. On the one hand, it is necessary to acknowledge the dimension of 'the political' as the ever-present possibility of antagonism, and this requires, on the other hand, coming to terms with the lack of a final ground and the undecidability that pervades every order. This means recognizing the hegemonic nature of every kind of social order and envisaging every society as the product of a series of practices whose aim is to establish order in a context of contingency. Those practices of articulation through which a certain order is created and the meaning of social institutions fixed, we call 'hegemonic practices'. According to this approach, every order is the temporary and precarious articulation of contingent practices. Things could always have been otherwise, and every order is therefore predicated on the exclusion of other possibilities. It is in that sense that it can be called 'political', since it is the expression of a particular structure of power relations. What is at a given moment considered the 'natural' order, jointly with the 'common sense' that accompanies it, is the result of sedimented hegemonic practices; it is never the manifestation of a deeper objectivity exterior to the practices that bring it into being. Every hegemonic order is susceptible to being challenged by 'counter-hegemonic' practices, i.e. practices that attempt to disarticulate the existing order so as to install another form of hegemony.

I submit that it is necessary to introduce this hegemonic dimension when one envisages the transition from Fordism to post-Fordism. In order to do this, we can find interesting insights in the interpretation of that transition defended by Luc Boltanski and Eve Chiapello. In their book *The New Spirit of Capitalism* (2005) they bring to light the role played by what they call 'artistic critique' in the transformation undergone by capitalism in the last decades of the 20th century. They indicate how the demands of autonomy of the new movements of the 60s have been harnessed in the development of the post-Fordist networked economy and transformed into new forms of control. The aesthetic strategies of the counter-culture: the search for authenticity, the ideal of self-management, the anti-hierarchical exigency, are now used to promote the conditions required by the current mode of capitalist regulation, replacing the disciplinary framework characteristic of the Fordist period. Nowadays artistic and cultural production plays a central role in the process of capital valorization, and it has become an important element of capitalist productivity.

From my point of view what is interesting in this approach is that it shows that an important dimension of the transition from Fordism to post-Fordism was a process of discursive rearticulation of a set of existing discourses and practices, allowing us to visualize this transition in terms of an hegemonic struggle. To be sure, Boltanski and Chiapello do not use this terminology, but theirs is a clear example of what Gramsci calls 'hegemony through neutralization' or 'passive revolution' to refer to the situation where, by satisfying them in a way that neutralizes their subversive potential, demands which challenge an established hegemonic order are recuperated by the existing system. To apprehend the transition from Fordism to post-Fordism in such a way helps us to see it as a hegemonic move by capital to re-establish its leading role and to restore its legitimacy.

By adding to the analysis offered by Boltanski and Chiapello the undeniable role played in this transition by workers' resistances, we can obtain a more complex understanding of the forces at play in the emergence of the current neo-liberal hegemony. This hegemony is the result of a set of political interventions in a complex field of economic, legal and ideological forces. It is a discursive construction that articulates in a very specific manner a manifold of practices, discourses and language-games of very different natures. Through a process of sedimentation, the political origin of those contingent practices has been erased and they have become naturalized. Neo-liberal practices and institutions can therefore appear as the outcome of natural processes, and the forms of identifications that they have produced have crystallized in identities which are taken for granted. This is how the 'common sense' which constitutes the framework for what most people perceive as possible and desirable has been established. To challenge neo-liberalism it is therefore vital to transform this framework, and this is precisely what the hegemonic struggle should be about.

An agonistic politics

To imagine how to wage a successful counter-hegemonic struggle it is also necessary to grasp what is really at stake in democratic politics. I have argued in previous works that once the ineradicable dimension of antagonism is acknowledged it becomes clear that one of the main tasks of democratic politics consists in defusing the potential antagonism that exists in social relations. This can be done by fostering an ensemble of institutions, practices and language games which will make it possible for conflicts to take an 'agonistic' form instead of an 'antagonistic' one (Mouffe 2000, ch. 4). Let me briefly indicate what I mean. While in an antagonistic type of political relation the conflicting parties perceive their opponents as 'enemies' to be destroyed, in the agonistic one they treat them as 'adversaries', i.e., they recognize the legitimacy of the claims of their opponents. This supposes that, although they are in conflict, they nevertheless see themselves as belonging to the same political association as their opponents with whom they share a common symbolic space within which their conflict takes place. What is at stake in the agonistic struggle is the very configuration of power relations around which a given society is structured. It is a struggle between hegemonic projects that cannot be reconciled rationally. The antagonistic dimension is therefore present, and it is a real confrontation, but one that is played out under conditions regulated by a set of democratic procedures accepted by the adversaries. An agonistic conception of democracy acknowledges the contingent character of the hegemonic politico-economic articulations which determine the special configuration of society at a given moment. They are precarious and pragmatic constructions that can be disarticulated and transformed as the result of the agonistic struggle. Society, according to such a perspective, is not to be seen as the unfolding of a logic exterior to itself, whatever the source of this logic could be: forces of production, development of the Spirit, law of history, etc. Society is always politically instituted, and the terrain in which hegemonic interventions take place is always the outcome of previous hegemonic practices; it is never a neutral one.

A central task of the agonistic hegemonic struggle has always been the production of new subjectivities, but in the present stage of capitalism such a terrain is more important than ever. Today's capitalism relies increasingly on semiotic techniques in order to create the modes of subjectivation that are necessary for its reproduction. In modern production, the control of the souls (Foucault) plays a strategic role in governing affects and passions. The forms of exploitation characteristic of the times when manual labor was dominant have been replaced by new ones which require constantly creating new needs and an incessant desire for the acquisition of goods. This is why in our consumer societies advertising plays such an important role. This role is not limited to promoting specific products but also entails producing fantasy worlds with which the consumers of goods will identify. Indeed, nowadays to buy something is to enter into a specific world, to become part of an imagined community. To maintain its hegemony the current capitalist system needs to constantly mobilize people's desires and shape their identity, and it is the construction of the very identity of the buyer that is at stake in the techniques of advertising. A counter-hegemonic politics must therefore engage with this terrain so as to foster other forms of identification. This is why today the cultural terrain occupies such a strategic place in politics.

Agonistic public spaces

How can cultural and artistic practices contribute to the counter-hegemonic challenge to neo-liberal hegemony? To tackle this issue we need to address the question of public space, and I will begin by indicating the consequences of the agonistic approach in this field. Its main contribution is to challenge the widespread conception that, albeit in different ways, informs most visions of public space conceived as the terrain where one should aim at creating consensus. According to the perspective that I am advocating, on the contrary, public spaces – which are always plural – represent the diverse battlegrounds where the different hegemonic projects are confronted, without any possibility of final reconciliation. My position is therefore very different from the one defended by Jürgen Habermas, who envisages what he calls the 'public sphere' as the place where deliberation aiming at a rational consensus takes place. To be sure, Habermas now accepts that it is improbable, given the limitations of social life, that such a consensus could effectively be reached, and he sees his 'ideal situation of communication' as a 'regulative idea'. However, for the agonistic hegemonic approach, the impediments to the Habermasian ideal speech situation are not empirical but ontological. One of its main tenets is indeed that such a rational consensus is a conceptual impossibility because it posits the availability of a consensus without exclusion, which is precisely what such an approach reveals to be impossible.

Despite some similarities in terminology, my conception of agonistic public spaces also differs from that of Hannah Arendt, which has become so popular recently. In my view, the main problem with Arendt's understanding of 'agonism' is, to put it in a nutshell, that it is an 'agonism without antagonism'. What I mean is that, while Arendt puts great emphasis on plurality and insists that politics deals with the community and reciprocity of human beings which are different, she never acknowledges that this plurality is at the origin of antagonistic conflicts. According to her, to think politically is to develop the ability to see things from a multiplicity of perspectives. As her reference to Kant's idea of 'enlarged thought' testifies, her pluralism is inscribed in the horizon of an intersubjective agreement. What she looks for in Kant's doctrine of aesthetic judgment is precisely a procedure for ascertaining intersubjective agreement in public space. This is why, albeit with significant differences in their respective approaches, Arendt, like Habermas, ultimately ends up envisaging public space in a consensual way.

To visualize the nature of public spaces in an agonistic manner has important consequences in the field of artistic practices, because it allows us to envisage how they can contribute to the hegemonic struggle. By bringing to the fore what the dominant consensus tends to obscure and obliterate, by making visible what neoliberal hegemony represses, critical artistic practices can play an important role in the creation of a multiplicity of sites where the dominant hegemony would be questioned. They should be seen as counter-hegemonic interventions, which, by contributing to the construction of new practices and new subjectivities, aim at subverting the dominant hegemony. From such a perspective all those who work in the field of art and culture constitute an important part of what Gramsci calls 'organic intellectuals'.

I want to clarify that such counter-hegemonic interventions cannot have as their objective to lift a supposedly false consciousness so as to reveal the 'true reality'. This would be completely at odds with the anti-essentialist premises of the theory of hegemony, which rejects the very idea of a 'true consciousness'. Identities are, according to this approach, always the result of processes of identification, and it is through insertion in a manifold of practices, discourses and language games that specific forms of individualities are constructed. What is at stake in the transformation of political identities is not a rationalist appeal to the true interests of the subject but the inscription of the social agent in practices that will mobilize its affects in a way that disarticulates the framework in which the dominant process of identification is taking place, so as to bring about other forms of identification. This means that to construct oppositional identities it is not enough to simply foster a process of 'de-identification' or 'de-individualization'. The second move, the moment of 're-identification', of 're-individualization' is crucial. To insist only on the first move is in fact to remain trapped in a problematic according to which the negative moment would be sufficient on its own to bring about something positive, as if new subjectivities were already there, ready to emerge when the weight of the dominant ideology was lifted. Such a view, which informs many forms of critical art, fails to come to terms with the nature of the hegemonic struggle and the complex process of construction of identities.

To conceive critical artistic practices as interventions in the hegemonic struggle also means that the political strategy cannot be one of exodus. Such a view, advocated by a diversity of post-Operaist theorists, comes in different versions but they all imply that in the conditions characteristic of empire, the traditional structures of power organized around the national state and representative democracy have become irrelevant and that they will progressively disappear. Hence the claim that we should simply ignore them and work towards the self-organization of the multitude. Those who follow this approach believe that one can ignore the existing power structures to dedicate oneself to constructing alternative social forms outside the state power network. This is why they refuse any collaboration with the traditional channels of politics, like parties and trade unions. They reject any majoritarian model of society, organized around a state, in favor of another model of organization of the multitude which they present as more universal, a form of a unity provided by common places of the mind, cognitive-linguistic habits and the general intellect.

We should note that it is the very idea of the 'public' that is increasingly put into question by those theorists because they see it as too much indebted to the idea of the state, which they take as its necessary corollary. Instead of the public we should, they say, think in terms of the 'common'. According to Virno the multitude dissolves the distinction between public and private, and Hardt and Negri have recently declared that in the transition from modern to postmodern politics, it is necessary to abandon the categories of public/private and that the mode of existence of the multitude should be envisaged in terms of the 'exercise of the common'.

We are clearly dealing here with two very different conceptions of politics, based on conflicting ontologies. While the strategy of exodus, based on an ontology of immanence, supposes the possibility of a redemptive leap into a society, beyond politics and sovereignty, where the multitude would be able to immediately rule itself and from which antagonism would have disappeared, the hegemonic strategy of 'war of position' acknowledges that antagonism is irreducible and that as a consequence social objectivity can never be fully constituted and that a fully inclusive consensus is never available. According to the immanentist view the primary ontological terrain is one of multiplicity, while for the hegemonic approach it is one of division, or failed unicity. Acknowledging the ineradicability of antagonism, the latter recognizes that every form of order is necessarily a hegemonic one and that a perfect realization of democracy is impossible.

No doubt when we examine the future of radical politics through the hegemonic approach, we get a less optimistic view than the one put forward by Hardt and Negri. But it is more optimistic than the view propagated by those who claim that there is no alternative to the existing order. Our societies are not inexorably moving towards an 'absolute democracy of the multitude', as Hardt and Negri would have it, but neo-liberal globalization does not represent the end of history either. The configuration of power relations which has been articulated through hegemonic political interventions can always be disarticulated through counter-hegemonic ones. More democratic hegemonic forms of order can exist, and we should fight to bring them about. What needs to be abandoned are dreams of an absolute democracy, or messianic illusions à la Agamben of a completely different kind of politics beyond law and violence. Those conceptions lead to impotence because they impede us from grasping the nature of politics and the necessity for organic intellectuals to engage with a multiplicity of agonistic democratic struggles to transform the existing hegemonic order.

References

Boltanski, Luc, and Chiapello, Eve. 2005. *The New Spirit of Capitalism.* London: Verso.
Gorz, André. 2004. Interview. *Multitudes,* no 15.
Hardt, Michael, and Negri, Antonio. 2000. *Empire.* Cambridge, MA and London: Harvard University Press.
———2004. *Multitude: War and Democracy in the Age of Empire.* 2004. New York: Penguin Press.
Laclau, Ernesto, and Mouffe, Chantal. 1985. *Hegemony and Socialist Strategy: Towards a Radical Democratic Politics.* London: Verso.
Mouffe, Chantal. 2000. *The Democratic Paradox.* London: Verso.
Virno, Paolo. 2004. *A Grammar of the Multitude.* New York: Semiotext(e).

14

DEMOCRACY IN A MULTIPOLAR WORLD (2009)

I have decided that the best way to address the theme of this conference, 'Interrogating Democracy in International Relations',[1] is to examine the implications of my agonistic approach for envisaging what democracy could mean in a multipolar world.

I will begin by presenting the basic tenets of the theoretical framework that informs my reflection on the political. It has been elaborated in *Hegemony and Socialist Strategy*, co-written with Ernesto Laclau (Laclau and Mouffe, 2001). In this book we argue that the two concepts needed to grasp the nature of the political are 'antagonism' and 'hegemony'. Both point to the need for acknowledging the dimension of radical negativity and the ever present possibility of antagonism which impede the full totalisation of society and foreclose the possibility of a society beyond division and power. They require coming to terms with the lack of a final ground and the undecidability that pervades every order; this means, in our vocabulary, recognising the hegemonic nature of every kind of social order and envisaging society as the product of a series of practices whose aim is to establish order in a context of contingency. The practices of articulation through which a given order is created and the meaning of social institutions is fixed are what we call 'hegemonic practices'. Every order is the temporary and precarious articulation of contingent practices. Things could always have been otherwise, and every order is predicated on the exclusion of other possibilities. It is always the expression of a particular configuration of power relations. What is at a given moment accepted as the 'natural' order, jointly with the common sense that accompanies it, is the result of sedimented hegemonic practices; it is never the manifestation of a deeper objectivity that would be exterior to the practices that brought it into being. Every order is therefore susceptible of being challenged by counter-hegemonic practices which attempt to disarticulate it in order to install another form of hegemony.

In *The Return of the Political* (Mouffe, 1993), *The Democratic Paradox* (Mouffe, 2000) and *On the Political* (Mouffe, 2005) I have developed this reflection on 'the political', understood as the antagonistic dimension which is inherent in all human societies. I have proposed to distinguish between 'the political' and 'politics'; 'the political' refers to the dimension of antagonism which can take many forms and can emerge in diverse social relations, a dimension that can never be eradicated; 'politics' refers to the ensemble of practices, discourses and institutions which seek to establish a certain order and to organise human coexistence in conditions which are always potentially conflicting because they are affected by the dimension of 'the political'.

The denial of 'the political' in its antagonistic dimension is, I have argued, what impedes liberal theory's ability to grasp the roots of violence and to envisage politics in an adequate way. Indeed 'the political' in its antagonistic dimension cannot be made to disappear by simply denying and wishing it away, which is the typical liberal gesture; such negation only leads to impotence, an impotence which characterises liberal thought when confronted with the emergence of antagonisms and forms of violence that, according to its theory, belong to a bygone age when reason had not yet managed to control the supposedly archaic passions.

The main problem with liberal rationalism is that it deploys a logic of the social based on an essentialist conception of 'being as presence' and that it conceives objectivity as being inherent to the things themselves. This is why it cannot apprehend the process of construction of political identities. It cannot recognise that there can only be an identity when it is constructed as difference and that any social objectivity is constituted through acts of power. What it refuses to admit is that any form of social objectivity is ultimately political and that it must bear the traces of the acts of exclusion which govern its constitution.

The notion of 'constitutive outside' can be helpful here to make this argument more explicit. This term has been proposed by Henry Staten (1985) to refer to a number of themes developed by Jacques Derrida through notions like 'supplement', 'trace' and 'différance'. Its aim is to highlight the fact that the creation of an identity implies the establishment of a difference. When dealing with political identities, which are always collective identities, we are dealing with the creation of an 'us' that can only exist by its demarcation from a 'them'. This does not mean of course that such a relation is by necessity an antagonistic one. But it means that there is always the possibility of this relation us/them becoming one of friend/ enemy. This happens when the others, who up to now had been considered as simply different, start to be perceived as putting into question our identity and threatening our existence. From that moment on, any form of us/them relation, be it religious, ethnic or economic, becomes the locus of an antagonism. What is important here is to acknowledge that the very condition of possibility for the formation of political identities is at the same time the condition of impossibility of a society from which antagonism would have been eliminated. Antagonism is therefore an ever present possibility.

An agonistic model

An important part of my reflection has been dedicated to the elaboration of what I call an 'agonistic' model of democracy. My objective is to provide what Richard Rorty would call a 'metaphoric redescription' of liberal democratic institutions which, I claim, is better able to grasp what is at stake in pluralist democratic politics than the two main models of democracy currently on offer, the aggregative and the deliberative ones. In a nutshell, my argument goes as follows. Once we acknowledge the dimension of 'the political', we begin to realise that one of the main challenges for pluralist liberal democratic politics consists in trying to defuse the potential antagonism that exists in human relations. Indeed, the fundamental question is not how to arrive at a consensus reached without exclusion, because this would require the construction of an 'us' that would not have a corresponding 'them'. Yet this is impossible because, as I have just argued, the very condition for the constitution of an 'us' is the demarcation of a 'them'. The crucial issue then is how to establish this us/them distinction which is constitutive of politics in a way that is compatible with the recognition of pluralism. Conflict in liberal democratic societies cannot and should not be eradicated since the specificity of 'modern democracy' is precisely the recognition and the legitimation of conflict. What modern liberal democratic politics requires is that the others are not seen as enemies to be destroyed but as adversaries whose ideas can be fought against, even fiercely, but whose right to defend those ideas will never be put into question. To put it in another way, what is important is that conflict does not take the form of an 'antagonism' (struggle between enemies) but the form of an 'agonism' (struggle between adversaries).

A well-functioning democracy calls for a confrontation of democratic political positions. If this is missing, there is always the danger that this democratic confrontation will be replaced by a confrontation between non-negotiable moral values or essentialist forms of identifications. Too much emphasis on consensus, together with aversion towards confrontations, leads to apathy and to disaffection with political participation. This is why a liberal democratic society requires a debate about possible alternatives. It must provide political forms of identifications around clearly differentiated democratic positions, or, to put it in Niklas Luhman's terms, there must be a clear 'splitting of the summit', a real choice between the policies put forward by the government and those of the opposition. While consensus is no doubt necessary, it must be accompanied by dissent. Consensus is needed on the institutions which are constitutive of liberal democracy and on the ethico-political values that should inform the political association, but there will always be disagreement concerning the meaning of those values and the way they should be implemented. In a pluralist democracy such disagreements are not only legitimate but also necessary. They allow for different forms of citizenship identification and are the stuff of democratic politics. When the agonistic dynamics of pluralism are hindered because of a lack of democratic forms of identifications, passions cannot be given a democratic outlet and the ground is laid for various forms of politics articulated around essentialist identities of nationalist, religious or ethnic type and for the multiplication of confrontations over non-negotiable moral values, with all the manifestations of violence that such confrontations entail.

Towards a multipolar world

My agonistic model has been elaborated to provide a proper understanding of the nature of a specific political regime: liberal pluralist democracy. However, I think that some of its insights, for example, the importance of offering the possibility for legitimate, 'agonistic' forms of conflict in order to avoid the explosion of antagonistic ones, can be useful in the field of international relations. Indeed the situation in the international arena is today in many respects similar to the one found in domestic politics, with its lack of an agonistic debate about possible alternatives. Since the end of the Cold War we have been living in a unipolar world, and the absence of legitimate alternatives to the dominant hegemonic order means that resistances against this hegemonic order cannot find legitimate forms of expression. This is why those resistances breed conflicts, which, when they explode, take antagonistic forms, putting into question the very basis of the existing order. As I have suggested in *On the Political* (Mouffe, 2005), it is the lack of political channels for challenging the hegemony of the neo-liberal model of globalisation which is at the origin of the proliferation of discourses and practices of radical negation of the established order.

Contrary to some currently fashionable views, I do not believe that the solution to our current predicament lies in the establishment of a cosmopolitan democracy. The problem, in my view, with the cosmopolitan approach is that, whatever its formulation, it postulates the availability of a world beyond hegemony and beyond sovereignty, therefore negating the dimension of the political. Moreover, it is predicated on the universalisation of the Western model and therefore does not make room for a plurality of legitimate alternatives. All those who assert that the aim of politics – be it at the national or the international level – should be to establish consensus on one single model end up foreclosing the possibility of legitimate dissent and creating the terrain for the emergence of violent forms of antagonisms.

In my view, the challenge that we are facing is therefore the following: if on one side we acknowledge that every order is a hegemonic order and that there is no possible order 'beyond hegemony', but on the other side we also acknowledge the negative consequences of a unipolar world, organised around the hegemony of a hyper-power, what is the alternative? My suggestion is that the only solution lies in the pluralisation of hegemonies. Abandoning the illusory hope for a political unification of the world, we should advocate the establishment of a multipolar, agonistic world organised around several big regional units with their different cultures and values. I am not pretending, of course, that this would bring about the end of conflicts, but I am convinced that those conflicts are less likely to take an antagonistic form than in a world where a single economic and political model is presented as the only legitimate one and is imposed on all parties in the name of its supposedly superior rationality and morality.

Let me clarify here an important point. By speaking of an 'agonistic' world order, I am not trying to 'apply', strictly speaking, my agonistic domestic model to the field of international relations. What I am doing is bringing to the fore some similarities between those two very different realms. My objective is to stress that what is at stake in both cases is the importance of acknowledging the dimension of 'the political'. We need to realise that, instead of trying to bring about a consensus that would eliminate the very possibility of antagonism, the crucial task is to find ways to deal with conflicts so as to minimise the risks of them taking an antagonistic form. But of course the conditions are very different in the domestic and the international domains. The kind of 'conflictual consensus' based on divergent interpretations of shared ethico-political principles that is necessary for the implementation of an agonistic model of liberal democracy cannot be expected at the global level, because such a consensus supposes the existence of a political community which is not available at the international level. Indeed, to envisage the world order in terms of a plurality of hegemonic blocs requires relinquishing the idea that they need to be parts of an encompassing moral and political unit. The illusions of a global ethics, global civil society and other cosmopolitan dreams impede our ability to recognise that in the field of international relations one can only reach prudential agreements, and that all attempts to definitively overcome the 'state of nature' between states by the establishment of a global covenant run into insurmountable difficulties.

I am going to refer to Norberto Bobbio's model of 'institutional pacifism' to illustrate my point because it provides a good example of those difficulties. Bobbio's (1995) cosmopolitan approach consists in applying Hobbes's contractualism to the relations between states. Utilising the Hobbesian distinction between *pactum societatis* and *pactum subjectionis*, he argues that what is needed to create a peaceful international order is, in a first move, that states establish among themselves a permanent association through a treaty of non-aggression, jointly with a series of rules in order to resolve their disputes. This stage of *pactum societatis* should be followed by their submission to a common power that would ensure their effective adherence to the agreed treaties, using force if necessary (*pactum subjectionis*). Bobbio distinguishes three stages: the first, the polemical stage, the situation in the state of nature in which conflicts are resolved only by force; the second, the agonistic stage that corresponds to the *pactum societatis*, which excludes the use of reciprocal force to resolve conflicts and settles them by negotiation; and finally, the pacific stage, which is when a *pactum subjectionis* is established with the existence of a Third Party able to enforce the agreements established in the agonistic stage. The pacific stage would see the overcoming of the state of nature in international relations, and Bobbio believes that, although we have not yet reached the stage of a *pactum subjectionis*, the creation of the United Nations was an enormous step forward in that direction. He proposes to make a distinction between two different judicial figures: 'one who, despite his superior authority, does not have the coercive power to enforce his decision (as still happens in international law today) and another whose superior authority grants him this power insofar as the pact of obedience has entrusted the use of legitimate force to it and to it alone. Only when the Judge has coercive power is the pacific stage wholly achieved' (ibid., p. 25). The current situation is one in which the United Nations finds itself in the position of a powerless Third Party Judge. This is due to the fact that states remain sovereign and have not yet abandoned their monopoly of force to a common authority endowed with exclusive rights of coercive power. For Bobbio, a peaceful international system requires the completion of the transition from the agonistic to the pacific stage by the concentration of military force in the hands of a supreme international authority.

Although inspired by Hobbes, Bobbio's project departs from him in two significant aspects. Hobbes, of course, asserted that the passage from a state of nature to a civil union was not possible in the field of international relations, and he repeatedly denied the possibility of both a *pactum societatis* and a *pactum subjectionis* among states. The pact of submission of which his *Leviathan* offers a model could only exist within a state. Moreover it was of an autocratic nature. Bobbio intends to go further. Not only does he want to apply this model to the relations among states, he also wants the Third Party to acquire a democratic form. This is why he insists that this entrusting of coercive power to a superior entity should be the result of a universal agreement founded on democratic procedures. He asserts that peace and democracy are inextricably linked and that, for the power of the international Leviathan not to be oppressive, it is important that the states, which are at the origin of the contract through which the 'superstate' holder of a legal monopoly of international force is established, are democracies constitutionally committed to the protection of the fundamental rights of their citizens. The problem of course is that not all existing states are democratic, and this leads him to difficulties that he openly acknowledges:

> I am well aware that my whole argument is based on conjecture inspired by the Kantian idea that perpetual peace is feasible only among states with the same form of republican government (the form in which collective decisions are made by the people) – supplemented by the idea that the union of states must also be republican in form … Like any conjecture, my thesis may be expressed only as an 'if-then' hypothetic proposition: 'If all the states were republican, if the society of all states were republican, then … ' 'If' is the stumbling block.
>
> (ibid., p. 38)

Bobbio is clearly caught in a vicious circle that he formulates in the following way:

> states can become democratic only in a fully democratised international society, but a fully democratised international society presupposes that all the states that compose it are democratic. The completion of one process is hindered by the non-completion of the other.
>
> (ibid., p. 39)

Bobbio is nevertheless hopeful for the future because, in his view, the number of democratic states is increasing, and he believes that the process of the democratisation of international society is therefore truly underway.

There are of course many people today who would disagree with such optimism, among them Robert Kagan, who, in his recent book *The Return of History and the End of Dreams* (2008), argues that the global competition between liberal and autocratic governments is likely to intensify in coming years. Kagan is of course a neo-conservative concerned with the maintenance of American hegemony, but many people on the left are also sceptical about the optimistic, 'smooth' view of globalisation.

The question, however, is not a matter of pessimism versus optimism, and it should be addressed in a different way. If, as I have argued, every order is by necessity a hegemonic one, it is clear that the political unification of the world advocated by Bobbio, if it was ever to happen, could only take place under the hegemony of a central power. Bobbio's figure of a democratic international Leviathan, created through a pact of submission by which all states agree through democratic procedures that a Third Party Judge will have the coercive power to resolve their conflicts, could only be a global hegemony. His hoped-for democratic world order would in fact be a unipolar world where, in the name of universalism, the Western model of democracy would have been imposed worldwide. This would have dire consequences, and, as I have already indicated, we are currently witnessing how attempts to homogenise the world are provoking violent adverse reactions from those societies whose specific values and cultures are rendered illegitimate by the enforced universalisation of the Western model.

It is time, I submit, to relinquish the very idea of a *pactum subjectionis* among states and acknowledge that peace in a pluralist world can only be reached through the establishment of a variety of *pactum societatis*, i.e. a multiplicity of pragmatic multilateral agreements which will always remain precarious and contingent. Against Bobbio's illusion that a pacific stage could ever be reached in the field of international relations, it is necessary to accept that the agonistic stage is the only alternative to the state of nature. To envisage what are, under the current conditions of globalisation, the most adequate forms of constructing such an agonistic order, this is the challenge that we are facing.

Which democracy for a multipolar/'agonistic' world?

What could be the place of democracy in such a multipolar order? This is the question that I want to address in the last part of my article. It is evident that a multipolar world will not necessarily be a democratic one and that several of its poles might be organised around different political principles. Since we have discarded the presence of an impartial Third Party Judge, able to impose what would be deemed the only legitimate order, a coexistence of political regimes is unavoidable. This is of course the situation that we are beginning to witness, with the first signs of the advent of a multipolar world in which China, certainly not a democracy, will no doubt play an important role. My position on this question is that a multipolar world composed of a variety of regimes would certainly be better than the current unipolar one because it is less likely to foster the emergence of extreme forms of antagonism.

But I do not think that we need to discard the possibility that democracy might become established worldwide. However, this question would have to be envisaged in a different way, abandoning the claim that this process of democratisation should consist in the global implementation of the Western liberal democratic model. Democracy in a multipolar world could take a variety of forms, according to the different modes of inscription of the democratic ideal in a variety of contexts.

As I have argued in *The Democratic Paradox* (Mouffe, 2000), liberal democracy is the articulation between two different traditions: liberalism, with its emphasis on individual liberty and universal rights, and democracy, which privileges the idea of equality and 'rule by the people', i.e. popular sovereignty. Such an articulation is not a necessary but a contingent one; it is the product of a specific history. Indeed, the liberal democratic model, with its particular conception of human rights, is the expression of a particular cultural and historical context, in which, as has often been noted, the Judaeo-Christian tradition has played a central role. Such a model of democracy is constitutive of our form of life and it is certainly worthy of our allegiance, but there is no reason to present it as the only legitimate way of organising human coexistence and to try to impose it on the rest of the world. The kind of individualism dominant in Western societies is alien to many other cultures, whose traditions are informed by different values, and democracy understood as 'rule by the people' can therefore take other forms, in which for instance the value of community is more pregnant than the idea of individual liberty.

The dominant view, found in many different currents of political theory, asserts that moral progress requires the acceptance of the Western model of liberal democracy because it is the only possible shell for the implementation of human rights. This thesis has to be rejected but that does not necessarily mean discarding the idea of human rights. It might in fact continue to play a role but on condition that it is reformulated in a way that permits a pluralism of interpretations. To elucidate this issue, we find important insights in the work of Raimundo Panikkar, who, in an article entitled 'Is the Notion of Human Rights a Western Concept?' asserts that, in order to understand the meaning of human rights, it is necessary to scrutinise the function played by this notion in our culture. This will allow us, he says, to examine later if this function is not fulfilled in different ways in other cultures. Panikkar urges us to enquire about the possibility of what he calls 'homeomorphic', i.e. functional, equivalents of the notion of human rights. Looking at Western culture, we ascertain that human rights are presented as providing the basic criteria for the recognition of human dignity and as being the necessary condition for a just social and political order. Therefore the question we need to ask is whether other cultures do not give different answers to the same question (Panikkar 1982, pp. 81–82).

Once it is acknowledged that what is at stake in human rights is the dignity of the person, the possibility of different manners of envisaging this question becomes evident, as well as the different ways in which it can be answered. What Western culture calls 'human rights' is in fact a culturally specific form of asserting the dignity of the person, and it would be very presumptuous to declare that it is the only legitimate one. Many theorists have pointed out how the very formulation in terms of 'rights' depends on a way of moral theorising which, while appropriate for modern liberal individualism, can be inappropriate for grasping the question of the dignity of the person in other cultures. According to François Jullien, for instance, the idea of 'rights' privileges the freeing of the subject from its vital context and devalues its integration in a multiplicity of spheres of belonging. It corresponds to a defensive approach which relinquishes the religious dimension and presents the individual as absolute. Jullien notes that the concept of 'rights of man' does not find any echo in the thought of classical India, which does not envisage man as being isolated from the rest of the natural world. While 'liberty' is the final word in European culture, for the Far East, from India to China, the final word is 'harmony' (Jullien 2008).

In the same line of thought Panikkar illustrates how the concept of human rights relies on a well-known set of presuppositions, all of which are distinctively Western, namely: there is a universal human nature that can be known by rational means; human nature is essentially different from and higher than the rest of reality; the individual has an absolute and irreducible dignity that must be defended against society and the state; the autonomy of that individual requires that society be organised in a non-hierarchical way, as a sum of free individuals. All those presuppositions, claims Panikkar, are definitively Western and liberal, and they are distinguishable from other conceptions of human dignity in other cultures. For instance, there is no necessary overlap between the idea of the 'person' and the idea of the 'individual'. The 'individual' is the specific way in which Western liberal discourse formulates the concept of the self. Other cultures, however, envisage the self in different ways.

Many consequences stem from those considerations. One of the most important ones is that we have to recognise that the idea of 'autonomy', which is so central in Western liberal discourse and which is at the centre of our understanding of human rights, cannot have such a priority in other cultures where decision-making is less individualistic and more cooperative than in Western societies. This in no way signifies that those cultures are not concerned with the dignity of the person and the conditions for a just social order. What it means is that they deal with those questions in a different way. This is why the search for homeomorphic equivalents is a necessary one. Societies that envisage human dignity in a way which differs from the Western understanding of human rights would also have a different way of envisaging the nature and role of democratic institutions. To take seriously 'value pluralism' in its multiple dimensions therefore requires making room for the pluralism of cultures, forms of life and political regimes. This means that, to the recognition of a plurality of understandings of 'human rights', we should add the recognition of a plurality of forms of democracy.

Next to human rights, another crucial issue for democracy is the question of secularisation. In fact, even in the West there is a long standing debate about the relation between democracy and the mode of existence of a secular society. As José Casanova (2006) has convincingly shown, an impasse has been reached in that debate between the European and the American approaches and the different ways in which they envisage the nature of a secular society and the link between secularism and modernity. On one side, there are the European sociologists who believe that the decline in the societal power of religious institutions and the decline in religious beliefs and practices among individuals are necessary components of the process of modernisation; on the other side, there are the American sociologists of religion who reject the theory of secularisation because they do not see any decline in the religious beliefs and practices of the American people. What is really at stake in this debate is the following question: should secularisation be seen as a necessary feature of modernity, and should it be seen as a precondition for modern liberal democratic politics? I am going to leave this question aside because the issue that I want to tackle is another one: even if we give an affirmative answer to this question in the context of Western democracy, does it mean that secularisation is a normative condition for all forms of democracy? Or should we not envisage the possibility of democratic societies where such a process did not take place? Casanova asks: 'Can the theory of secularisation as a particular theory of historical development be dissociated from general theories of global modernisation? Can there be a non-Western, non-secular modernity?' (ibid., p. 10). I would like to make this question even more precise and ask: can there be a non-Western, non-secular modernity with a non-secular form of democracy? If, as many people assert, the European concept of secularisation is not particularly relevant for the United States, it is clear that it is even less relevant for other civilisations with very different modes of social structuration. What could be its relevance, for instance, for worldly religions like Confucianism or Taoism? As Casanova notes, their model of transcendence can hardly be called 'religious', and they do not have ecclesiastical organisation. In a sense they have always been 'worldly' and do not need to undergo a process of secularisation. One could say, for instance, that China and the Confucian civilisational area have been secular '*avant la lettre*' (ibid., p. 13).

The best way to avoid those pitfalls is to acknowledge the possibility of multiple modernities and to accept that the path followed by the West is not the only possible and legitimate one and that non-Western societies can follow different trajectories according to the specificity of their cultural traditions and of their religions. Once it is granted that the set of institutions constitutive of liberal democracy – with their vocabulary of human rights and their form of secularisation – are the result of a contingent historical articulation in a specific cultural context, there is no reason to see their adoption worldwide as the criterion of political modernity and as a necessary component of democracy. A pluralist approach should therefore envisage the possibility of other forms of articulation of the democratic ideal of government by the people, articulations in which religion would have a different type of relation with politics and in which human rights (provided we want to keep this term) would be conceived in ways which depart from their formulation in the individualistic liberal culture.

To be sure, in many parts of the world we find intellectuals and activists who are engaged in precisely that kind of reflection, working to elaborate a vernacular conception of democracy inscribed in their respective cultural and religious traditions. In the case of Islam, for instance, Noah Feldman has shown that what is at stake is how to envisage a constitutional order grounded in the *sharia* and devoted to the rule of law. He examines different attempts to visualise how a democratic Islamic state, a state governed through Islamic law and Islamic values, could reconcile divine sovereignty with the democratic principle of popular sovereignty. Mainstream Islamism, he notes, has accepted the compatibility of the *sharia* and democracy but differences exist concerning the mechanisms of reconciliation. The most prominent solution is

> for the constitution of the Islamic state to acknowledge divine sovereignty rather than establish popular sovereignty and then use it to enact Islamic law. On this theoretical model, the people function somewhat as the ruler did in the classical constitutional order: they accept the responsibility for implementing what God has commanded.
>
> (Feldman 2008, p. 119)

According to some interpretations, this democratically elected legislature responsible for enacting the provisions of the *sharia* would need to be supervised by a con-stitutionalised process of Islamic judicial review. Feldman is aware of the difficulties that the establishment of such a democratic Islamic state will encounter, but he insists that it would be an error for the West to see it as a threat to democracy and to try to destroy those who are advocating it.

The situation is no doubt different in other parts of the world, and in each case the solution will have to take account of specific circumstances and cultural traditions. But all those who want to develop vernacular models of democracy face the same problem with respect to the West: its refusal to acknowledge forms of democracy different from the liberal democratic one. Western powers are adamant that the only legitimate democracy is their current interpretation: multi-party electoral democracy, accompanied by an individualistic conception of human rights, and of course by free market policies. This is the model that they claim to have the moral duty to promote, or impose if necessary. The disastrous con-sequences of the imposition of such a model can be seen worldwide. To take the case of Africa, for instance, several authors have pointed out that the catastrophic conditions existing in many African countries are the consequence of the inadequate political system that was bequeathed to them by their former colonisers. Independence often left them not as stable national states but as a patchwork of ethnic fiefdoms, burdened with parliaments based on those of the former colonial power. In countries with so many ethnicities with their own languages, customs and cultures, multi-party democracy has led to political frag-mentation and bitterly divided politics. Many specialists recognise that forms of democracy more adapted to African customs are needed and that governments of national unity might be better suited for holding those countries together and fostering their development.

As far as Asia is concerned, the situation is again different. There one of the challenges might be to reconcile the democratic principle of popular sovereignty with Confucianism and Taoism. The idea of 'Asian values' is often rejected on the grounds that it is used as an excuse by authoritarian rulers to justify their domination. In some cases there might indeed be some truth in this claim, but this should not lead to the dismissal of the legitimacy of such a notion. In the end, those issues should be decided by the people concerned, and it is not up to us Westerners to tell them how to organise their own societies. The thought that I would like to share with you in concluding is that we should acknowledge that the world is a pluriverse and realise that to accept a diversity of political forms of organisation will be more conducive to peace and stability than the enforcement of a universal model.

Note

1 Held on 25–26 October 2008 at the London School of Economics.

References

Bobbio, Norberto. 1995. Democracy and the International System. In *Cosmopolitan Democracy*, eds. Daniele Archibugi and David Held. Cambridge: Polity Press.

Casanova, José. 2006. 'Rethinking Secularization: A Global Comparative Perspective'. *Hedgehog Review* (spring/summer).

Feldman, Noah. 2008. *The Fall and Rise of the Islamic State*. Princeton, NJ: Princeton University Press.

Jullien, François. 2008. *Le Monde Diplomatique*. February, p. 24.

Kagan, Robert. 2008. *The Return of History and the End of Dreams*. New York: Knopf.

Laclau, Ernesto, and Mouffe, Chantal. 2001. *Hegemony and Socialist Strategy: Towards a Radical Politics*. London: Verso.

Mouffe, Chantal. 1993. *The Return of the Political*. London: Verso.

——2000. *The Democratic Paradox*. London: Verso.

——2005. *On the Political*. London: Routledge.

Panikkar, Raimundo. 1982. 'Is the Notion of Human Rights a Western Concept?' *Diogenes* 120.

Staten, Henry. 1985. *Wittgenstein and Derrida*. Oxford: Basil Blackwell.

15

AN INTERVIEW WITH CHANTAL MOUFFE

Questions by James Martin

JM: This volume is part of a series concerned with innovators in political theory. Your work evolved out of a distinctly Gramscian Marxist tradition but over the years has incorporated insights from feminism and post-structuralism and, more recently, you have engaged Anglo-American political theory. Given this rich and complex articulation of traditions, where exactly do you see your innovations lying?

CM: One of the innovations that my work has introduced in political theory consists in having articulated crucial insights from Gramsci with the work of some post-structuralist thinkers like Derrida and Lacan. This is a shared enterprise with Ernesto Laclau that began with our collaboration in writing *Hegemony and Socialist Strategy*. Our aim was to elaborate an adequate conception of the political around two key concepts: antagonism and hegemony. In my posterior work, I developed this approach by introducing the distinction between antagonism and agonism to propose a new understanding of the nature of democratic politics.

With Anglo-American political theory, my relation is completely different. My engagement with it has been of a critical nature. In fact, when I began to discuss authors like John Rawls, it was because, after having criticized Marxism for its lack of understanding of the political, I strongly felt that the solution for the Left was not to turn to Liberalism, as it was so often the case in the 1980s, particularly in France. I wanted to show that there was no place for the political in liberal theory.

It is in that context that I began to be interested in the work of Schmitt. I find his critique of liberalism really powerful and I think that there is a lot that we can learn from it. I want to stress, however, that I strongly disagree with his conclusions about the impossibility of a pluralist democratic regime. My aim has always been – as the title of one of my essays indicated – to 'work with Schmitt, against Schmitt', using his critique not to dismiss the liberal tradition but to reformulate some of its insights in a properly political way. I argue that to be able to envisage liberal pluralist democracy in an adequate way, we have first to acknowledge the ineradicability of antagonism and the impossibility of reaching an inclusive rational consensus in politics. We also need to grasp the process of formation of political identities and the crucial role played by affects in this process. I use the term 'passions' to refer to the affective dimension which is at play in collective forms of identification, a dimension which contemporary political theory has been at pains to eliminate from democratic politics. In my view the main shortcomings of liberal democratic political theory proceed from its rationalism and its individualism. I have attempted in my work to remedy those deficiencies by developing an alternative approach that takes account of the role of radical negativity and uses the insights of psychoanalysis to apprehend the way collective political identities are constructed through processes of identification.

JM: You have drawn upon Gramsci's theory of hegemony and developed it beyond a strictly Marxist frame of reference, connecting his strategically oriented concepts (such as 'war of position' or 'organic intellectuals') to terms like 'discourse', 'undecidability' or 'antagonism'. In your view, is the Gramscian heritage entirely separable from its Marxian roots?

CM: Our use of Gramsci's theory of hegemony in *Hegemony and Socialist Strategy* is definitively 'post-Gramscian' because we reject the privileged role that he attributes to the working class. But I think that it is in a sense faithful to the spirit of Gramsci, who, I would dare to suggest, would probably have developed his thought in a similar direction if he had been confronted with the changes brought about by the development of post-Fordism. To use his concepts of 'war of position' or 'organic intellectual' in a creative way, we should try to adapt them to new situations and different contexts, not to insist that their meaning was fixed once and for all in the conjuncture in which Gramsci elaborated them.

Indeed, what I find remarkable in his work is his capacity to understand the way conditions are changing and not to be prisoner of any orthodoxy. Gramsci was very receptive to different intellectual perspectives, and, as Norberto Bobbio has shown, he did not dismiss the liberal tradition. He was very interested in pragmatism and appreciated the work of William James. I am sure that he would have been willing to incorporate the critique of essentialism found in several currents of post-war philosophy. In fact, many of his insights chime with such a critique. So I do not believe that what we are doing by inscribing Gramscian concepts in a post-structuralist vocabulary is separating the Gramscian heritage from its Marxist roots but developing its potential in new directions. In any case the question of 'fidelity' to Marxism is a disputed issue and many traditional Marxists already considered Gramsci as being too revisionist.

JM: Your work has evolved in a period that spans major international transforma-tions from the collapse of Communism, the end of Apartheid in South Africa, the rise of neo-liberal 'globalization' as well as resistance to it, to world politics in the aftermath of '9/11'. How important is it to you that political theorists are responsive to struggles and conflicts in the wider context? Do you see you work more as an engagement with the possibilities of the prevailing situation than with 'ideas' as such?

CM: My work has always been driven by a desire to understand what is happening in the world, so as to be able to intervene in it. I truly believe in the power of ideas, otherwise I would not have chosen to be a theorist. I first studied philosophy and for several years I taught epistemology at the National University of Colombia in Bogotá. This was under the influence of Althusser with whom I had studied in Paris. However, I quickly felt that what I was doing had not enough connection with political and social issues, so I came back to Europe to study politics. But I was not satisfied by the discipline of political science which I found too empirical. Finally, it is by combining philosophy and politics in political theory that I encountered an approach that suited me. It allowed me to develop ideas that could play a role in politics by clarifying issues important for political intervention.

When I decide to examine a specific issue, my original motivation is always a political one. For instance, in the case of *Hegemony and Socialist Strategy*, our aim was to understand the reasons for the incapacity of Marxism to grasp the nature of the new social movements and to put forward a project able to articulate a diversity of demands, which were not class-based. We argued that this incapacity was due to its class-essentialist ontology and to its economistic approach, which did not allow it to recognize that political subjects were discursively constructed. It is in order to overcome those limitations that we had recourse to post-structuralism. The arguments of the book were elaborated at two levels, political and theoretical, but the original impulse was a political one. I could say the same for all my posterior writings. The initial spark is always provided by a given political conjuncture. My critique of deliberative democracy, for instance, comes from my conviction that it is vital for democratic politics to acknowledge the role of affects in politics and not to abandon this terrain to the right. In *On the Political*, I have shown how the crisis of the Left today is due to a lack of understanding of the necessary 'partisan' nature of politics and a mistaken emphasis on consensus. I think that the rise of right-wing populist parties in Europe is linked to the fact that Left parties were unable to offer alternatives to neo-liberal hegemony because they were searching for a 'consensus at the centre'. They have accepted the claim that there was no alternative to the current neo-liberal form of globalization and are only trying to manage it in a 'more humane' way.

JM: You advocate what you call an 'agonistic public sphere'. The emphasis here is on acknowledging disagreement and transforming antagonists into adversaries, rather than fashioning consensual agreements. What do you regard as the limits to agonism? Is there a strict difference between antagonism and agonism?

CM: It is precisely in order to challenge the idea that democratic politics consists in trying to reach consensus through deliberative procedures that I have developed my agonistic approach. My argument is that democratic politics requires the existence of an 'agonistic public sphere' where a confrontation can take place between conflicting hegemonic projects. Once it is acknowledged that antagonistic conflicts are ineradicable and that a rational consensus is impossible in politics, the task of democratic politics is to provide the institutions and practices that will allow for those conflicts to take an agonistic form in which the opponents are not treated as enemies to be eradicated but as adversaries. As I have repeatedly stressed, the antagonistic dimension does not disappear in an agonistic relation and adversaries are, so to speak, 'legitimate enemies'. They are aware that, in the conflict in which they are engaged, the different positions can never be reconciled – hence the antagonistic element – but they recognize the legitimacy of their opponents in fighting for the victory of their position. This is where the difference lies between an antagonistic relation and an agonistic one. At the theoretical level it is therefore impossible to completely distinguish antagonism from agonism. Agonism is a form of 'tamed' or 'sublimated' antagonism but the antagonism is always there and can always emerge at a given moment. When we envisage the question at the political level, however, it is necessary at a given moment to be able to distinguish between antagonists and adversaries. Indeed, the demands of the antagonists cannot be part of the agonistic struggle. As I have argued, there must exist between adversaries a 'conflictual consensus' consisting in agreement on the ethico-political principles that inform the political association but dissensus about their interpretation. Those who do not share those ethico-political principles are not adversaries but enemies whose demands are not considered as legitimate. Of course, such a distinction is not easy to make. In most cases it results from a political decision based on pragmatic considerations and it is for that reason that it should always be open to contestation.

JM: The concept of 'the political' figures greatly in your work from the 1990s onwards. You draw much of your understanding of this concept from Carl Schmitt and his distinction between 'friend' and 'enemy'. Do you see scope for any further differentiation within the concept of the political?

CM: According to my approach, 'the political' refers to the antagonistic dimension that exists in human societies. It manifests itself in conflicts that do not have a rational solution. This is indeed a conception that chimes with Carl Schmitt's concept of 'the political' as the friend/enemy discrimination. Like Schmitt, my position belongs to what Oliver Marchart calls the 'dissociative' view of the political, which emphasizes the dimension of conflict and that he distinguishes from the 'associative' view, which envisages the political as 'acting in concert'.

I have also proposed to distinguish between 'the political' and 'politics' in order to bring to the fore the difference between the ontological and the ontic levels. According to my approach, the political is not located at the level of concrete practices. It is an ontological assertion about the existence of radical negativity. Politics, on the other side, is located at the ontic level and it consists in the various practices through which a specific order is established in order to organize human coexistence according to different ethico-political principles.

It is at the level of politics that one can make the distinction between enemies and adversaries. In other words, this radical negativity, which impedes the totalization of society, can express itself at the ontic level through different forms of conflicts: either as friend/enemy (let's call it the properly 'antagonistic' one) or as agonism which is a conflict between adversaries. As I have already indicated, the antagonistic dimension does not disappear in agonism, it is merely tamed or sublimated. One of my key theses is that the challenge for democratic politics is to provide the institutions which will allow for conflicts to take an agonistic form. Otherwise those conflicts might emerge as antagonisms that could destroy the political association.

JM: Throughout your writings – from before *Hegemony and Socialist Strategy* through to your critique of 'third way' politics – you have been deeply critical of social democracy in Europe. Can parliamentary politics ever realistically form part of the radical democratic strategy you advocate?

CM: It is true that one can find through all my writings a critique of social democracy but it is never a total rejection of social democracy. The project of radical democracy that we put forward in *Hegemony and Socialist Strategy* could be understood as a radicalization of social democracy. At the time of writing the book in the early 1980s, we were critical of the welfare state because of the bureaucratic way it had been implemented and for its incapacity to take account of the demands of the social movements. We argued that social and economic rights needed to be deepened and extended, so as to include more areas of social life. But we were adamant that this process did not require a revolution and that it could be envisaged as an immanent critique of liberal democratic institutions. At that time social democratic hegemony had not yet been destroyed by Thatcherism and it was still possible to envisage the Left project in terms of the radicalization and deepening of the social-democratic values.

Today the situation is of course different and indeed much worse. With the almost unchallenged hegemony of neo-liberalism, many of the gains of social democracy have been taken away. We find ourselves in the paradoxical situation of having to defend the very institutions that we criticized before for not being democratic enough. And we also have to defend them against the self-proclaimed 'centre-left' that, under the pretence of 'modernizing' it, has liquidated social democracy. Despite their shortcomings the Labour governments previous to Thatcherism were certainly more progressive than New Labour. The current centre-left politics has accepted the terrain established by decades of neo-liberal hegemony and they have abandoned any attempt to challenge the neo-liberal form of globalization.

One of the tasks today is to recover and radicalize the social democratic ideals. I see this struggle on the mode of what Gramsci called a 'war of position', a struggle aiming at challenging the diverse nodal points through which the current hegemony is secured. Contrary to the view which is very fashionable today, that the 'multitude' should withdraw from existing traditional politics and auto-organize itself away from the state and the political institutions, I am convinced that parliamentary politics has a role to play in a radical democratic strategy. Of course, parties need to be drastically transformed in order to make them more representative of the democratic demands. But they do represent an important arena where the citizens can become engaged in the adversarial struggle and they provide a necessary terrain for the establishment of a truly agonistic politics. This is why the 'war of position' requires the creation of a synergy between parliamentary and extra-parliamentary struggles, the working together of traditional political institutions like parties and trade unions with the different social movements.

JM: You have called for the Left to recognize the role of passions in forging democratic identities. But is not this a realm far more suited to the Right and its appeal to purportedly incontestable attachments – or what Gramsci might call 'common sense'?

CM: The idea that the mobilization of passions is more suited to the right and that the Left should not engage with the domain of affects is precisely the view that I am challenging. I believe that it is one of the causes of the current incapacity of Left parties to make people identify with their project and arouse their enthusiasm. The claim that democratic politics should aim at reaching a rational consensus through procedures of deliberation that would secure the impartiality of the results is in my view a profoundly mistaken conception of the nature of democracy. If we accept, as I contend, that politics is inherently partisan and that the creation of a 'we' necessarily requires the determination of a 'them', the crucial issue cannot be the creation of a completely inclusive 'we' without a corresponding 'them'. As I have argued using the notion of the 'constitutive outside', this is indeed a conceptual impossibility. What is at stake in democratic politics is the nature of the 'them' and the way it is constructed. In that respect, the insights of psychoanalysis are absolutely crucial and they bring to the fore the central role played by affects and desires in the construction of collective identities. I agree with Yannis Stavrakakis that the discursive approach needs to make room for the element of 'jouissance' in order to grasp the nature and resilience of the attachments around which specific identifications are established.

With respect to meaning the of the Gramscian notion of 'common sense', I would like to insist that it is always the result of a given hegemony, whose system of values has become so sedimented that their political origin has been erased. This is how a certain conception of the world and specific ideas about what is possible and desirable appear as the expression of the 'natural order'. There is nothing 'natural' in the common sense and it can always be transformed through counter-hegemonic practices. We have indeed witnessed in Britain with Thatcherism, how a social democratic 'common sense' had been replaced by a neo-liberal one. This neo-liberal common sense has imposed the view that there is no alternative to neo-liberal globalization, that it is a fate to which we have to submit. It is crucial for the Left to be able to disarticulate this hegemony and to bring about another form of common sense. For such a strategy to be successful requires acknowledging the affective dimension present in the current forms of identifications and providing alternative forms of attachments. I do not want to deny that rational arguments might contribute to this struggle, but they certainly do not play the central role. I am convinced that rhetoric, by addressing more complex layers of our personality, can have much more impact in providing new forms of subjectivity.

JM: Recently, you have discussed the place of art and artists in the formation of a radical democratic hegemony. What kind of critical contribution do you believe artists or, indeed, popular culture generally, might play in this politics? How receptive do you find artists to your ideas?

CM: I have always been particularly interested in the role of cultural and artistic practices because it is one of the places where subjectivity is constructed. If we accept that identities are never simply given but that we are always dealing with identifications, then we need to pay special attention to those places where identification is formed. I think that the fields of culture and art are very important in this regard. Indeed, no hegemony could be established without their contribution since they constitute a privileged terrain for the construction of the 'common sense'. But in the conditions of post-Fordist capitalism, their role has become absolutely decisive because it relies increasingly on semiotic techniques to create the modes of subjectivation necessary for its reproduction. To maintain its hegemony, the current capitalist system needs to constantly mobilize people's desires and shape their identity. This is done in part through advertising but the mass media play a crucial role. This is why the cultural terrain occupies a strategic place in today's politics.

Many cultural producers have become aware of this situation and I think that this is the reason for the interest that my work has encountered in those circles. At first, I was very surprised to be invited by museums and a variety of artistic institutions but then I began to understand how my agonistic conception of the public space allowed artists to visualize the political nature of their practices. Many people told me that they had first tried to use Habermas's idea of the public sphere to situate their interventions in a political context but that it left them unsatisfied. In the agonistic approach, on the contrary, they found a way to envisage what role they could play in a counter-hegemonic struggle.

I prefer to speak of 'critical' artistic practices to refer to the practices whose objective is to challenge the dominant hegemony because when we acknowledge that cultural and artistic practices always play a role in the constitution and the reproduction of hegemony, it becomes clear that they always have a political dimension. The distinction between political and non-political art needs therefore to be abandoned since there is no art which is completely apolitical. From an agonistic perspective, critical practices are those that aim at fomenting dissensus, at bringing to the fore the alternatives repressed by the dominant hegemony. What is at stake is the transformation of the way we perceive our common world, the emergence of a different common sense and the construction of new subjectivities. This can be done in a variety of ways and I am definitively in favour of a pluralist understanding of how to envisage the nature of critical artistic practices. Some people want to privilege the sublime over the beautiful, which they dismiss as being reactionary. I consider this to be a mistake because beautiful art can be very subversive. Others present transgression as being the most radical gesture in art. But transgression is not necessarily subversive and in fact market forces love transgression, they thrive on it.

JM: Recent events such as the 2011 'Arab Spring' demonstrate the continued enthusiasm for democratic struggles around the world. What do you see as the significance of these events?

CM: What is happening in the Middle East is very important and those popular revolts will no doubt have far-reaching consequences. But it is too early to know what will be their outcome. In the meantime it is interesting to see how they are celebrated from many different sides which are trying to present them as the proof that their approach is the right one. In the USA, the neo-conservatives claim that those revolts justify the strategy of democratization of George W. Bush; for Alain Badiou they are the manifestation of the 'communist idea' and he pretends that they have nothing to do with democracy; Hardt and Negri, for their part, present them as a typical expression of the Multitude. Clearly what they do challenge is the essentialist perspective according to which Arab societies were destined to be governed by autocrats.

But the kind of order that will replace these autocrats is still undecided. A really progressive outcome will require that the actors of those revolts are able to establish chains of equivalence among their various demands and that they find ways of institutionalizing their multiple struggles. One thing is to bring down an autocrat or an unpopular government, another one is to build a democratic alternative. In fact, the 'Arab Spring' provides a very good example of the issue that I was discussing earlier when I was criticizing the strategy of 'exodus' for not acknowledging the necessary phase of institutionalization and for dismissing the role that parties can play in the transformation of the configuration of power relations and the establishment of a different type of state.

To be sure, this question is not only relevant for the Middle East, and it is crucial for the revolts that are currently happening in Europe. While being very sympathetic to the movement of the 'indignants' in Spain, I am really concerned when I hear them claiming that they want a participatory democracy without leaders and parties and that the objective of those direct participatory forms should be to reach an inclusive consensus. This is no doubt well meant but, as we have already witnessed in the regional elections, so far the result of such an anti-political approach has been to bring about the defeat of the socialists of the PSOE (Partido Socialista Obrero Español) and their replacement by the right-wing Partido Popular. There is no doubt that existing centre-left parties are completely incapable of confronting the challenges posed by the neo-liberal model of globalization, but the solution is not to do away with representative democracy, hoping that this will open the way to the advent of the 'absolute democracy' of the multitude advocated by Hardt and Negri.

JM: As you note, some have recently advocated a return to the idea of 'communism' as a way to subvert the dominance of neo-liberal thought and practice. How do you respond to this?

CM: While agreeing with the necessity to challenge the widely accepted claim that the disastrous failure of the Soviet model forces us to reject the entirety of the emancipatory project, I do believe that there are important lessons to be learned from this tragic experience and this calls for a serious rethinking of some central tenets of the communist project. It would indeed be too easy to simply declare that 'really existing socialism' represents a flawed realization of an ideal that remains to be truly implemented. To be sure, many of the reasons for which it went astray could be avoided and the current conditions might provide a more favourable terrain. But some of the problems that it encountered cannot be reduced to a simple question of application and they have to do with the way this ideal was conceptualized. To remain faithful to the ideals that inspired the different communist movements, it is necessary to examine how they conceived their goal to understand why those ideals could become so disastrously misled.

I am convinced that it is the very idea of 'communism' that needs to be problematized because it is strongly connoted with the anti-political vision of a society where antagonisms would have been eradicated and where law, the state and other regulatory institutions would have become irrelevant. According to my agonistic approach, pluralist democratic politics starts with the recognition that 'the people' is divided and that the democratic rule of the people can never be absolute. Every form of order is the expression of a given hegemony, which means that it is the rule of specific form of construction of 'the people'. This is why democracy requires the existence of institutions allowing for an existing hegemony to be contested. It is in that sense that I argue that there is a necessary populist dimension in democratic politics since what is at stake is the construction of a people. The crucial issue is how this people is going to be constructed and this is what the agonistic struggle is about. It is a serious mistake to identify populism with right-wing politics and to believe that the Left should avoid engaging with such a terrain. What we urgently need today is the development of left-wing populist parties able to give an institutional expression to the democratic demands of the numerous groups aspiring to an alternative to the current hegemony of neo-liberalism.

INDEX

HARVARD UNIVERSITY

http://lib.harvard.edu